# Dealmaking

# Dealmaking

*Using Real Options and
Monte Carlo Analysis*

RICHARD RAZGAITIS

**WILEY**

John Wiley & Sons, Inc.

For general information on our other products and services, or technical support, please contact our Customer Care Department within the United States at 800-762-2974, outside the United States at 317-572-3993 or fax 317-572-4002.

Wiley also publishes its books in a variety of electronic formats. Some content that appears in print may not be available in electronic books.

For more information about Wiley products, visit our web site at www.wiley.com.

*Library of Congress Cataloging-in-Publication Data:*

Razgaitis, Richard.
     Dealmaking : using real options and Monte Carlo analysis / Richard
   Razgaitis.
          p.     cm.
        ISBN 0-471-25048-1 (cloth : alk. paper)
        1. Negotiation in business.   2. Monte Carlo method.   I. Title.
   HD58.6 .R392 2003
   658.4'052—dc21

                                                            2002155493

Printed in the United States of America

10 9 8 7 6 5 4 3 2 1

*This book is dedicated to*
*the late Bruce Sidran,*
*former colleague, friend, and a great negotiator,*
*and in his memory, to his wife Debbie*
*and daughters Pamela, Melanie, and Michelle.*
*He left us with more than memories.*

# Preface

The ideas, principles, and tools contained in this book have emerged from literally thousands of discussions, interactions, and negotiations with friends, colleagues, and business prospects and partners. The context in most cases was creating value from technology by some form of collaborative enterprise. However, the foundational negotiation issue in these encounters was our present, respective representations of a conceived future. (It is we humans who are unique in existence that can conceive, and are even compelled to conceive, of the future.)

In this book I seek to create a methodology for negotiation by creating a present representation of possible futures in a way that can characterize risk, capture value, and communicate opportunity. Someone has said that every commitment to pursue a given future "it" hinges on answering three questions:

1. Is it real?
2. Is it worth it?
3. Can we achieve it?

This book expresses the belief that there exists methods and tools that can, with judgment, aid in this discovery.

# Acknowledgments

To acknowledge all the contributions to the ideas contained here is an impossible task. I have been benefited by more people than I can possibly recall, but I thank you all. I do want to recognize friends and professional fellow travelers in the Licensing Executives Society (www.les.org), and at InteCap (www.intecap.com). In particular, I would like to acknowledge Brian Oliver, Dan McGavock, Mike Lasinski, Jeff Snell, Jeff Brown, Dan Wald, and Kevin Arst, professional colleagues at InteCap who at one time or another willingly helped refine my thinking, though any limitations are mine alone.

I have dedicated this book to Bruce Sidran. It was my privilege to have Bruce work for me for 3 years at Bellcore (now Telcordia, a division of SAIC) and later to work for him as a consultant. His creativity, enthusiasm, wry humor, and people skills taught me a lot about a lot of things. His passing to the forces of leukemia just in his forties was a loss to us all and especially to wife Debbie and his dear family. To his daughters especially, you knew him as a great dad and special friend; and he was a special professional man too. There are not many days when I don't think of him, and miss his voice.

# About the Author

**D**r. Richard Razgaitis is a Managing Director at InteCap, Inc. He has over 35 years of experience working with the development, commercialization, and strategic management of technology, 20 of which have been spent specializing in the commercialization of intellectual property. He has participated in the licensing in and licensing out of numerous technologies, including advanced materials, manufacturing systems, software, and communications products. He has negotiated numerous commercialization agreements with clients in the United States, Europe, and the Far East ranging from Fortune 500 to small startup companies. Dr. Razgaitis is a Trustee and the Treasurer of the Licensing Executives Society USA/Canada (LES) and of the Licensing Foundation of LES. He is also a board member of the National Inventors Hall of Fame Foundation.

# Contents

# Dealmaking

# CHAPTER 1

# Introduction

**N**egotiation books appear to proliferate almost at the rate of self-help titles; that is to say, they emerge with astonishing frequency and number. So, why this one?

## WHY ANOTHER NEGOTIATING BOOK?

The prevalent category of negotiating books belongs to the motivational "YOU can do it!" genre. Those books focus on possibilities, an extremely important word in such books, and the secrets (another important word) of realizing those possibilities, secrets that were previously known only to a special priesthood but now, for the modest sum of $19.95, can be yours. Indeed. Such negotiation content is typically laden with tips and tricks, such as the infamous "eyebrow wink," which, when properly done, appears to guarantee not only tremendous financial success but also prosperity in every other human encounter. These books often are woven together within a theatrical construct of actors and scripts, props and plots, staging and intermissions, climax, and postproduction stage party.

As an adjunct to the "YOU can do it!" category, "Tips, Tricks, and Theatre" negotiating books might be distinguished as their own subgroup. Within the broader self-help genre, negotiation has submerged within it a special application of pop psychology directed to personal development and getting others to do what you want by persuasion, tomfoolery, and, of course, the ever-powerful eyebrow winking.[1]

Another prevalent category of negotiating books centers on the use, or misuse, of language, symbols (semiology[2]), meaning, and human psychology. The application context of such books ranges from family matters, to the arena of politics and compromise, union and other class contracts, world geopolitics, and hostage negotiations. These books tend to look at negotiation as a very complex process, which, if one is considering the job of being the next Middle East peace negotiator, is an enlightened perception. They also deal extensively with historical matters and the related circumstance of rigidly framed perceptions of what is at stake and what is negotiable and what is not.

A third category of negotiating books addresses game or bargaining theory. These books discuss an important subject within the field of modern economic theory. They include such topics as Bayesian Equilibrium and Nash Bargaining and Equilibrium (named after John Nash, now made famous by the recent movie and biography *A Beautiful Mind*). These theories and books tend to be highly symbolic (algebraic) developments of theoretical cases of various negotiating environment models. Such books often attempt to illuminate why people gravitate toward, or accept, various negotiated outcomes based on underlying economic theory mathematically expressed.

This negotiating book does not belong to any of the previous categories. It is a book about practical business negotiations. It focuses on those matters that are, or can be, quantified, modeled, and valued, which is most of what business is about. However, it deals with the important situation in which there is substantial future uncertainty of the value of an opportunity. So, this book is not about negotiating for a carload of paper clips, however important that may be.

Although the discussion, tools, and methods of this book are intended to be of general application, a common context of negotiation, and of this writing, is the transfer of rights and related assets for a technology. However, by the term "technology" it is meant to encompass the broad meaning intended by its Greek root, *techne*,[3] which designates the craft, skill, and know-how associated with making some product or performing some service. This meaning of technology would apply to patented, but not yet commercialized, superconductivity inventions as well as to business models and associated know-how and market presence for a business process such as an internet-based auction service. The envisioned negotiation outcome could range from a nonexclusive transfer of limited rights to such technology to some form of partnership or joint venture to an outright sale (assignment). Likewise, the payment structure could vary across a wide spectrum from royalties on the buyer's future use, to equity in a NEWCO, to some form of annual or event-triggered payments, to a single lump sum payment on closing (or to some combination of structures).

The underlying purpose of this book is to empower negotiation for business-to-business dealmaking of business *opportunities* using analytical tools and planning procedures. One of the important elements of such empowered negotiation is knowing what you should want, in specific circumstances, and specifically why it is reasonable to hold such a view so that it can be communicated to internal stakeholders and people on the other side of the negotiation. It is such a reasoned view that can become the sufficient basis for ones own convictions, and hope and, importantly, for infecting others. This focus on practical tools and procedures that can be justifiably used in a business context distinguishes the book from a vast catalog of other negotiation books. Our goal then is to develop the tools of analysis with a business preparation process that will lead to a kind of dealmaking, here termed ⁱDealmaking.

## ⁱDEALMAKING™

The term *business negotiation* usually conjures up an adversarial process in which prospective buyers wishing to pay zero joust with aspiring sellers wishing to sell for millions and billions. Here, we wish to consider a richer range of meaning for the negotiation context. Business, as in life, operates on choices made in the face of multiple alternatives, including the alternative of making no immediate choice. In any fiscal quarter a business is likely to be confronted with multiple investment opportunities in support of its current technologies, products, and customers; its supporting infrastructure; and new technologies, products, and customers. How should such varied choices be made? In almost every instance, such opportunities and choices are not simple binary, take it or leave it, considerations. Rather, they are commonly available as a range of possible options. In many instances the business enterprise is itself the owner of the opportunity, such as a new technology invented by the research and development (R&D) department. In such circumstances the *negotiation* character of the decision-making process is not always recognized as it should be. For our purposes, each of these opportunities represent not just choices but negotiations in which two parties, whether of the same business entity or not, consider the full range of opportunities for the purposes of making optimal choices using tools and methods presented in this book.

The word *negotiation* can itself be ambiguous. Does it mean only the face-to-face back and forth associated with gaining agreement with the other side? Does it encompass planning for such face-to-face discussion? Is it just compromising?[4] What about the activities and work products used in marketing the opportunity? Term structure? Valuation? Is it not, as it is sometimes said, *all* business is negotiation?[5] As will be discussed in greater detail later, we shall use the term *dealmaking*, for four elements of a business process that leads to business-to-business agreements: Conceiving, Communicating, Comprising,[6] and Consummating—these 4Cs of dealmaking will be defined later in this chapter. *ⁱDealmaking* is a shorthand term we use to encompass these 4Cs in a special, very important type of dealmaking, as discussed in the following sections.

## HIGH SIGNIFICANCE, HIGH AMBIGUITY CONTEXTS

Another way of envisioning the scope of this book is shown in Exhibit 1.1. As illustrated, dealmaking opportunities can be segmented by potential value (high and low) and ambiguity of key business terms (again high and low):

- For *low* potential value and *low* ambiguity, dealmaking should occur with a minimum investment of analysis and preparation, but is supported by the substantial availability of business information, such as revenues, margins, market, new production growth potential, and so on.

- For *high* potential value and *low* ambiguity, dealmaking warrants a significant investment to confirm the abundant business information and rationalize it for valuation, negotiation preparation, and agreement purposes.

- For *low* potential value and *high* ambiguity, the power (and complexity) of tools/methods such as Real Options and Monte Carlo may not be warranted.

- For *high* potential value and *high* ambiguity, we have the "sweet spot" for ¹Dealmaking: There is both a lot at stake and traditional data and methods are likely to be inadequate. This quadrant is often characterized

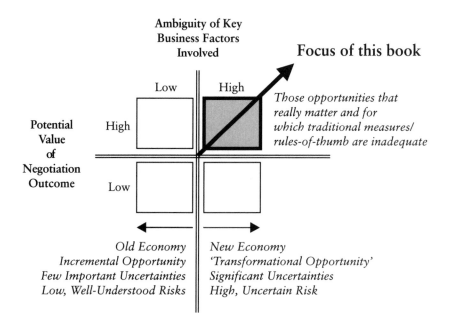

**EXHIBIT 1.1** High Value, High Ambiguity Opportunities

by colloquialisms that express the high potential opportunity with the corresponding, inherent uncertainties in the underlying technology, market, or business operation: "transformational," "game-changing," revolutionary, disruptive, new paradigm or paradigm shift, step change, upset (or "tipping point"), "killer app" (deriving from "killer application," often used in software, or quantum leap[7]). When such terms are used they are a strong indication that the opportunity is *high* potential value and, though it may not be overtly recognized, *high* ambiguity (low certainty) often because the transformational model is not achieved by some incremental, obvious new product adoption and growth pattern.

In the late 1990s, with the emergence of the Internet and World Wide Web (WWW), the rapidly increasing power at a rapidly decreasing cost of personal computing, the emergent ubiquity of mobile communication (phones, pagers, PDAs, and laptops), and the corporate information technology (IT) revolution in content availability, data mining, and networking (ethernet, LANs, VPNs, etc.) created a maelstrom of *transformational* business ideas. For a while it appeared that *every* new business idea promised to revolutionize how we lived and worked. These ideas were clearly touted as high opportunity and even the ardent believers generally admitted that they had attendant high uncertainties. At work was another force: time ultraurgency. These opportunities were so compelling, it was thought, and so competitively pursued that there was little time to analyze, quantify, or even—it seemed—to think. It was said that no one could do "Ready, Aim, Fire!" It had to be "Ready, Fire! Aim," or, as it was in many cases, just "Fire! Fire! Fire!" and hope you hit something worth the effort. Even our vocabulary reflected the new urgency by the then common usage of "Internet time." Its initial use was in circa 1994. During that year, the *Wall Street Journal* used the term in its writings just 4 times; in 2000, it was used 43 times.[8] The term conveyed an idea that expressed a behavior that reflected a core belief: The rates of change were so dramatic that time for reasoning was scarce or even nonexistent and the opportunities for success so abundant that the absence of reason was insignificant. Put another way, doing something, anything, had higher value creation opportunity than could be captured by any reasoning process requiring more than the proverbial 15 minutes.

In such absence of reasoned analysis, how were opportunities valued and chosen? Well, the obvious global answer as one surveys the smoldering ruins in 2002 is "not very well." But, specifically, pursuers of such high value/high ambiguity opportunities used two primary methods: (1) simplistic rules of thumb and (2) unstructured auctions. Among the examples of simplistic rules of thumb was the use of $2 million per software "developer" employed in valuing a potential software acquisition target. So, using the first method, if you were considering buying a software company with nominal revenues, but nowhere close to net earnings, with 500 "developers," you would be prepared to pay $1 billion.

The second method was the use of informal auctions. Potential sellers of opportunities had multiple pursuers. This situation enabled them in many cases to play one bidder off against the other in an informal auction process that they, the seller, controlled. This auction was informal because in most cases the buyers did not know who the other interested parties were, or even if there were truly other interested parties or actual bids. In addition, there were no standardized rules of engagement such as exist, for example, in stock or commodity exchanges or even bankruptcy court auctions. The motives of greed for gain and fear of lost opportunity led many buyers to bid and pay for opportunities far in excess of what they now appear to be worth. The examples of such overpayment are legion. Are auctions really markets, and are markets not reliable? The answer to both questions, in the case of informal auctions when there is a frenzy of buyers with money chasing the 'next big thing' is "no." Could not a potential buyer have, instead, resorted to advanced valuation tools and methods such as are considered in this book? The general belief was "no" because, it was widely believed, that by the time they completed even a cursory analysis the opportunity would have been sold to a buyer unfettered by such concerns who simply looked it over and topped the previous and all competitive bids.

Selecting one illustrative proxy for this point is difficult because there are so many to choose from. Exhibit 1.2 presents an easy to understand example, namely, the public recommendations by a well-known brokerage firm (Merrill Lynch) with respect to a high-flying Internet (dot.com) startup (InfoSpace).

Consider the following as a benchmark for a poor return-on-investment standard. One can purchase a 12-pack of say, Coke® for about $3.00 in no-deposit states or for $3.60 in the 5 states requiring deposits of 5 cents per aluminum can. After consuming the Coke, one's "return" would be 95 percent loss of invested capital in a no-deposit state (each can is $\frac{1}{29}$ of a pound and a pound of recyclable aluminum cans is worth about 40 cents) or 83 percent loss of capital if you live in NY, CT, MA, VT, ME, IA, or OR; for those in Michigan (10 cent deposit) the loss of capital would be only 71 percent, and for Californians (2.5 cents) 91 percent. So, we might say that, on average, the "just-drink-your-investment" experiences a loss of invested capital of 90 percent. For many Fire-Fire-Fire dealmakers, they would have done better in terms of enjoyment *and* return on invested capital to have purchased Coke, *the soft drink itself*—not the company—than many of the 1995–2000 merger and acquisition (or equity) investments, our most recent mania, many of which have exhibited declines in value exceeding the just-drink-your-investment benchmark.

We now know that there are allegations that brokerage houses compromised their judgment on stock value by their desire to win investment bank-

**BEFORE A FALL . . .**

Merrill Lynch initiated coverage of InfoSpace in December 1999 with a rating of 'accumulate-buy' and a price objective of $160. The company's share price fell much faster than its rating.

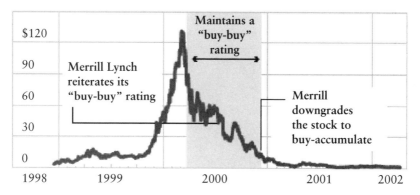

Sources: *Thomson Financial/Datastream; New York Attorney General's office affidavit*

**EXHIBIT 1.2**    Buy Recommendations by Merrill Lynch for InfoSpace

*Source: Wall Street Journal:* Europe (staff produced copy only) by Ravzin, Philip. Copyright 2000 by Dow Jones & Co. Inc. Reproduced with permission of Dow Jones & Co. Inc. in the format Trade Book via Copyright Clearance Center.

ing business, which may have been joined with less than well-considered merger and acquisition and other dealmaking advice. Whether, or to the extent, that is so, such recommendations would not have been effective if the public markets in large part did not find such counsel credible. The point is that investors and dealmakers, with all the reasoning opportunity in the world, believed such prognostications, to their (in many cases) financial detriment.

Negotiation preparation either by rules of thumb or informal auctions can lead to very damaging results. However, business is about exigency; a scholarly, methodical, patient inquiry into all matters relevant to a potential negotiation is simply not a practicable option. What is needed are reasonable, powerful, quick-to-apply and interpret tools and methods that can assess opportunities and prepare for negotiation. So urgency in preparation is important, but not to the exclusion of a rational, defendable analysis. Developing a rapidly deployable methodology using valuation tools is what iDealmaking and this book are about. As we shall see, the principle tools we apply are Monte Carlo and Real Options.

## THE "SO WHAT?" QUESTION

In most business situations one frequently deals with the "so what?" question. If we consider for a moment the internal decision of whether to go forward with some particular investment project, it can be argued that the level of analysis should take into account that all that is needed is the answer to the question of should we go forward or not. A common and powerful tool for making such determination is discounted cash flow analysis leading to a net present value (NPV). Although we treat this subject beginning in Chapter 4, it is useful here to recognize the significance of dealmaking on such decision making. In the case of internal project investment decisions, we can perform a simplistic NPV analysis to sort out those obvious opportunities that have strongly positive NPV values and accordingly should be undertaken, and those that have strongly negative values and should be killed. For purposes of decision making, the only opportunities that justify more careful analysis, such as the use of Monte Carlo or Real Options, are those for which the NPV is near zero. These are the tough calls that hinge on a refined analysis.[9]

In dealmaking, as opposed to internal investment analysis, near-zero NPV projections commonly occur. Consider for a moment a seller and buyer each using the same data on which they make projections and the same overall business assumptions; their calculation of NPV will be identical but for small differences perhaps in some secondary assumptions. In this situation, the seller will try to capture in its sales price the entire positive NPV under the argument that so long as the opportunity has any positive value, a buyer should say "yes" to the deal and terms proposed. Thus, sellers are by their self-interest offering terms that create near-zero NPVs for the buyer. If there are multiple prospective buyers who then engage in a formal or informal bidding context, they will each be driven to increase their bids up to the limit of a zero or near-zero NPV.

So it is common in dealmaking contexts that the decision to proceed or not, from both the seller's and buyer's perspectives, ends up being a close call. In contrast then to many internal investment decision-making situations, the natural contest and context of negotiations warrants the use of the tools and methods we discuss in this book.

## VALUATION, PRICING, AND NEGOTIATION

Negotiation is a business process, like sales and R&D. It is closely related to another business process, namely, that of *valuation*. A simple way of thinking of these two processes is: negotiation is getting someone else to accept your valuation as part of a transaction. This perspective is of a one-direction sequence whereby a valuation process has determined "the number" and handed that number off to the negotiation process to realize such number (or better) by whatever means necessary.

A richer, and better, understanding of the interrelation is that negotiating is the process by which both parties come to a transactable agreement based on independently performed valuations. This view recognizes that although the negotiation process was preceded by a valuation, the process of negotiation will likely cause a revaluation. Also, any negotiation occurs in the context of two valuations, ours and theirs. For an agreement to be reachable, the key parameters of the respective valuation processes must, through the process of negotiation, come to some commonality of terms.

So valuation from our perspective of the deal is an important step of negotiation planning. But valuation from the perspective of the other side is also important to planning. Finally, valuation needs to be an active component of the negotiation itself.

## TANGIBLE AND INTANGIBLE CONTENT/VALUE AND THE NEW ECONOMY

The subject matter of many business negotiations is changing as fundamentally as the economic structure of the businesses themselves, from being about the value of tangible things such as machines and buildings, to the right to use intangibles such as information and technology. This shift in underlying business value is often characterized by the term *New Economy*. Although a full discussion of what constitutes such a New Economy deals with broad issues of economic theory and is beyond the scope of this book, it is useful for us to consider some concrete examples. Just 100 years ago (in 1901) the first U.S. company to emerge with a market value of $1 billion ($1.4 billion in authorized capitalization) was U.S. Steel. ($One billion in 1901 is approximately equivalent to $30 billion in 2003.) It achieved such valuation primarily through property, plant, and equipment (PPE), three traditional measures of industrial, tangible value. U.S. Steel, which became USX in 1986, was an icon of the new industrial age and the Old Economy; U.S. Steel in 1901 owned 213 manufacturing plants, 41 mines, 1,000 miles of railroad and employed more than 160,000 people. U.S. Steel's book value, as measured by accountants and reported on the company's balance sheet was substantially determined by its PPE and closely reflected such market value.

One hundred years later, in 2001, the most valuable company in the United States was Microsoft, an icon of the information age and the New Economy, when it reached a market capitalization[10] (or market cap) of $400 billion. Its book value, however, was less than $100 million, reflecting its relatively modest PPE ownership of land, buildings, and various capital equipment (office furniture, computers, communications networks and devices, and certain equipment associated with its making and shipping CD-ROMs and manuals). How can a rational market ascribe a value to Microsoft that is 4,000 times its book (tangible) value? The answer lies in the very significant *intangible* value associated with Microsoft's copyrighted software, which is just a string of 1s and 0s, bits, in an archived Microsoft facility; know-how and patents; and its trademark and tradename value.[11]

Yet another measure of the transformation of the U.S. economy is evident in transportation. In the first decade of the 20th century, ca. 60 percent of companies traded on The New York Stock Exchange were railroads, entities that stored and shipped things with mass. During the first decade of the twenty-first century our market economy is led by companies like Microsoft, IBM, Cisco, SBC that store and ship massless data bits.

Think of the effect on a negotiation to buy or sell some component of the respective assets of a U.S. Steel in 1901 versus Microsoft in 2001. In the case of U.S. Steel we would be characterizing something tangible using available standards of reference for transactions of other like tangibles to guide both our valuation and negotiation preparation.

## THE ¹DEALMAKING PROCESS

As introduced previously, ¹Dealmaking can be considered by thinking about 4Cs: Conceiving, Communicating, Comprising, and Consummating. Conceiving is the business activity of deal imagining. What would a deal look like that would be good for us, and for the parties we conceive to be on the other side of the transaction? Why should we do this? (And, perhaps, why not?) What strategic, or tactical, underlying purpose motivates such deal conceiving? What is the prize that we seek? What is the answer to the skeptic's 'so what' question, which could be sarcastically expressed by "big deal!" meaning, really, "small deal" or deal not worth the time and investment? What motivates us, really, to want to go through all this? So, deal Conceiving is about answering the strategic intent and underlying purpose questions, and it includes deal planning as to resources and time required and organizational issues. It also includes developing both a Plan A and a Plan B, issues that we will return to in Chapter 11.

Communicating, our 2nd C, includes the obvious activities of managing information flow on my side of the dealmaking, and to the other side. But it also includes all the issues associated with deal-marketing. How will the opportunity, or my reaction to a presented opportunity, be communicated? What aspects can be communicated without a confidentiality agreement? When and how does a confidentiality agreement become necessary? How do I package the written description (sometimes known as the Offering Memorandum, or a less formal Opportunity Memorandum, or simply 'the Book')? How do I decide to whom it gets presented and in what way it is presented? How can I do active learning based on the feedback from initial discussions? How will I manage all the varied levels of communication needs on the deal team and with others in my organization who have varying needs to know deal status and dealmaking planning? How do I communicate the deal price and terms or structure, or counter offers on price and terms or structure, and how do such relate to underlying deal value? ᶦDealmaking Communicating includes the plan for how one's interest in the dealmaking process and sought-for outcome will be made known to the other side in a defendable, persuasive way. We will consider these matters in Chapter 10.

Comprising, our 3rd C, is about configuring a deal that creates optimum value for both the seller and the buyer. ᶦDealmaking Comprising is the process of making adjustments in the course of the back and forth of communications to make the terms more favorable for all sides. "Compromising," which suggests retraction of one's terms, could be one way of such "comprising." However, in many circumstances adjustments can be made in the prospective terms of the agreement that make its value more attractive to the other side without harming the interests or value of one's own side. Comprising, then, is not just conceding some thing of value to our side but could be conceiving an alternative deal structure that is of more value to the other side while of constant or even greater value to our side. The metaphor we will use for enabling this process is the Box and the Wheelbarrow: The Box is the content and terms of what the seller is offering, and the Wheelbarrow is for the structure and magnitude for what the buyer is paying. We will introduce the Box and Wheelbarrow in Chapter 3, and return to matters of pricing such elements in Chapter 9.

Finally, Consummating, our final C, is about gaining agreement with all affected parties both internally and on the other side. This may involve revisiting Conceiving, to imagine an entirely different deal structure or even a Plan B. It almost always involves Comprising as in putting the seller's offer (the Box) and buyer's offer (the Wheelbarrow) in alternative more beneficial frameworks and perhaps values. It certainly involves Communicating to understand and express the issues and difficulties impeding agreement in ways that can, if at all possible, lead to new ways of meeting needs and objectives. For high-complexity situations with diverse interests and views across and amongst each side, negotiations can become interminable. It is normally valuable and necessary to have as an aspect of Consummation a strategy for achieving some form of closure.

Underlying all these Cs is the use of tools and methods of analysis and valuation. Such method based analysis is the heart of ᶦDealmaking. Chapters 4, 5, 6, and 7 develop such tools and methods of discounted cash flow and

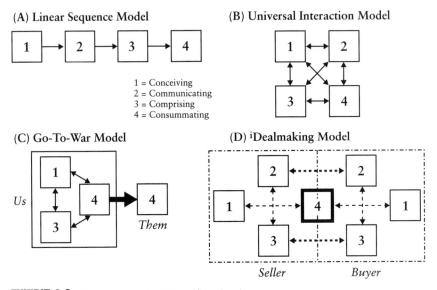

**EXHIBIT 1.3**    Sequencing the 4Cs of ᶦDealmaking

net present value analysis, scenario conception, Monte Carlo methods and analysis, and the use of Real Options methods.

Breaking down ᶦDealmaking into these 4C elements leads to the question of do they, or how do they, interrelate? Shown in Exhibit 1.3 are several inaccurate portrayals and one that might be helpful.

Shown in (A) of the above exhibit is the "Linear Sequence" model of the 4Cs, namely: You finish Conceiving, then, and only then, you go to Communicating, and so forth, much like a stage-gate project development, or pinball, process. However, as we shall see, these processes are interrelated and intertwined that even though Conceiving commonly occurs first, it is not a one-time process.

Shown in (B) is the opposite configuration, namely all the elements interact with one another throughout ᶦDealmaking. This is closer to being a realistic portrayal but is still incomplete.

In (C) we see the go-to-war perspective, namely: the Conceiving, Communicating, and Comprising all take place internally, get locked-and-loaded, and like a missile is sent to hit a target (and often with intent to kill).

The most-useful portrayal is shown in (D). The first three Cs should be developed as an interacting unit for the purpose of reaching agreement with an outside party, but instead of it being a fixed triangle of a deal it should be developed more as a lock and key arrangement that fits with a mirrored configuration on the other side. The Consummation is really about all the Cs fitting together on both sides.

## ORGANIZATION OF THE BOOK

In Chapters 2 and 3, we consider some of the important background issues of negotiation planning. In Chapter 4 we illustrate scenario building using discounted cash flow (DCF) and NPV calculations based on both risk-adjusted rates and probability trees. We also introduce Monte Carlo modeling. Then in Chapter 5 we cover in detail the Monte Carlo method of valuation and negotiation planning

In Chapter 6 we introduce the concept of Real Options. Also we cover the important idea of Black-Scholes option pricing. Then in Chapter 7 we cover in detail the Real Option method of valuation and negotiation planning.

In Chapter 8 we explore the twin ideas of knowledge and certainty for the purpose of gaining an understanding of how to comprehend the results of the methods and tools just considered. Then in Chapter 9 we consider pricing and term sheets. Chapter 10 covers negotiation perspectives and planning.

Finally, in Chapters 11 and 12 we consider the very important idea of having a "Plan B," and some concluding observations.

### NOTES

1. For the inveterately curious, the eyebrow wink is the act of lifting one's eyebrow on approaching another person to establish contact and rapport. It has been studied in many cultures, including that of apes, and is generally taken as friendly precursor to verbal and physical contact. Political consultants, in particular, counsel their clients to do "eyebrow pushups" to "open up the face."

2. Semiology is the study of signs and their meanings, such as costuming of person or office.

3. Aristotle defined *techne* as a capacity to do or make something with a correct understanding of the principle involved. So this book may be thought, I hope, as a *techne* about the business process of negotiation of *techne* opportunities. (*Techne* itself comes from the Indo-European root *tekth* meaning to weave or join, which is the source of the Latin word *texere* meaning to weave or build.)

4. Ambrose Bierce in his devious book of definitions, *The Devil's Dictionary* (1881–1906), defined "compromise" as: "Such adjustment of conflicting interests as gives each adversary the satisfaction of thinking he has got what he ought not to have, and is deprived on nothing except what was justly his due."

5. In fact the very word negotiate originates from the Latin word to transact business in contrast to acts of leisure: *neg-* (Latin for "not") and *otium* (for "leisure").

6. *Comprising*, for putting things together in certain beneficial ways, not *compromising* which can mean simply giving up something important in the interest of some other point of harmony. This distinction will be addressed later in the book.

7. The widely used phrase "quantum leap" is surely the most ironic. A quantum is the *smallest* unit of energy change in the universe. So "quantum leap" is oxymoronic.

8. "How Internet Time's Fifteen Minutes of Fame Ran Out," *Wall Street Journal*, October 28, 2002, p. B1.

9. There is a common corporate trend for skewing the numbers to make them conform to what some project champion, perhaps you, wants to do anyway. A favored project may have embedded in it a web of assumptions that cause it to have a highly positive NPV, and conversely for an unfavored project. Unless there is some independent, unbiased control over the assumption "dials," an investment committee can easily be presented with the easy decision making caused by a portfolio exhibiting a bimodal distribution of good and bad investments. This tactic can easily create a feedback loop much like the game of liar's poker: How much can I skew my project's assumptions to make its NPV sufficiently large that it is committed to without scrutiny into the kited numbers used to bias the decision?

   Even in this circumstance, Monte Carlo or Real Options can be warranted because of the limitations of discounting all future cash flows by a single discount value, a subject discussed in Chapter 4.

10. Determined by the number of shares outstanding multiplied by the market price per share.

11. In both the U.S. Steel and the Microsoft examples, I have used market capitalization as the measure of company value. A more complete picture of total enterprise value would use the sum of equity and debt. In the case of Microsoft, debt is negligible compared to its equity value.

# Negotiation People, Language, and Frameworks

In this chapter we develop a language to use for negotiation and the rest of the analysis in this book. First we establish a naming convention for the people involved on both sides of the negotiation.

## NEGOTIATION PEOPLE

One of the most ancient, and foundational, questions is: *Who* is there "out there?" The study of this famous question is known as *ontology*. In pop psychology books on selling or negotiating, this question is addressed by contrasting various personality types such as "analytical" versus "entre-preneurial," or role types such as "gate keeper" versus "decision maker." Here, we look at this important matter from the perspective of direct deal responsibilities.

In most negotiation contexts there are often seven different people "out there":

1. Lawyers
2. Profit and loss managers
3. Business developer ("bus dev"), deal creator
4. Deal manager
5. Financial analysts
6. Inventors, content creators
7. Those impossible to classify

First, we have lawyers. Agreements in our culture and time have sufficient complexity, and normally importance, that require that they be reduced to writing in formally structured documents. Further, such writing must be done in a way that independent third parties, judges and juries and other dispute resolvers, can, at any later time, divine the intentions and duties of the parties. Ultimately, the words and sentences of most agreements will receive the thought and reflect the fears of lawyers. Their skills are exceedingly useful in creating language that is understandable, which is surprisingly difficult to do (as someone once said: "English resists meaning"). They also often bring a "what if" questioning as to a seemingly endless stream of possible adverse turns of events. (In human psychology this focus on the possibility of adverse events is known as "awfulization"; if someone personally close to you has this trait, and you remain cheerful and unswayed in your optimism, you may be a candidate for sainthood.) The underlying aspiration for such awfulization is to avoid adverse surprises (risks) and as much as possible avoid all duties and obligations by shifting them to the other side. This situation is the legal equivalent of the analyst we discuss later who similarly, in the extreme, aspires to deals that give nothing but get everything.

Next we have managers. Although everyone is a manager, what is meant here are those persons who have profit and loss (P&L) responsibilities. Frequently, they are either the owners of the selling company's books of what is being dealt, or will be the owners on the buy side. After the deal is done, they are the ones who will enjoy, or suffer, a substantial portion of the economic gain, or loss, flowing from the deal, and the attendant glory or shame.

The business developer in this context is understood to be the deal creator (or generator). He or she is the point person for wanting this deal done, and could be the P&L manager, or (as discussed later) the deal manager or even the inventor; in different circumstances any of these seven people could be the deal creator.

In the middle of our list is the deal manager. He or she is the person who is responsible for making the deal happen. In this sense he or she is a project manager, which is a useful concept for reasons to be discussed later. I have used the singular on purpose as there normally is, and in any case should be, just one person who is the deal manager. That person may have a support team whose members are sometimes termed "second-chair" negotiators, but for a concerted negotiation to lead to a deal, there should always be one person who is the recognized project leader.

Next are the financial analysts. They have a very specific interest in the numbers of the deal. Financial analysts span a wide range of perspectives and roles. Some reflect the treasury and accounting functions in the buying and selling companies. Some "work the numbers" for the respective business units affected in a P&L sense by the deal being envisioned. Still others are focused on the numbers directly related to the deal itself (deal numbers). It is sometimes cynically joked that companies have three sets of books: one to deceive investors, one to deceive the tax collectors, and one to deceive themselves. (Lately, this joke has lost its humor value.) In dealmaking, there are often three (it is hoped not deceiving) sets of numbers: those from the chief financial officer's (CFO's) perspective of the company's books, those from the P&L manager's scorecard, and those of the deal manager. As is discussed later, these first two sets of numbers—the CFO's and the P&L manager's—frequently influence the deal value, but it is the deal value that is negotiated and forms the terms on which agreement is reached; how those terms affect P&L and company financial statements are consequences of a deal, but should not be the cause of the deal terms.

Next we have the people whose content, key contributions, or even inventions are the very subject of the deal. In many instances, their participation in the negotiation is important to their respective sides of the negotiation because they assist in developing financial and business models of the future, as is discussed later. They are also important in the communication of the opportunity to the other side and in the due-diligence process that has as its primary objective an accurate understanding of the present stage of development, the important future uncertainties, and a characterization of the future risks. As discussed in Chapter 3, they also play an important role, often with the P&L managers, in developing the content of what will be sold or bought. Such content can be configured to include multiple technologies and associated forms of intellectual property (patents, trade secrets and know-how, copyrighted content and software), physical assets (plant, property, and equipment), and key people who may serve as deal resources and even as postdeal transition resources or who may become permanently associated with the implementation of the opportunity.

Finally, others are often involved in the deal who are impossible to classify. They can be inside or outside consultants, a trusted pair of eyes and ears sent by the chief executive officer (CEO); or some not otherwise gainfully employed person who in some unknown way has an ability to get him- or herself included in various deliberations and worksteps, and others.

Although we are all to some degree captive to our education and training, in general the roles played are not perfectly correlated to our formal degrees. A lawyer may be the deal manager or the P&L manager. The financial analyst could have been, in an earlier life, an inventor. Deal managers arise from many different career paths. We each bring both our histories and our duties to the job at hand. It is generally helpful to know who shows up and who they are in the matter, and well-managed deal teams normally require these multiple perspectives and insights.

Deals are balances. One kind of balance is between risk, generally taken as a possibility or probability of an adverse outcome, versus the possibility of highly successful realizations. Generally, the two people focused on the risk side of the balance are the lawyers and the financial analysts. Typically by training, disposition, and responsibility, these two team members are prone to identifying risk, "awfulizing" it, and developing propositions to transfer it to someone else, avoid it by some other means, or otherwise minimize it. They are usually the voice of caution in dealmaking. In many circumstances, they may prefer or appear to prefer "no deal" as the preferable option. Characterizing them as pessimists is probably too sweeping because it may not be reflective of their personalities as much as their responsibilities. A more accurate concept, using a presently invented word, is that they are "pessi-missive," meaning that it is their *mission* in the subject negotiation to cause the team to consider the probabilities and consequences of undesired and even worst-case outcomes. (Pessimism derives from the Latin word *pessimus,* which means "worst"). Opportunities are fragile things. Overbearing pessimism can extinguish good opportunities, especially during the early stages before they have established some momentum.

On the other side of the risk–opportunity balance normally are the business developers and inventors (though inventors on the buy side can be negatively biased against not-invented-here opportunities). Their natural inclinations are to discount risk often expressed by the confidence that solutions exist to any potential exigencies and a "nothing ventured, nothing gained" can-do optimism. Using a coined word, we can characterize their role on the team to be "opto-missive," meaning it is *their* mission to reason toward the opportunity that can reasonably be realized while recognizing that nothing is certain, as they say, but death and taxes. (Optimism derives from New Latin *optimum,* meaning "greatest good.") There has to be a present visceral belief in a future good to sustain the momentum toward deal realization.

Well-managed negotiating teams have effective considerations of voices on both sides of the risk–opportunity axis. As is discussed in later chapters, the formulation of scenarios and probabilities requires characterizing both downside and upside possibilities. Between the worst and highest such possibilities there are many rational intermediate possibilities whose value and likelihood are important deal considerations. A team overweighted with risk considerations by "pessi-missives" will undervalue their selling opportunities and underbid, and thereby likely lose, excellent buying opportunities. Overweighting with "opto-missives" can result when present in sellers in unreasonable deal expectations, in buyers overpaying and even pursuing opportunities that should not be embraced. Great dealmaking teams are just that, teams comprised of voices that play an important role but do not dominate the balance.[1]

Another balancing axis is past versus future perspective. Profit and loss managers are commonly the owners of historical positions or results and, accordingly, bring a historical perspective to an opportunity analysis and a concern for how a deal may affect existing financial books. One common historical perspective is the cost associated with the subject opportunity as contained, for example, on the seller's books, or as the prospective transaction will immediately impact the buyer's books or the buyer's previous representations. On the buy side, the P&L manager often is concerned with the implications of investments previously made whose value could become infertile as a consequence of the proposed deal. Although the axiom "all sunk costs are irrelevant" is widely accepted, the business developers on a negotiating team tend to be fervent in its acceptance because of their innate future orientation. Generally these people are hired—and make their reputations—on making something new happen. What is in the past is, for them, not their primary concern. Everyone brings his or her history to the present considerations, but on a deal team, there are often those primarily concerned about "retro-spective" impacts and those focused on "pro-spective" opportunity. (*Specio* is Latin for "to see" or "to know," and is the root of the word "science.") The "retro-spective" view is important for harmonizing the present deal in the context of previous decisions and present situation.

The absence of such harmonization can make dealmaking difficult. Two current examples of this situation have to do with corporate venture capital investments and corporate real estate holdings. In both cases, investments were made under late 1990s assumptions that are sadly out of harmony with early twenty-first century realities. The respective owners of such intellectual and real property assets are faced with holding onto them even when they are no longer part of their strategic plan or current requirements, or taking their lumps by selling for a present value far below their book value. Lucent, for example, is reported to have sold its Marlboro, Massachusetts, facility in 2002 for just $28 million, which is about half of its replacement cost and only about one-third of what it would have sold for at the most recent peak just three years earlier.[2] According to the cited *Wall Street Journal* article, Lucent was reportedly pleased with the outcome because the sale "reduced our overall cost structure and [made] the most efficient use of our capital." Although no doubt disappointed that their realization was below what recently could have been, changing the past is not an available option. Harmonizing the present perception of future opportunity with the past is always an available option. Such harmonization is sometimes a key dealmaking event.

A graphic illustrating these two axes is shown in Exhibit 2.1. Although the past, and the "retro-spective" view, is unchangeable, it can affect the present perception of a proposed deal. From the seller's perspective dealmaking may require several aspects of "retro-spective" reconciliation. One area of concern is how the selling price compares with existing numbers on the company's books. In many situations, the public books of a public company will be unaffected either because the subject deal value does not meet a test of materiality or because the selling asset had not been shown at any value. However, the books that are used to run the business and measure internal performance could reflect values that will need to be aligned in some way with the deal value. For instance, if the deal calls for a modest upfront payment and then progress, milestone, annual, or royalty payments in the future, the immediate financial realization on such operating books could be

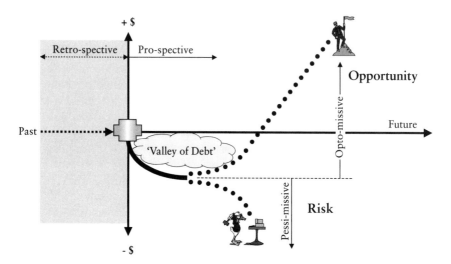

**EXHIBIT 2.1**    Two Axes of Dealmaking

significantly less than, say, research and development (R&D) or business de-velopment costs that have been collected in a project account or charged against the operating expenses of a business unit or division. Such an immedi-ate shortfall could affect year-end bonuses and other judgments management may reach about stewardship of company investment resources. If someone in the seller's organization fears taking a hit financially, or otherwise, because of the immediate impact of a transaction, that historical perspective will in-fluence negotiation planning and perhaps ultimate deal terms or even deal prospects. Another kind of "retro-spective" issue is the meaning ascribed to the sale itself. Does this event mean that some "we" failed in our commercial-ization efforts? Was our plan more ambitious than our delivery? Does this say anything about the fidelity, or reliability, of our previous promises and fore-casts? Might this transaction now call into question future revenue or earning projections of the selling company because they included significant contribu-tions from the now about-to-be-sold asset? Does this say anything to our in-ventors and business developers about our company's growth prospects, or confidence in its marketing skills or in its complementary technology, or in its liquidity? Does this sale mean certain careers are ending or being sidelined? So, despite the mantra of "sunk costs are irrelevant," if these costs, and plans, are associated with people, then these issues, and others, are likely matters that a deal manager must manage as part of the overall process, primarily by resort-ing to future total benefit being greater than doing no deal or a different deal.

Likewise the buyer may have important "retro-spective" issues. Does this purchase reflect a failure on the buyer's R&D team? If so, why is it spending so much on its R&D? Did the buyer miss the market opportunity and is it now paying a premium to cover its mistake? Given the checkered history of mergers, is the buyer paying for something that has a high probability of disappointment? Given the checkered business history of the period 2000 through 2002, does the buyer know what it is doing and is it paying a fair price? Is this transaction inconsistent with a strategic vision or business plan previously put forth to investors or employees or customers or suppliers? Will this be taken as a competitive threat to a key ally?

Looking toward the "pro-spective" future, there is often a negative return position for the buyer before there is the anticipated positive return; such negative return is shown by the area in Exhibit 2.1 annotated as "the valley of debt," as in "Though I walk in the valley of death . . . ," humorously adapted from the 23rd Psalm. The "pessi-missive" view tends to focus on those outcomes that never survive such "debt valley." The "opto-missive" view sees that wonderful, high-earning outcome when every variable breaks just in its favor.

The primary point here is that all four of these voices are normally present and their presence properly balanced makes for an effective dealmaking team. When any one perspective overwhelms an appropriate, balanced consideration for its opposite, then it is likely that the dealmaking team will have a distorted perspective on the opportunity, to its detriment.

## A QUEST

The concept behind and embodied within the word *quest* has a long and rich history in literature. In medieval times (ca. 1100 to 1400 A.D.), a special class of warriors known as knights would embark on missions known as quests. In a business context, the dealmaker is much like a knight. He or she is in a very real sense on a quest for an optimal commercial opportunity, either on the sell or buy side. The key elements faced by a person on a quest are:

- Uncertainty as to the exact final result sought
- General belief that that which is being sought will be recognized ("I'll know it when I see it")
- Singularity of purpose (the quest is always the magnet drawing one forward)
- Journey experience (the object of the quest is a pursuit, rather than just answering mail)
- Distractions (to the quest)
- Opposition/enemies (the quest will require a battle or a contest of some sort)

■  A charge (authorization) to perform that represents a duty for which one is accountable

There is a famous, largely legendary, story distinguishing two of our key concepts in the context of a quest. It is the story of Roland and Oliver, who were charged with defense of Charlemagne's southern flank. Because the story dates to circa 800 A.D., and despite recent copyright extensions by the U.S. Congress to accommodate various powerful suppliants, the copyright has expired and is, so far, freely available on the World Wide Web. In this story we see the mythos of two contrasting responses to the struggles and dangers of a quest. Roland in his brashness evidences (from the Latin) *fortitudo* (courage and determination in the face of adversaries), but not *sapienza* (wisdom). Oliver, Roland's right-hand man, and lifelong friend, in contrast, displays both *fortitudo* and *sapienza*. The story illustrates the catastrophe that results from *fortitudo* without *sapienza* as Roland, in ignoring Oliver's wise counsel, engages the enemy and, despite his courage and warfare skills, leads his side to utter defeat and his own death and the death of his partner, Oliver, and many others.

We are raised in a culture of thinking of the "right answer" and the "right way" to get there. College classes, after all, are filled with homework problems and examinations. They are graded in some form of right and wrong. Those who get a lot of "wrongs," do not generally make it through the education process. So we are engrained to pursue the "right" method to obtain the right answer. A quest has a different architecture. The problem is often quite ambiguous. Instead of it being neatly defined at the start, it is more of a "I'll know it when I see it" situation. Instead of the right method, there is the greater significance of the right character qualities in our pursuit and motives. The right answer becomes the outcome of discovering that problem, conquest, or challenge that the person charged with the quest was uniquely called to do, and accomplish by the best of his or her character and abilities.

In many business activities, especially of large bureaucratic companies, such sense of adventure and wonder has been extinguished in our longing for certainty or at least predictability. (In contrast, people who are drawn to entrepreneurship find its appeal because, in contrast to common business environments, every day can seem questlike.) In negotiations, here characterized as ¹Dealmaking, this questlike search for the to-be-discovered best opportunity is one of its key traits.

A final thought on the idea of a quest. There are two conflicting joys in life: successfully predicting how things will turn out and discovery of not previously known successes. Financial analysts, especially those with a strong accounting affection, and such feelings of attraction are possible, generally find more joy in the first situation, namely, accurately predicting how things will turn out. There is the delight of analysis, complete and accurate. For those with this bent, preparing for dealmaking is the enjoyable part; it is dealing with the messiness of human encounter and compromise that is tortuous and torturing. However, for those whose joy lies in discovery, the delight is the pursuit, and the sooner the better; for those with this bent, preparing is painful, but horsetrading, gamesmanship, and inventing new opportunities or new twists on existing opportunities is where the fun lies. Dealmaking is really about both these inclinations; it provides us a preparatory framework, but it is a framework that enables in-progress discovery and adaptation. So, for those more comfortable with predeterministic analysis, we seek to expand that perspective to include ways of enhancing or discovering opportunity stemming from the analysis, and for those more comfortable with the "I'll know it when I see it school," we seek to empower you with tools and methods that will enable you to pursue in a more directed way and to be able to make wiser choices in the heat of pursuit. And, on this point, our objective is, after all, a deal done as Aristotle noted:

"For dogs do not delight in the scent of hares, but in the eating of them, nor does the lion delight in the lowing of the ox, but in eating it." Book 3, Chapter 10.

## THE NUT, THE NUMBER, THE BOGIE, AND THE TOE TAG

There is an interesting term that is used in fields as diverse as theatrical productions and rental property management and it is "the Nut." The Nut, and one wonders of its origin, is the cash-inflow number that must occur to cover just the ongoing expenses of operation. A more elegant accounting term would be "break-even cash inflow," but the somberness of the Nut is useful to our discussion. Looming over the seller in many dealmaking experiences is this very Nut, namely, that monetary figure that must be recovered on the particular deal to clear the books, or to rescue some P&L situation within the seller's organization.

Sometimes this break-even cash inflow is known as the Bogie, which has never made sense to me. (Is it a stroke over par? Doesn't getting a Bogie, which supposedly is a good thing, mean that I'm still falling behind?)[3] Sometimes it is known as the "toe tag," meaning that you as the dealmaker will get that number or it will become your body's identifier.

Regardless of the term of art that is used, the dilemma of the must-have number is that it casts a shadow over value and deal options because of requirements, needs, or expectations external to the deal event or even to its intrinsic value. In a sense it is the global politic that, in certain circumstances, can override all other considerations.

Who owns the Nut? Sometimes it is the P&L manager who will be credited with the proceeds from the transaction. Sometimes it is the CFO, or even the CEO, who will absorb such proceeds and report an overall profit number to shareholders and investors. Sometimes it is the deal manager who, for some reason, needs, or feels the need, to create a career number. Sometimes it is just a number that has emerged out of an inventor's head as an appropriately spectacular signifier of his or her contributions. On the buy side, *the number,* as might be anticipated, is some extraordinarily low figure that reflects the great bargain expectations placed on the deal manager. In either situation, the power of the ¹Dealmaking methods and tools to be discussed is the ability to create a rational framework against which such external, and often unfounded, asserted values can be tested, contrasted, and corrected. There is an old joke about propaganda published by the former Soviet Union in its official newspaper *Pravda*: "Comrade, this latest material is so good we're believing it ourselves." The goal of the deal manager is to overcome these backdrop expectations that often are the metaphorical equivalent of propaganda by creating a business model that becomes defendable and ultimately believable by both sides of the negotiation.

## QUANTIFICATION, RATIONALITY, AND HYPERRATIONALITY

What are we to conclude from this discussion of the quest and the problem of the Nut? Can we, should we, just wander our landscapes and if it feels good do it? No, there is math and method. Implicit in the idea of math and method is rationality, namely, that the quantification that emerges from the mathematical and structural approaches described in this book guides one to the best choice in any given set of circumstances. Hyperrationality is sometimes used to characterize an analytical approach in which only factors that can be expressed numerically and processed mathematically are considered because nonmathematical matters are deemed unimportant or irrelevant. Underlying this pattern of reasoning is the search for certitude. Exhibit 2.2 depicts a graphic that illustrates "certainty world."

On the left side of this figure is shown the two conclusions that can be reached: (1) pursue the opportunity because it will be worth it or (2) avoid the opportunity because it will not be worth it. On the top of the figure are shown the two outcomes: (1) it turned out that the opportunity was worth pursuing or (2) the opportunity was not worth pursuing. In "certainty world," there is an absolute conformance between my a priori belief reached by a rational analysis and the ultimate outcome, namely, 100 percent of the time when I concluded the opportunity was worth it or it was not, it ultimately was so. Does certainty world exist? Yes. One domain is mathematics. We do

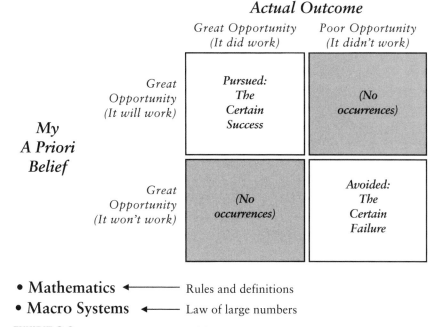

• **Mathematics** ←——— Rules and definitions
• **Macro Systems** ←——— Law of large numbers

**EXHIBIT 2.2**　How a Certainty World Looks and Works

not admit to the possibility that mathematical operations, say, adding up a column of numbers, performed at different times or by different individuals will reach different answers. Another certainty world, or at least nearly certain world, is a consequence of the law of large numbers. If we flip a coin once, there is only a 50 percent chance that any prediction will be correct. But if we flip it, say, a million times, then it is virtually certain that 50 percent of time it will be heads. Opportunity analysis in support of negotiation, alas, does fall in one of these domains though there can be individual circumstances that come close, especially ones that have very little opportunity to succeed such as, say, the invention for a nuclear-powered bicycle.

Exhibit 2.3 is "uncertainty world,"[4] in contrast to Exhibit 2.2. As before, the left side of the diagram shows the two a priori conclusions and the top side the two outcomes. In uncertainty world the a priori beliefs exhibit perfect randomness with respect to outcomes, in contrast to the perfect correlation evidenced in certainty world. There are domains that effectively exhibit such uncertainty. Coin flipping, as previously mentioned, just once bears no correlation between any method of analysis and ultimate result for single flips. The stock market, as an opportunity investment vehicle, approximates this uncertain world as well because the cost to exercise the opportunity has been

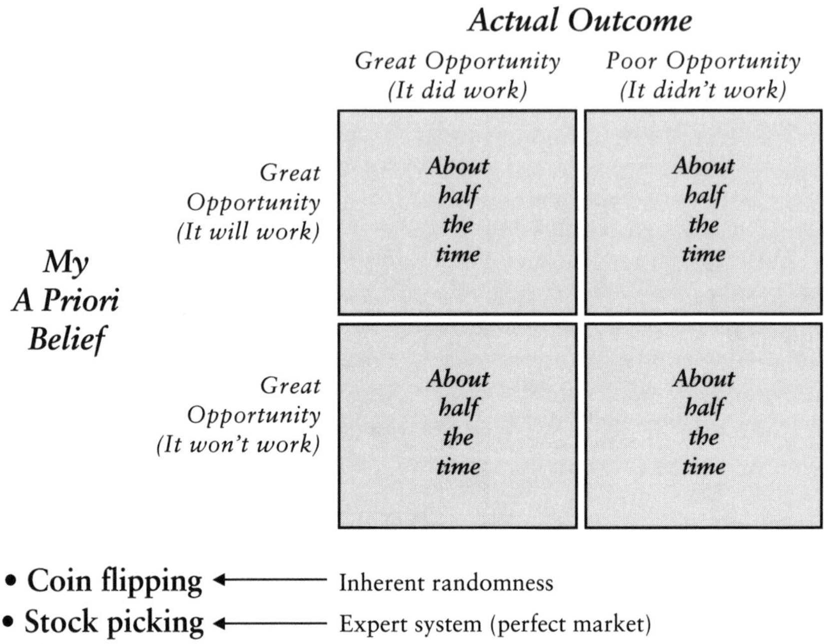

*Actual Outcome*

|  | *Great Opportunity*<br>*(It did work)* | *Poor Opportunity*<br>*(It didn't work)* |
|---|---|---|
| *Great*<br>*Opportunity*<br>*(It will work)* | *About half the time* | *About half the time* |
| *Great*<br>*Opportunity*<br>*(It won't work)* | *About half the time* | *About half the time* |

*My*
*A Priori*
*Belief*

- Coin flipping ⟵——— Inherent randomness
- Stock picking ⟵——— Expert system (perfect market)

**EXHIBIT 2.3**   How an Uncertainty World Looks and Works

determined by an expert system (the market) that, on average, works extremely well. So there may be individuals who claim they can "beat the market," meaning they can find by systematic means undervalued stocks and, thereby, experience greater than average market returns. Most such individuals are experiencing rolling "heads" 5 or 10 times in a row and concluding omniscience.[5]

Finally consider the situation depicted in Exhibit 2.4. Here is the broad condition intermediate between the extremes of certainty and complete uncertainty world. A priori convictions, done rationally and well, do have predictive value with actual outcomes, but not to the extent of certainty. Depending on the fact circumstances and the analytical tools and skill, such predictive power can be reasonably taken to be highly likely or marginally likely. As might be expected, it is this world that governs new technologies, new products, new markets, and dealmaking in general. This book expresses the conviction that the greater the power contained within predictive methods, together with the skillful use of tools and judgment, the more likely we are to be able to characterize the relative probabilities and the respective significance of the outcome for such probabilities and, thus, the better we will be able to plan, present, and negotiate opportunities, whether we are buying or selling.

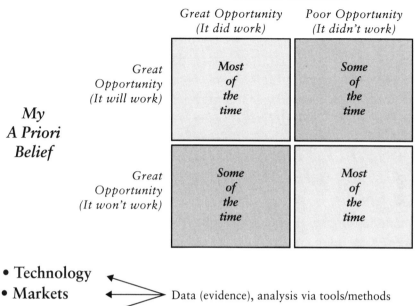

**EXHIBIT 2.4**   How a Probability World Looks and Works

Aristotle, as he addresses so many topics, does this one, too:

> It is the mark of an educated man to look for precision in each class of things just so far as the nature of the subject admits; it is evidently foolish to accept probability reasoning from a mathematician and to demand from a rhetorician scientific proofs.
>
> Book 1, Chapter 3, *Nicomachaen Ethics*

We return to this issue of certainty versus probability at the end of this book. In the meanwhile, let us note that not everything important can be quantified and multiplied, but in business that is where we start. Although our scope is not to create a devotional for deal managers, collected here are some thoughts, ranging from those of Cicero to Stengel, believed useful for reflection:

- They don't pay you to juggle just one ball (or one view, perspective, or voice).

- One of your principal jobs is the management of meaning.

- In any conflict situation it's hard to tell whether they're attacking you or helping you.[6]

- Bernard Baruch: "Only a mule and a milepost never change their mind."

- John D. Rockefeller: "The man who starts out with the idea of getting rich, won't succeed; you must have a larger ambition."

- "The tyrant is a child of Pride. Who drinks from his great sickening cup, recklessness and vanity, until from his high crest headlong he plummets to the dust of hope."

  *Oedipus Rex:* Sophocles

- Casey Stengel: "The secret of managing is to keep the guys who hate you away from the guys who are undecided."

- "The Six Mistakes of Man" according to Roman philosopher Markus Tullius Cicero (106–43 B.C.) writing more than 2,000 years ago in the closing years of the Roman Republic:

  1. "The delusion that personal gain is made by crushing others.

  2. The tendency to worry about things that cannot be changed or corrected [or that it has to be perfect].

  3. Insisting that a thing is impossible because you cannot accomplish it [by yourself].

  4. Refusing to set aside trivial differences [yes, even then].

  5. Neglecting development and refinement of the mind, and not acquiring the habit of reading and studying [learning new tools/methods, willingness to listen to the power of a better argument].

  6. Attempting to compel others to believe and live as we do [negotiating as bludgeoning into submission the other side, and dissent]."

## NOTES

1. It is appropriate to repeat a well-worn pith attributed to James Branch Cabell (1879–1958): "An optimist proclaims that we live in the best of all possible worlds; and a pessimist fears that this is true."

2. "Office Buildings Sell at Bargain Prices," *Wall Street Journal*, October 29, 2002, p. A2.

3. "Bogie" as used, likely derives from a military context in which it is used for the enemy targeted.

4. By "uncertainty" here is meant *complete* uncertainty. As is discussed in detail in this book, uncertainty is a common situation even in high probability circumstances.

5. Consider the following scam. Send 100 million people an e-mail, which regrettably is quite easy and cheap to do, and create 10 10-million-person groups and predict a high-volatility stock for each group for which you offer your insight that it will experience a significant rise in value over the next week. Say only 1 of your 10

predictions comes true. Then divide that group of 10 million into 10 groups of 1 million each and repeat the prediction with new stock selections. Again, assuming that just 1 of your second 10 predictions comes true, you have a population of a million people who are starting to think you are a genius. Keep the process going and you will likely have thousands of people who will believe you can really beat the market.

6. I am indebted to Bob Smith, head of HR for Battelle Memorial Institute, for the first three quotes.

# The Box and the Wheelbarrow: What Am I Selling (or Buying)?

In this chapter we discuss the important grounding subject of defining what is being sold and what is being paid. There is an old joke that describes the issue: A saleperson at the end of a particularly busy day proudly relates that "I made 10 sales calls today, and I could have made 15 but somebody asked me what I was selling."

Among the most important questions that can be asked is this: What am I selling (or if I am on the buy side: What am I buying)? This question may also be expressed as: What is the deal? It is surprising how often the answer to this question is not congruently and clearly understood even by either side of a negotiation. And it is common that misunderstandings between the two sides extend down to the core issues of what is for sale or what or how will consideration be provided for the sale.

No dealmaking process, ideal or not, can be rationally launched without a working definition of what is for sale and what the payment structure will be. These two sides of an agreement, one provided by the seller and one provided by the buyer, are here metaphorically termed the "box" and the "wheelbarrow."

## THE BOX

In merger and acquisition (M&A) dealmaking involving, for example, the entire assets of publicly traded companies, the box may be large, complicated, but innately clear: it's everything. In many other contexts, especially those involving substantially intangible assets, a more appropriate model is licensing. Although the size of the licensing box may be smaller than an M&A box, it is often subject to greater flexibility in the configuration and, thereby, its potential ambiguity. Accordingly, the context and examples given in this chapter derive primarily from license dealmaking involving real, intangible, and people assets.

The critical starting point of any valuation is defining exactly what is being offered for negotiation.[1] Yet, it is not uncommon that long into a marketing campaign, or deep into a negotiation, it becomes frustratingly obvious that the parties have not had a common or even similar idea of what is being offered. Here we wish to consider what a seller may offer and a buyer may seek in an agreement. In the next section we reverse the view and consider what a seller may expect and a buyer may offer in consideration for such agreement.

The box defines what is being offered by the seller as "the deal." It is the sell-side value. It is what the seller carries to prospective buyers in which he or she opens the box and extracts each deal element so the seller can grasp what is being offered and not offered. What might such a box contain? Clearly, we begin with the right to practice the technology or make the product(s) being offered. But even this simple idea contains two very important terms that must be defined: technology and right.

1. *Technology.* What exactly is the technology being transacted (sold or licensed)? Here, the world technology derives from the Greek word "techne" that means craft or skill, and is used broadly to refer to the know-how and skills that are needed to make the contents of the box work and create value. How does technology relate to any formal ownership rights, such as patents (if any), that might be in the box? For instance, does technology mean that the buyer can use the claims of the licensed patents, however it is able to do so, and only that? Or, is the scope of the technology only incompletely encompassed by the issued patents? What about pending patent applications whose ultimate claims are not known at the time of the negotiation? What about improvement inventions that might arise at the seller's research and development (R&D) labs or that the seller may acquire rights to in the future? What does improvement really mean in relation to the technology?

2. *Right.* This is another term capable of having a rich range of meanings. What is the uniqueness of the transacted right? Is it exclusive or an outright assignment? If so, what are the terms? Does it apply to all potential applications (fields of use)? All territories? For all time? Does exclusive preclude the seller's right to practice? Is the right to sublicense included in such an exclusive right? What about the right to assign?

It is common that sellers are willing to consider alternative boxes with respect to the technology and right issues. Two things are important about changing boxes: How does the change affect value? How does the change affect deal doability?

1. *Valuation.* Any change in the contents of the box should, in general, cause a change in the value of the rights offered to the box's contents. Accord-

ingly, without locking on a definition of the content of the box, it is not possible for valuation to take place by either the seller or buyer. One is tempted to conceive of creating an a la carte menu by which each element in the box is individually priced, such that any buyer can self-price the deal by the selections it makes, something like this: nonexclusive royalty is 2 percent; with exclusivity there is a 3 percent adder (5 percent total), the sublicensing right is 1 percent; 2 year's worth of improvements cost an additional 2 percent but 5 years of improvements are on special today for only 3 percent; and so forth (or the equivalent in present-value, lump-sum payments).

2. *Doability.* In negotiating situations, the number of possible elements is so large, and their value can so interact with the presence (or absence) of other elements, that to create such a valuation model would require an overwhelming level of analysis. Although such an approach works for restaurants and custom-built homes, the idea of a single box with a la carte pricing that incorporates all the possible deal variations is simply impractical for technology licensing.

Fortunately there are practical ways of considering box alternatives. The obvious solution is for the seller to prescribe only one box and value it accordingly—as Henry Ford said, you could have any color of a Model-T automobile, as long as it was black. Such a one-size-fits-all approach is likely to be rejected by potential buyers as including more than they want to pay for or less than they need. In many cases, a potential buyer will have very particular interests and values and will seek a licensing box unique to its business situation.

If an a la carte box cannot reasonably be valued, and a one-size-fits-all box has low or no deal doability, what is to be done? As a starting point for marketing and negotiations, the seller creates a baseline box of what he or she conceives is an appropriate configuration of its interests and its target buyers, but with an analysis of one or two alternatives to establish a range of values and an estimate of value sensitivity. Regardless of these choices and complications, the box must be defined before the valuation process can begin if its result is to have a rational basis.

So far, we have considered technology and rights as two elements of the box. What else is there? Well, the list is long indeed. Following are brief descriptions of additional possible elements that could be appropriate to and included in such a licensing box:

■ *Patents and other intellectual property (IP).* This element could include pending patent applications, formalized trade secrets, copyrighted content and software, and even trademarks.

■ *Proprietary technical information (PTI).* Although this element can be grouped under IP trade secrets, it is useful to consider the wealth of technical information that is typically created by a seller as being broader than the more restrictive legal term of trade secrets. Included in such PTI could be laboratory notebooks, unpublished white papers, project plans, management presentations, a selected compendium of published articles whose results are pertinent and valuable to the offered technology, assessments of competing technologies, market assessments including customer surveys or focus panel results, and the like.

■ *People.* There could be individuals employed by the seller who would be interested in joining the buyer and so continue to stay involved with the technology. The seller can agree to permit the buyer to recruit selected individuals and even provide inducements to key employees to go with the technology. As part of such transfer, the seller can provide the buyer, and the people transferring employment, the right to use all their "head IP" as it relates to the subject technology. Such seller commitments are subject, always, to the willingness of such people to become transferring employees of the buyer's company, but incentives can be committed to by either the seller or buyer or both.

■ *Hardware.* The technology can be expressed in a wide range of physical forms from special raw materials, to models, R&D prototypes, development breadboards, test samples, and so forth, all the way to saleable inventory.

■ *Facilities.* This element can range from the offerings of a complete operable production plant embodying the licensed technology or a factory that manufactures the licensed technology as a product, down to specialized facilities/infrastructure that can be removed, shipped, and reinstalled at the buyer's location. Alternatively, a lease arrangement could be used whereby the buyer would use the seller's facilities on a short-term or long-term basis.

■ *Software.* The seller could have software programs that model the performance of the technology and are useful in R&D or production design or production control.

■ *Customers.* Commercial accounts could be transferrable to a buyer. In other cases, there could be trials with potential customers or expressions of intent to buy that could be available.

■ *Suppliers.* The seller could have identified and even qualified certain vendors who can supply needed materials or services, with the attendant specifications. The seller itself could agree to be a supplier of a needed component (an element that could be a source of high deal value to the seller).

■ *External contracts.* There could be sources of funding, including R&D funding by third parties such as a government agency, that the buyer would then receive as part of the agreement. Likewise, commercial services that are currently provided by the seller could be transferred to the buyer.

- *External licenses.* The seller may have operating permits, government approvals, or other licenses to the subject technology collecting revenues that can be transferred. Alternatively, licensed rights to third party patents could be included here, or under "other IP" and could be an important source of deal value if the seller has the right to sublicense or assign.

- *Patent prosecution and maintenance.* If the patents are assigned (sold), then their prosecution and maintenance normally becomes the responsibility of the buyer. If the patents are only licensed, then the buyer or the seller could undertake the financial obligation, or it could be shared.

- *Infringement enforcement.* A common concern is what happens after the deal is done if a third party infringes or appears to infringe licensed claims? A seller-licensor could agree to enforce the licensed patents to ensure the buyer's exclusivity. If nonexclusive, the seller may accept the responsibility to take action against unlicensed third parties who compete with the buyer. In either case there may be some threshold of infringement before the seller would be obligated to take action.

- *Infringement defense.* A different infringement concern by the buyer has to do with the risk associated with its freedom to practice what it licensed from the seller. The seller could indemnify the buyer against claims by the third party against the buyer for a specific product.

- *R&D/consulting services.* The seller could provide R&D services (commonly termed *tech transfer assistance*) for a transition period or for an indefinite period. A prescribed level of such services could be included in the license or the commitment to provide such services under specified terms.

- *Regulatory support services.* There could be circumstances whereby the use of the technology will require some form of regulatory approval and the seller could be of assistance to the buyer in seeking or transferring such approval.

- *General representations and warranties.* It is, of course, common for the seller to warrant that it has the right to sell or license what it is offering to the buyer. But the seller could offer additional representations and warranties.

Although few agreements have all these elements, it is useful to both the seller and buyer to consider what can, should, and should not be included to maximize the relative value of the opportunity to both parties, particularly for technologies with significant commercial potential. It is especially useful for the seller to create a summary of what is in the box—or boxes, in the case of multiple scenarios. This practice allows all the affected individuals within the seller's organization to possess a common understanding of the dimensions of a potential deal. In any case, such a specification is necessary to create a baseline on which a valuation can take place. Further, it is also useful in communicating with potential buyers so that an early understanding can be reached, or the box appropriately adjusted, to accommodate the deal being envisioned.

These possible elements are not equally important, nor are they unrelated to each other. The IP is, for example, closely tied to both the technology and rights; it would not be uncommon that a license deal would have only these core elements in the box.

## THE WHEELBARROW

The previous section focuses on the value provided by the seller to the buyer, using the metaphor of the box, as the contents for the technology, the rights to use, and the related value-affecting aspects of an all-encompassing deal. Here, we consider how the buyer may provide value to the seller. As before, a metaphor is useful.

The wheelbarrow is used to characterize what the seller is offering, or envisioned to offer, as value in exchange for the contents of the box. It is the buy-side value or consideration. In some cases, such buy-side consideration is very simple: a one-time, lump-sum payment, cash, check, or wire transfer, for the box. In most cases, and the normative situation in iDealmaking, the wheelbarrow is much more complicated than that of a one-time payment.

One frequent measure of value of a license-based deal is the royalty rate, as in "this deal is for a 5 percent license." Actually, a royalty rate by itself is an incomplete description of value. The seller is rightfully concerned about the size of the check that it expects to receive, not the royalty rate used in calculating the amount owed under the license, regardless of the rate, and regardless of whether it is usage based, time based, or event based. To effectively capture the concern of the seller (and buyer), the term wheelbarrow has been used in reference to the buyer hauling cash to the seller in a wheelbarrow. Accordingly, while a royalty rate is a common negotiation point for those agreements in which both parties are motivated to pay over time in proportion to actual commercial use, both parties are ultimately concerned with the size of the wheelbarrow.

The seller provides a box of technology, rights, and other deal elements, whereas the buyer provides, in the form of one or many wheelbarrows, value payments to the seller. There are two common forms of value contained in such wheelbarrows: a single payment, such as "the buyer paid $10 million for the license," and a royalty rate.

1. *Lump-sum payment.* A single-payment license, commonly termed a *lump-sum* or *paid-up transaction*, is the simplest valuation structure. It represents a check, or more commonly a wire transfer, usually made simultaneously with executing the license. It represents the only payment that the buyer will make. However, even in this simplest of arrangements there may be other important forms of value provided by the buyer, such as granting the seller access to certain patents belonging to the buyer (cross licensing), a supply agreement whereby the buyer agrees to provide products made by the licensed technology, or even some other technology, under more favorable terms than are commercially available. Thus, even for such simple, single-payment licenses, the wheelbarrow may contain something notable beyond the closing payment.

2. *Royalty license.* A pure royalty-based license, also known as a *running royalty license*, is the inverse of the single-payment license: the single-payment license is a fixed sum paid upfront for unlimited (or in accordance with the terms of the license), subsequently free use, whereas the pure royalty license has only payments due on use (make, use, or sell) and only on such use. However, a critical factor in determining value is the royalty base against which such royalty rate is applied. A common negotiation involves a determination of the appropriate base. Consider the situation of a quick disconnect that is being licensed for use on the terminals of an automobile battery. The seller may argue that the appropriate royalty base is the selling price of the automobile because such terminals are, say, used only on batteries in automobiles. If the buyer is a battery maker, such an approach will be unacceptable regardless of how low the royalty rate is because the battery maker has no control, or even knowledge, of the selling price of the automobile with the battery in it. Further, the battery maker is likely to argue that the connector royalty should not be based on the selling price of the battery itself because the connector is only a small part of the battery and, in fact, does not contribute to the basic function of the battery. The buyer is likely to propose a royalty base on the selling (or fair market) price of the connector component itself. The negotiated royalty rate will be done in conjunction with the negotiation on the appropriate royalty base: A 1 percent royalty based on the selling price of the battery, for example, could alternatively be a 25 percent royalty based on the connector's cost or fair market value, and yield the same cash amount in the wheelbarrow.

In addition to these two common elements, following are eight other possible elements that can be used in any combination in the wheelbarrow to provide value to the seller:

1. *Upfront payment(s)*. A common value element is the use of one or multiple upfront or license fee cash payments. Upfront payments are unconditional and precede the anticipated commercial use by the buyer. One such payment is made on closing or within a specified number of days of closing (e.g., 30 days). Additional upfront payments could be made at specified dates, such as on the first and second anniversary of the license. In this case, the term *upfront* is used to specify payments that are committed at deal execution but may be deferred to specific dates after closing. As used here, such form of value is unconditional and additional. It is unconditional in the sense that regardless of the buyer's later decision not to use the licensed technology or even termination of the license, such payments are still due. It is additional in that other subsequent forms of value payments, such as royalties, are a separate contributor to the wheelbarrow of payment. One important negotiation issue is the ability of the buyer to credit such payments against future royalties owed; not surprisingly, sellers gravitate to no and buyers to yes. The reasonable answer lies in the calculation of the royalty: If the full value of the license has been ascribed to the royalties, and some of the running royalties have been moved to be fixed, upfront payments, then the answer should be yes because they are, in fact, prepayments. However, if the royalties were calculated to represent the license value remaining after the upfront payments, then the answer should be no.

2. *Annual payments*. Another form of fixed-cash payments is the use of annual payments payable on each anniversary of the license for as long as the license is in effect. Sometimes this form of payment is referred to as *license maintenance fees* or *minimum royalties* (or simply *minimums*). Normally the use of minimums is restricted to those periods when earned royalties can reasonably be expected and the magnitude of the minimums is scaled on some proportion of the magnitude of expected royalty payments, and such payments are commonly credited against earned royalties during that period (and such credits may or may not be applicable to subsequent periods).

3. *Milestone payments*. Such payments are specified amounts that become due on the crossing of some milestone event. In the area of pharmaceuticals, such milestones could be the entry into each phase of clinical testing, or any regulatory approval. Other kinds of milestones could be key R&D achievements, or the commitment to building a commercial plant of specified minimum size, or the first commercial sale. A special type

of milestone payment would be a payment due upon termination of the license.

4. *Option payments.* One form of option payment is an initial payment made by the buyer to allow it to conduct additional R&D, or market assessment or other feasibility activities, to enable it to make an informed licensing decision. Such a payment has the effect of compensating a seller for withholding the licensing opportunity from the market during the option period. Other types of option payments are possible. One example is the option to maintain exclusivity of the license beyond a certain date. Another example would be to acquire an additional field of use or territorial right. Yet other examples would be to acquire a companion technology, to buy out the license (a one-time payment to end all future royalties), and to make other payments to buy down the royalty rate (a payment that lowers the effective royalty for all subsequent sales). We will consider the use of option payments in detail in Chapter 6.

5. *Royalty payment adjustments.* Many creative adjustments have been used with a baseline royalty rate. A *wedding cake royalty* is one that decreases in rate with increasing sales, such as 5 percent on the first $5 million, 3 percent on the next $10 million, and 1 percent for all additional sales. Such sales could be annual—that is, with each anniversary the royalty again begins at 5 percent in this example—or cumulative (i.e., total sales since the onset of the license). Alternatively, an *escalating royalty* could be used in which the royalty rate actually increases with increasing sales, under the reasoning that higher sales would correspond to higher licensee profitability. This approach might also be used to restrict or control the output of the buyer's licensed goods. A *multimarket royalty* is another approach, in which different, specified royalties are used for individual products (fields of use) or territories.

   Yet another strategy calls for certain sales to be royalty free (possibly to aid market introduction or some other purpose). Sellers might seek to include in the same or an alternative royalty calculation something called *convoyed sales*, additional products or services that the licensee might anticipate selling as a result of selling the goods embodying the licensed technology.

   Similar to a milestone payment, a *kicker* is a royalty premium paid on the occurrence of some milestone. For example, the baseline royalty rate might be set at 5 percent, but if the performance of the technology exceeds some specified level, there is a 2 percent kicker, making the royalty paid actually 7 percent. Of course, the opposite could be negotiated by the buyer, such that there is a 3 percent "deflator," making the royalty paid 2 percent if the technology meets only some lower standard. Other adjustments in royalty rate could be based on market share, payments made to third parties for the right to practice, patents needed to practice the licensed technology, step-downs in rate if the licensee elects to convert its license from exclusive to nonexclusive or if certain (but not all) patents expire, the making public of licensed trade secrets, the passage of a specified period of time, or even the profitability of the relevant product line or company (though such a provision can be perilous to the seller because of accounting complexities). Another complex royalty adjustment can exist with respect to the royalty base itself. In some licensing situations, the sales made by a certain buyer of a technology might be primarily as a result of one or more patents in the box.

Alternatively, such patents could be relatively minor contributors to a later sale by that same buyer. The parties could deal with this situation by adjusting the royalty base and possibly the rate itself to deal with each of these possible future situations. A final example is that of *sublicensing royalties*. The royalty amounts paid to the seller under the buyer's sublicenses could be different from that which would have been paid by the buyer for its own making/using/selling. This could be done by apportioning the gross amount of such sublicensing revenues between the buyer and seller.

6. *IP rights.* A *grant-back* is one type of IP right in which the buyer can provide rights to its own improvements to the subject technology to the seller, either for the seller's own internal use or to enable the seller to offer additional technology to its other technology licensees. Another example of IP rights provided by the buyer would be rights to patents or other forms of IP owned by the buyer but unrelated to the subject technology; such an arrangement is commonly termed a *cross license*. Another form of this type of value would be an agreement to provide the seller with a product that it, in turn, could sell based on the subject technology, or even some unrelated technology. Publicity by the buyer of the seller's role as a technology provider could create value to the seller in the form of goodwill and market recognition.

7. *Commitment to purchase goods/services.* The buyer could agree to purchase goods made by the seller at terms that are commercially favorable to the seller in a so-called supply agreement. Another example would be the buyer's commitment to purchase professional services, such as R&D in the area of the licensed technology or some other area; such an arrangement is common when the seller is a university and the buyer is a large company. Depending on the terms of these types of commitments, it could be value neutral to the parties, a value provided by the buyer, or even a value provided by the seller.

8. *Equity.* The provision of a share of ownership in the buyer can create a source of considerable value, or even the total value in lieu of any cash

payments, royalty, or any other form of value in consideration for a license. Another variation is that the seller has an option to purchase a specified number of shares at a prescribed price per share by a prescribed date, or similarly the right to convert fixed or royalty payments into equity. Another form of equity value could be provided by the buyer by its infusing capital into the seller in exchange for shares in the seller's company. Such a cash infusion could provide the seller with a strategic advantage with respect to other fund-raising activities. Based on the circumstances, such a transaction could be value neutral, or value favoring the seller, or value favoring the buyer.

Although these eight elements do not exhaust the possibilities, they do reflect the commonly used means of creating a wheelbarrow of value to the seller in the domain of technology licensing. As with the box, it is unlikely that there are many agreements that include all possible elements, but the flexibility afforded by the inclusion of an element and its specific implementation can be important in reaching an agreement. Agreements with only unconditional payments, such as paid-up licenses, or licenses with only fixed periodic or event-driven payments, may have higher valuation risks because the certitude of such payments in the face of an uncertain commercial future. Generally, though, these agreements result in a simpler document, both in construction and in implementation. Conversely, agreements whose value is primarily dependent on conditional elements (e.g., royalties) may have less valuation risk but higher complexity in document construction and ultimate implementation. In general, for less important and less valuable technologies, the parties tend to gravitate to simpler wheelbarrows (and boxes). However, as current trends continue into the twenty-first century, technology owners will increasingly recognize their fiduciary responsibility to maximize their return on assets, and as time to market urgency increases, sellers will be more inclined to license out even their crown jewels for appropriately large wheelbarrows. Likewise, we can expect all buyers to consider quite literally the world of technology in-licensing of boxes based on externally created technologies for the prospect that they can become strategic new businesses and, thereby, warrant highly crafted license-in arrangements.

## ᶦDEALMAKING'S SPINE

In movie making there is a term of art known as the movie's *spine*. The idea is this: Each movie needs a spine, or general axis, that holds the 120-minute experience together so that we can grasp the story as some coherent whole. The absence of a spine can create hilarity in comedy sketches as we try to follow illogical, even incomprehensible disjunctures of thought that spin one onto another expressly for the purpose of winding us around life's experience without trying to lead to one coherent whole. There are also plays in the postmodern genre that intentionally present stories without a spine because they are trying to reflect the postmodern view of lack of meaning. Perhaps the most famous of such plays is *Waiting for Godot* by Samuel Beckett (1906–1989) in which the avowed purpose of the play, Godot's appearance, not only never occurs but one is left wondering whether it was ever really envisioned or even whether Godot exists.[2]

The spine of a deal is the connecting framework of the seller, the buyer, the box, and the wheelbarrow in one comprehensible story. A primary "spinal" tool is the term sheet.

## THE TERM SHEET

The *term sheet*, sometimes known as "heads of agreement," is a short writing that codifies the box and the wheelbarrow to enable an initial test of serious intent and common understanding between the parties.

As discussed earlier, dealmaking involves the business process of determining a provisional value of the box; a strategy for monetizing, or value-realizing, such box value; marketing and initial discussions; negotiation; and deal commitment. A term sheet together with the specification of the box and wheelbarrow is the glue that holds these processes together. It is also the vehicle by which the processes interrelate. As the market responds that it finds incomplete, or overladen, the proposed box, the seller may revise its strategy, its box, or its valuation. As prospective buyers propose different structures for payment (wheelbarrows), the seller may re-vision the box or the strategy. All of these factors may lead to new marketing candidates for a dealmaking discussion. These interrelationships are shown in Exhibit 3.1.

## METHODS AND TOOLS

In subsequent chapters, we develop analytical methods that enable us to conduct ¹Dealmaking. The two principle methods are Monte Carlo and Real Options. The term *method* is meant to convey an analytical process within some computational construct. This construct is expressed in a financial model by a spreadsheet, such as Microsoft's Excel and with separate software tools such Crystal Ball (a Monte Carlo software product by Decisioneering, Inc.) and Real Options Analysis Toolkit (a Real Options software product also by Decisioneering, Inc.).

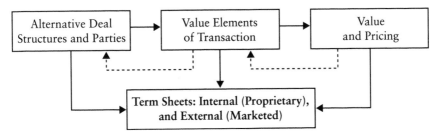

**EXHIBIT 3.1** The Interrelationships of Valuation, Marketing, Negotiations, and the Term Sheets

In addition to such overarching methods, we consider a variety of tools that assist our analysis. One such tool is a way of using "risk-adjusted hurdle rates" to discount future cash flows. Another tool we consider and use with the Monte Carlo method is a so-called tornado diagram that provides a way of discerning the more important assumptions.

## NOTES

1. The text in this discussion of the box and wheelbarrow has been adapted from Richard Razgaitis, "Technology Valuation," in *Licensing in the 21st Century*, (New York: John Wiley & Sons, 2002), Chapter 2.
2. "Nothing happens, nobody comes, nobody goes, it's awful." The character Estragon from Act 1. Godot, no doubt, represents God in this classic of postmodernist religious skepticism. It is a play without plot, or character, or dialogue coherence. It is the object of the box and wheelbarrow to do everything possible to have negotiation plot, character, and dialogue that is both purposeful and coherent.

# CHAPTER 4

# Discounted Cash Flow Analysis and Introduction to Monte Carlo Modeling

In this chapter we first review traditional methods of discounted cash flow (DCF) analysis for the purpose of establishing a common framework for financial modeling and understanding the strengths and limitations of this important method. Then we introduce Monte Carlo modeling, which begins with a DCF analysis but, as will be seen, greatly extends our ability to forecast the effects of uncertainty. In Chapter 5 we develop a comprehensive approach to Monte Carlo modeling in the context of preparing for and in the midst of negotiations. Then, in Chapter 6, we return to this DCF method to introduce the method of Real Options.

## DISCOUNTED CASH FLOW ANALYSIS

DCF analysis is the most basic tool in financial forecasting of business opportunities. To illustrate DCF analysis and as a further framework of later work, we use the following simple financial model.

A new product is to be introduced a year from now with an initial revenue forecast of $10 million, with a projected year-over-year (i.e., *compound*) growth rate in such revenue of 15 percent. Compound annual growth rate is usually abbreviated CAGR. The costs associated with making and selling the product (direct) and an allocation for general overhead (indirect) costs are projected to be as listed in Exhibit 4.1, namely, 80 percent of projected revenues beginning in Year 2 as shown by C/R = 80 percent, where C/R is cost-to-revenue ratio. Subtracting all such direct and indirect costs leads to a value commonly termed EBIT, for earnings before interest and taxes. In Exhibit 4.1 and throughout this book, C-EBIT is used to designate cumulative-EBIT. (At this point, for simplicity of illustration, we will assume such EBIT and C-EBIT is the same as net cash inflow to the enterprise; later we will identify the common adjustments made to EBIT to determine true cash flow.)

**EXHIBIT 4.1**    Five-Year DCF Example

| | Start | Year 1 | 2 | 3 | 4 | 5 | Total |
|---|---|---|---|---|---|---|---|
| **Revenues** *CAGR = 15%* | | $0.00 | <u>$10.00</u> | $11.50 | $13.23 | $15.21 | $49.93 |
| **Costs**      *C/R = 80%* | | <u>$8.00</u> | $8.00 | $9.20 | $10.58 | $12.17 | $47.95 |
| **EBIT** | | –$8.00 | $2.00 | $2.30 | $2.65 | $3.04 | $1.99 |
| **C-EBIT** | | –$8.00 | –$6.00 | –$3.70 | –$1.06 | $1.99 | |
| **C-EBIT/R** | | –100.0% | –75.0% | –46.3% | –13.2% | 24.8% | + |

Also listed in Exhibit 4.1 are two values that are underlined: $8 million in Year 1 and $10 million in Year 2. These values are underlined to identify them as specific assumptions rather than calculated values based on, for instance, the assumed CAGR. The $8 million is the cost of completing the development of the product, readying it for manufacture, and general product launch; when such costs precede the revenues anticipated from the sale of product, they are usually termed *investments*. The italics used for CAGR and C/R designate these as assumed (or input) values that are used in calculating the various cell values in the spreadsheet.

The customary big picture question is simply: Is this investment depicted in Exhibit 4.1 worth making? In other words, based on these forecasts we will after 5 years earn $1.99, say, $2, in excess of our Year 1 investment of $8. Is a return on investment of approximately 25 percent (from the ratio $1.99/ $8.00) a smart thing to do? Put in the context of a deal, would a buyer be wise to pay a seller $8 for the right to pursue the opportunity projected in Years 2 through 5 and netting, if such forecast is realized, $2 beyond the $8 paid for the opportunity?

In DCF analysis the customary measure used to answer such a question is by the analysis of the projected returns (EBITs) *discounted* to account for the effects of the cost of capital, the risk associated with the potential project, and the availability of alternative investments and returns. The basic valuation equation for performing such *discounting* arises as follows. We use $A$ to designate the value of an asset now, namely, the time of project start. $B$ is used to designate the value of a projected cash flow where $B1$ is for the cash value at the end of Year 1, $B2$ for Year 2, and so forth. The projected future value of such an investment $A$ is characterized by a rate of growth (or return) designated by $k$, such that:

$$B1 = A + k \times A = A \times (1 + k) \tag{4.1}$$

which simply says that the effect of Year 1 should be to experience an increase in value above $A$ by an amount proportional to $A$ with such proportionality reflected by $k$. For this reason in simple savings situations $k$ is designated as the *interest rate*.

The effect of Year 2 should further grow, or compound, the projected value of $B1$ by another year's interest, as follows:

$$B2 = B1 \times k \times B1 = B1 \times (1 + k) = A \times (1 + k)^2 \qquad (4.2)$$

where the factor $(1 + k)$ occurs twice, once for each of the two years.

So, in general, we have the following expression:

$$Bn = A \times (1 + k)^n \qquad (4.3)$$

where $A$ is the value of the cash asset at the *start* of the project, namely, the beginning of Year 1, and is known as the *present value*, and $Bn$ is the projected value at the *end* of Year $n$, and where $k$ is the annual compounding rate.

Solving this equation for $A$ yields the following essential equation:

$$A = Bn / (1 + k)^n \qquad (4.4)$$

In a DCF analysis this important equation is expressed in words as follows: The present value $(A)$ of any future lump-sum cash inflow $(Bn)$ is the absolute magnitude of such projected cash flow at the end of Year $n$ $(Bn)$ divided by the discounting factor $(1 + k)^n$, where $k$ is more commonly termed the *discount rate* because it has the effect of discounting (reducing) such future projected cash inflow to a smaller present value.

In business valuations, one does not normally experience cash inflows on discrete dates, let alone on the 12-month anniversary of the start of a project. Rather, they are expected to occur throughout each year. The way this situation is commonly handled in DCF analysis is to use what is known as the mid-year convention, namely: We assume that the effect of continuous cash inflow throughout any given Year $n$ can be approximated by assuming all the cash flows for such year to occur at midyear (July 1st) of Year $n$; this is the equivalent of replacing the value of $n$ in the exponent with $(2 \times n - 1)/2$, so if $n = 5$, such a midyear correction results in an exponent value of 4.5, which means that we discount Year 5 cash flows from a point 4.5 years from the start instead of 5.0 years.[1]

Using the midyear convention for Equation 4.4, yields:

$$A = Bn / (1 + k)^{((2n - 1)/2)} \qquad (4.5)$$

Equation 4.5 is used throughout this book to discount to present value future cash flows that are expected to occur throughout a Year $n$. When used in this way, $k$ can be more accurately characterized as the risk-adjusted hurdle rate, or RAHR. This designation reflects the role that $k$ plays in the previous equations. Recall that $Bn$ is a projected future cash inflow, and $A$ is the *present value* of all the future values of $Bn$ based on our projection of all the perceived risks and uncertainties associated with the projected value of $Bn$. So such value of $k$ is a risk-adjusted rate. Why "hurdle"? This term conveys the idea of a threshold value that must be reached in order for the projected investment to make sense, as is made clear later.

Using the above Equation 4.5 with the example expressed in Exhibit 4.1 is shown in Exhibit 4.2. This table shows how Equation 4.5 is used in this way to discount each year's cash flow, outflow in Year 1, and inflows in Years 2 through 5 in the four DCF rows corresponding to the respective RAHRs. The term *net present value* (NPV) is used when we are computing the net effect of projected cash outflows and inflows; if we are considering only cash inflows, we use the designation PV for present value of the sum of such inflows. Recall that $A$ was used for the present value of $Bn$, where $n$ designated any future year or time; so the PV of a sum of inflows is simply the sum of the values of $A$ for each individual $B$.

Discount calculations are listed in Exhibit 4.2 for four different values of RAHR: 0 percent, 5 percent, 10 percent, and 8.83 percent. As the value of RAHR increases, it has the effect of decreasing the PV of any given projected future cash inflow. This result makes sense because the use of a higher value of RAHR corresponds to a perceived higher risk that such inflow will be

**EXHIBIT 4.2**  Five-Year DCF Example Incorporating Various Values of RAHR

|  |  | Start | Year | | | | | Total |
|  |  |  | 1 | 2 | 3 | 4 | 5 |  |
|---|---|---|---|---|---|---|---|---|
| Revenues *CAGR = 15%* |  |  | $0.00 | $10.00 | $11.50 | $13.23 | $15.21 | $49.93 |
| Costs *C/R = 80%* |  |  | $8.00 | $8.00 | $9.20 | $10.58 | $12.17 | $47.95 |
| EBIT |  |  | −$8.00 | $2.00 | $2.30 | $2.65 | $3.04 | $1.99 |
|  |  | NPV |  |  |  |  |  |  |
| DCF | *RAHR = 0.00%* | $1.99 | −$8.00 | $2.00 | $2.30 | $2.65 | $3.04 |  |
|  | *RAHR = 5.00%* | $0.76 | −$7.81 | $1.86 | $2.04 | $2.23 | $2.44 |  |
|  | *RAHR = 10.00%* | −$0.21 | −$7.63 | $1.73 | $1.81 | $1.89 | $1.98 |  |
|  | *RAHR = 8.83%* | $0.00 | −$7.67 | $1.76 | $1.86 | $1.97 | $2.08 |  |

realized. The calculation for an RAHR of 0 percent shows that Exhibit 4.1 was just a special case of Exhibit 4.2.

The sum of the five DCF values corresponding to Years 1 through 5 is shown in the column headed NPV. Because each project year's DCF is expressed in terms of present value, they can all be simply summed as they are expressed on the same basis (namely, for the time of the project start date).

For a $k$ (or RAHR) value of 5 percent, these calculations show a positive NPV of $0.76. Using such DCF analysis, the interpretation given to this value is as follows: If the appropriate risk-adjusted hurdle rate is 5 percent, then this project, as now projected, has a net positive value and so should be undertaken because it is expected to return cash flows that exceed the hurdle value of 5 percent. So if, for example, one has access to capital at a cost of 4 percent (the required rate of return to investors providing such capital), and one concludes that the appropriate RAHR for the subject opportunity is 5 percent, then one should invest in the project because, on average, such an investment should exceed the estimated RAHR and provide a one percentage point (one "point") return above one's investment capital costs. In fact, one should be trying to find as many such projects as possible so long as the investment capital at less than 5 percent is available and projects exist with a positive NPV with an appropriately scaled RAHR of 5 percent.

However, for an RAHR of 10 percent, Exhibit 4.2 shows a negative NPV of −$0.21. This result simply means that this project as forecast will not meet a return rate of 10 percent and if this is the appropriate hurdle, then it should not be undertaken.

The final example in Exhibit 4.2 shows the RAHR value corresponding to an NPV of exactly zero, namely 8.83 percent,[2] which is the threshold value of RAHR for which the project transforms from worth doing to not worth doing, always under the assumptions that the RAHR is the appropriate value considering all the risks and investment capital is available at less than such RAHR. This scenario is sometimes known as "living on the spread," meaning one invests out capital expecting a rate of return (RAHR) that exceeds one's cost of capital. Banks that pay 2 percent for demand deposits and charge 6 percent for housing loans live on the spread of four points.

Later, in Chapter 4, we consider how one might determine an appropriate value of RAHR.

So in DCF analysis, the basic tool for determining the worth of a project is developing projections of all the cash outflows and inflows, year by year for the duration of the project, and discounting each such cash flow by Equation 4.5 using an appropriate value of RAHR. If the sum of all the year-by-year DCF values is then positive, the project should be done, and the value of the NPV can be thought of as *excess value* because it is the PV above the hurdle amount established by such RAHR.

## SCENARIO (DCF) ANALYSIS

When considering the future, as discussed earlier in this book, one is confronted with many possible circumstances that can affect every element of a projection. With DCF analysis one is forced to make discrete, single-valued assumptions for each such valuation element or factor in order for the calculation to proceed. Such discretization takes place in three general ways.

One way is simply by the assumed specific value of revenue, or cost, that is ascribed to any given year. Considering again Exhibit 4.2, in Year 5 we projected revenues of $15.21 and costs of $12.17. These discrete values are projected from a range of possibilities that could occur. For instance, considering just the revenue value, we assumed a starting value of $10.00 for Year 2, growing at a compound rate (CAGR) of 15 percent; these two values prescribe the value of $15.21 for Year 5 by simple mathematics. However, if the first revenues in Year 2 were only $9.00, with the same CAGR, the projection for Year 5 is then $13.69. Alternatively, if the CAGR had been assumed as 17.5 percent starting with $10.00 for Year 2, the Year 5 projected revenue would be $16.22. It is also possible that the year of product introduction could slip so that the $10 is achieved in Year 3 not Year 2; this would result in a Year 5 projected revenue of $13.23. Instead of using the previous starting revenue plus CAGR approach, one could simply make year-by-year projections of expected revenue say: $10, $11.5, $13.0, and $14.5, for Years 2 through 5, respectively. This direct approach can be done, for instance, by projecting the increase in sales associated with getting another customer account, or by the expected increased revenues associated with an additional sales person to be added in each year, or by making the product available with another feature set, or some other means. For instance, it can be assumed that each customer buys $0.5 in a year. So in the first year of sales, it is assumed that we will have 20 such customers yielding a revenue of $10. Then in Year 3, we are in effect projecting that we sustain a net increase of three customers in each subsequent year causing year-over-year increases in revenue of $1.5, resulting in $14.5 for Year 5. But, it may be very reasonable to assume that we can grow at five net customers a year, so in Year 5 we will have a projected revenue of $20.0. So just by the preceding analysis, we could select a Year 5 revenue of:

- $15.21 ($10 starting in Year 2, CAGR of 15 percent)
- $13.69 ($9 in Year 2, CAGR of 15 percent)
- $16.22 ($10 in Year 2, CAGR of 17.5 percent)
- $13.23 ($10 in Year 3, CAGR of 15 percent)
- $14.50 ($10 in Year 2, with three net additional customers per year at $0.5 each)

- $20.00 ($10 in Year 2, with five net additional customers per year at $0.5 each)

So the $15.21 value that was originally used for the Year 5 revenue in Exhibit 4.2 is a selected value from a range of possible choices based on different perspectives of what might happen in the future. Each cell value has this same feature, namely, from the universe of possible values that could occur a single-value selection has been made that represents "best thinking" usually expressed as representing "expected value."

A second way discretization when DCF analysis is used is through the use of different RAHR values such as shown in Exhibit 4.2 for 5 percent, 10 percent, and 8.83 percent. The idea here is to portray the sensitivity of a project go/no–go decision with respect to the underlying RAHR value. The Exhibit 4.2 analysis shows that for an RAHR of 5 percent the project is worth doing because the resulting NPV is positive. However, the NPV goes negative for any value of RAHR greater than 8.83 percent, so there is only a 2.83 point margin above 5 percent by which the project exhibits a positive NPV. It is easily possible with DCF analysis to include such consideration of different values of RAHR applied to a given projection of cash inflows and outflows just to illustrate the effect of different hurdle rates associated with different risk perceptions.

The third way of disecretization with DCF analysis is through the use of scenarios. A scenario is a self-consistent, conceived future outcome. For instance, we could envision a polymer technology acquisition (or license) that could have important commercial applications in (1) medical disposables, (2) machinery housings, and (3) structural brackets. Further, we could believe that such applications could use our sales channel based in North America (A) but with strong representation in Western Europe (B), and the Far East (C). This viewpoint is illustrated in Exhibit 4.3 as a matrix of nine cells, where each of the three territories, shown in the columns, will exhibit sales from product categories shown in each of the three rows.

Scenario analysis makes discrete classifications of the wide range of future possible business outcomes. In this example, we could envision a polymer

|  | (A) North America | (B) Western Europe | (C) Far East |
|---|---|---|---|
| (1) Medical Disposables |  |  |  |
| (2) Machinery Housings |  |  |  |
| (3) Structural Brackets |  |  |  |

**EXHIBIT 4.3** Scenario Analysis of Three Applications in Three Markets

technology that, if successfully developed, will meet new levels of impermeability, high-temperature resistance, and strength, at costs equal to the present, poorer-performing polymers. Further, our analysis of certain market
needs focuses on its potential application for medical disposables (benefited by improved impermeability and high-temperature resistance), machinery housings (benefited by high-temperature resistance and strength),
and structural brackets (benefited by higher strength properties). With these
optimistic assumptions we can create a coherent, high-outcome scenario
that projects that the polymer technology will be successful in all three
markets and in all three territories (assuming, for instance, that environmental restrictions or other local governmental requirements do not inhibit
the application of the technology for any of these products in any of the
territorial segments). Once this high-outcome scenario has been defined,
together with all the underlying assumptions and supporting data justifying such assumptions, then a projection can be created for each of the nine
cells in Exhibit 4.3 and the DCF analysis can proceed as before. It may be
possible to aggregate all the revenues and costs for all three applications
and territories so that a single DCF analysis can be done. If the cost ratios
vary from application to application, or territory to territory, or the growth
in revenues likewise depends on the specifics associated with a particular
cell in Exhibit 4.3, then one needs to perform a separate DCF calculation
for each such distinct situation and then add them together. The most complex situation would be if a separate DCF analysis were required for each
of the nine cells.

Next, we can consider a much more conservative perspective of the range
of applications of the polymer technology. For instance, we could observe that
the key breakthrough we have demonstrated and characterized is the property
of chemical impermeability and, although higher-temperature operation
and higher strength appears to be also realizable, there are some additional
challenges to be overcome. Further, it is noted that there are competitive alternatives emerging that could provide comparable temperature and strength
performance. These clouds on the horizon cause us to believe that there is a
real possibility that the only product application that we will achieve market
success with is medical disposables. Finally, based on previous experience we
may conclude that the ability to penetrate medical markets in the Far East is
unlikely to bear fruit. We call this set of cautious beliefs the low-Outcome
scenario. Here we might just use the previously developed calculations unchanged, but taking only the values for cells 1-A and 1-B (medical in North
America and Western Europe).

As you can expect, there is usually a middle level set of assumptions, often
called the base scenario. This scenario is generally considered to be the most-
likely outcome. In some cases it is determined by a corporate protocol for

being somewhat conservative so there is a reasonable likelihood that what occurs exceeds such base prediction; people do not like to be disappointed.

Depending on the specific situation, one can create any number of such scenarios. Two is the minimum, and three is common, but four or five would not be unreasonable. The basis for choosing the number is driven by the number of distinct, rational possible future outcomes that can be characterized and analyzed by generally self-consistent assumptions, and the justified level of effort given the magnitude of the opportunity.

Once all such scenarios are defined and modeled, the next step involves assigning relative probabilities. This step is sometimes called creating a "decision tree," but it is more accurately the construction of a "probability tree." Suppose that our analysis of each of the scenarios based on Exhibit 4.3 leads to the following NPV: high (optimistic scenario) $600, base $200, and low (conservative scenario) $75. We now need to exercise a further judgment as to the relative probabilities of each of these scenarios. For a three-scenario approach such as this one, the base is typically taken as being the most-likely outcome with an overall probability of at least 50 percent. This high weighting of the base condition is the valuation equivalent of the philosophical tenet of "the privilege of the normal case."[3] Assuming an equal probability for the high and low (which is a common framework), then our assumption is 25 percent probability of the high scenario, 50 percent base, and 25 percent low. Often the base scenario is constructed to have a higher than 50 percent probability. So we can consider the following scenario constructs distinguished by the relative weighting attached to the base scenario:

- 2x Base: (2:1 to either high or low): 25 percent high, 50 percent base, 25 percent low
- 3x Base: 20 percent high, 60 percent base, 20 percent low
- 4x Base: 16.7 percent high, 66.7 percent base, 16.7 percent low
- 6x Base: 12.5 percent high, 75 percent base, 12.5 percent low
- 8x Base: 10 percent high, 80 percent base, 10 percent low

Exhibit 4.4 illustrates the relative weighting of the three scenarios for each of the previous base weightings (2x to 8x), where the general relationship is given by the following equation:

$$\text{Base } (\%) = 100/((2/\text{BW}) + 1) \tag{4.6}$$

where BW is the base weighting. Clearly using a base weighting of 8x, which can be conceived of as an example of the "80:20 Rule," assumes low probabilities for the high and low scenarios (i.e., 10 percent each) compared to a 3x base weighting (20 percent each). Choosing the appropriate base

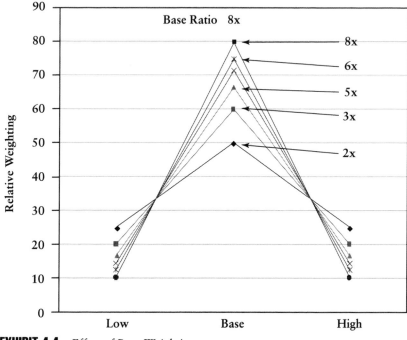

**EXHIBIT 4.4**    Effect of Base Weighting

weighting is dependent on the nature of the assumptions on which the high and low scenarios were calculated. We return to this point later.

Assuming that our three-scenario example was constructed such that a 3x base weighting is appropriate, we can use our previously assumed NPV values as shown in Exhibit 4.5 to calculate a probable overall NPV. Such probability trees have a great appeal in financial analysis partly because of their simplicity and graphical clarity, but also because they can weight the outcome in accordance with the character of assumptions that were made in creating particularly the high and low scenarios. As shown, with the assumed outcome probabilities in accordance with 3x base weighting, namely, a 60 percent probability for the base scenario, and 20 percent for each of the high and low scenarios, the predicted NPV for the opportunity is $255. Such 3x selection makes sense only in the context of the specific assumptions made for each of the three scenarios. If, after further analysis, or even simply reflection, we conclude that the probabilities associated with the high and low scenarios are substantially less than the 20 percent level associated with the 3x base weighting, and, say, more appropriate to a 10 percent probability as given with an 8x base weighting, we can readily adjust our calculation for expected NPV as follows:

NPV = $600 × 0.1 + $200 × 0.8 + $75 × 0.1 = $227.5

which is about 11 percent less than the $255 calculation of Exhibit 4.5.

Alternatively, we may consciously create a high scenario that is much more optimistic in any or all of its underlying assumptions than was used here resulting in, say, a high scenario NPV of $1,200 (instead of $600). However, our probability weighting for such amplified high scenario should now be decreased from 20 percent to some lower value, reflecting the reduced likelihood that this outcome will occur. So, earlier when we asserted that if we had the power to restart the universe so we could repeat our business opportunity from start to finish 1,000 times, 200 of those times we would have experienced the $600 outcome, 600 times the $200 outcome, and 200 times the $75 outcome. Now we have to conclude that the revised high scenario will occur much less frequently than 200 times. Let us assume that its probability of occurrence is reduced by the exact proportion of its increased projected value over the previous high scenario, namely: If there was a 200 times out of 1,000 probability for a $600 outcome, a $1,200 outcome would occur 200 × 600/1,200 = 100 times out of 1,000 (namely, only 10 percent of the time). Now, we have to reallocate the remaining 900 times between the base and low scenarios. Since these are in the ratio of 3:1 (600 to 200), for 900 times of outcomes then apportions 675 for the base and 225 for the low.

**EXHIBIT 4.5**   Illustration of a Scenario Probability Tree Used with DCF Analysis

| Scenario | NPV | Probability | Value |
|---|---|---|---|
| High | $600 | 20% | $120 |
| Base | $200 | 60% | $120 |
| Low | $75 | 20% | $15 |
|  |  | 100% | $255 |

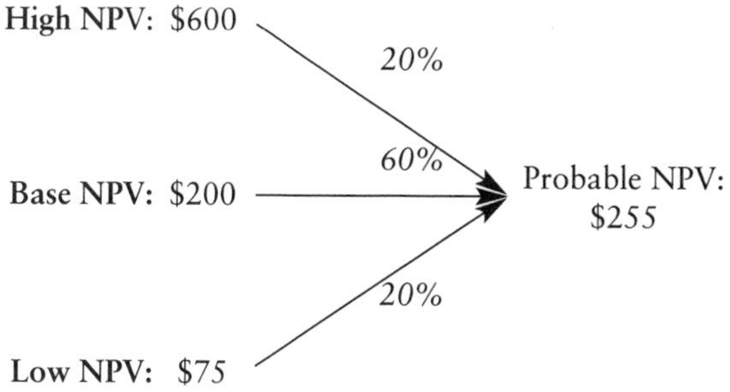

High NPV: $600

20%

60%  →  Probable NPV: $255

Base NPV: $200

20%

Low NPV:  $75

Using these values to calculate the predicted overall NPV we get:

- High-scenario probability contribution = $1,200 × 0.10 = $120
- Base-scenario probability contribution = $200 × 0.675 = $135
- Low-scenario probability contribution = $75 × 0.225 = $17
- TOTAL = $272, which is larger by about 7 percent than the $255 value we previously calculated.

So, is this outcome a good thing? Is this right? One possibility is that we have simply been inconsistent in how we have assigned our probabilities. If we assume that the initial calculation resulting in the $255 value is correct, then our revised high-scenario probability must be adjusted as summarized in Exhibit 4.6. As shown, the revised probabilities corresponding to the same predicted outcome are: 8 percent, 68 percent, and 23 percent. This result is most easily found by using the Goal Seek function in the Excel spreadsheet.

What this means is that if we believe the original probability estimate was sound, then the appropriate probability for such revised high scenario must be only 8 percent. However, if we had no basis for assuming the original calculation of $255 was correct, and we have some basis for assuming that the revised high scenario is appropriately weighted by a 10 percent probability, then one is led to the conclusion that the original estimate of the overall NPV was too low at $255, and should have been $272. Accordingly, we could justify recomputing a higher probability for the high scenario in that former case ($600) to adjust the outcome to correspond to $272.

**EXHIBIT 4.6**   Relative Probabilities Corresponding to $255 Expected Value

| Scenario | NPV | Probability | Value |
|----------|-----|-------------|-------|
| High | $1,200 | 8% | $101 |
| Base | $200 | 68% | $137 |
| Low | $75 | 23% | $17 |
|  |  | 100% | $255 |

High NPV:   $600
8%
Base NPV:   $200
68%
Probable NPV: $255
23%
Low NPV:   $75

In the same way, one can continue to construct other, alternative scenario high/base/low triads (or "tercets," drawing on an analogy of a poetic idea expressed by three-line, or three-thought, stanzas) and computing the NPV from each such combination based on the assumed probabilities associated with the nature of the underlying assumptions of each of the scenarios. Then, by comparing the predicted overall NPV values for such tercet, one can reach judgments as to the reasonableness of the scenario assumptions and respective probabilities. This often leads to an iterative process that may revise some of the assumptions underlying one (or more) of the outcomes of tercet-assumed scenario, and/or adding a fourth possibility to the scenario (making it a quatrain, a stanza of poetry comprised of four lines/thoughts).

The number of possible outcomes one could consider is almost unbounded. For instance, one could subsegment each of the three territories into individual countries, or further into states or counties or zip codes or individual blocks or individual points of sale (such as companies expected to be customers of the product or service). A workbook template can be created using separate worksheets for the calculation of each individual component of the analysis. Continuing with our example, one worksheet could reflect the analysis of the medical disposables in North America, looking at as many individual cells as reasonable judgments can be made. For each subset of product and territory, one would again make estimates of the high, medium, and low outcome over the product life, for a tercet analysis. Then by using the base-weighting formula, or individual weightings of the high and low scenarios in case one desires unequal weightings, an NPV value can be determined for the entire worksheet. Finally, all the worksheets can be aggregated onto a summary worksheet together with all the key assumptions.

When a scenario analysis is extended to such fine-scale detail it is often called a "bottom-up" analysis, to distinguish it from the "top-down" approach of just considering a few, macro level categories using more global assumptions. Such a bottom-up analysis can be illuminating because it leads to a consideration of the perceived value to each selling opportunity and the alignment with marketing and sales activities that will ultimately be necessary to realize the projected NPV. Even when the investment is made in a bottom-up analysis, it is usually useful to perform an independently developed top-down analysis to serve as a reasonableness check, particularly if one has data of other product introductions into such broad market categories.

However, the overall difficulty with this scenario approach may be that it is so ungrounded in reasonable estimates of the respective outcome probabilities in forecasting each of the scenario probabilities that one can produce a mountain of possible answers without a rational means of sorting through or weighing them to ascribe an overall opportunity value that can be persuasive to one's own organization, let alone to the other side of a negotiation. If there is commercial experience available to guide the framework of the calculation so, say, there is a way of defining a set of assumptions that, based on prior experience, is achieved a certain percentage of the time for each scenario in the tercet, then one can identify a calculation such as a particular, best-suited base weighting that should be the best reflection of the expected value. However, in many cases the subject opportunity and business environment are not reliably comparable to an available data set. This can lead to the temptation to tweak the assumptions and/or weightings so the projected NPV conforms to the a priori belief (apriorism), or hope. We deal with this temptation later in the book.

In all the previous scenario analysis examples, we have omitted the method of calculating the NPV values. As discussed earlier in this chapter, the NPV is determined by summing all the DCF values, each determined by discounting the estimated gross, future cash flow by the appropriate discount rate (RAHR) and timing. In scenario analysis, how should the RAHR be established? Recall that in traditional DCF analysis the value of the RAHR is, by its very definition, risk adjusted based on the specific opportunity being considered. In scenario analysis, we are performing such risk adjustment by the use of relative probabilities. Accordingly, the DCF calculation should use a smaller discounting than given by RAHR. One possible discount rate is the marginal cost of capital that will be required to enable the investment in the opportunity. This discount rate assumes that all other calls on corporate capital have been fixed and are immutable. Only this project, our project, is under consideration. If the decision is made to go forward based on this analysis, the investment capital will have to be secured. For large companies, such capital call can be considered as a claim on an already obtainable pool of investment resources available through debt, equity, and retained earnings. The cost of such available capital is a well-established benchmark for each company and is known as the weighted average cost of capital (WACC). For a large investment (relative to a company's existing capital resources), it may be appropriate to consider a project capital call as drawing on some existing company line of credit, or requiring a loan, or even the securing of additional equity investment such as by the sale of treasury stock. Such a discount rate can be called a marginal hurdle rate (MHR), namely, a hurdle rate based solely on the company's marginal cost of capital. Most commonly, the baseline hurdle rate would be the company's WACC. Using the WACC rate treats the investment decision in the subject opportunity as though all the capital of the company has been secured, resides internally in some accessible account, and this project, like any other, can draw on the account under the average terms of the corporation. Such discount rate is termed the WHR for WACC Hurdle Rate. The WHR, or MHR, is established by the market, based on a perception of value of risk above a risk-free standard rate, usually taken to be the available return on the 10-year U.S. treasury bond, which over recent years has fluctuated over the past 10 years between 4 and 8 percent (in Q4 of

1994). The market-required rate of return on corporate debt exceeds such 10-year treasury bonds by the amount the market expresses as its appropriate compensation for its risk. For a corporate bond category known as "Moody's Baa,"[4] the August 1, 2002 rate was 7.58 percent, reflecting a risk premium of 3.32 points above the then current 10-year treasury. The risk premium associated with equity is higher than with debt because of the increased risk associated with a lower likelihood of recovery in the event of bankruptcy. Estimates of the equity risk premium have aroused recent controversy because of the general higher price-earnings (P/E) ratios of public companies and the high volatility in share prices. Various measures of such premium based on the historic difference in equity returns compared to treasury bills over the past 75 years result in estimates of 4 to 8 points.

A third hurdle rate is a standard established by the company conducting the valuation and is used as a baseline for evaluating projects or opportunities requiring investment. This hurdle rate is normally based on the company's WACC plus an increment, such as five points, to provide a safety margin because a company not able to provide returns in excess of its WACC is initiating a death spiral; such incremented WACC rate can be designated CHR for company hurdle rate. Exhibit 4.7 illustrates how, for example, the NPV value of $200 used as the base value in Exhibit 4.5 could have been calculated based on a hurdle rate using the company's WACC (namely, WHR for 15 percent).[5] This example also shows how a more-typical 10-year projection can be used together with an estimate of terminal value at the 10th year, assuming, as it does, that the project is likely to have commercial value beyond the projection period.

All three of these hurdle rates (WHR, MHR, and CHR) are based on an opportunity and risk profile typical of the company as a whole. Each investment opportunity, however, has its own perceived upside opportunity and downside risk that may differ substantially from the company-average values and that can be estimated by the previously described use of an RAHR. One of the primary attractions of scenario analysis is the separation of the risk factor from the rental rate of money factor, namely the effect of the difference between RAHR and WHR. As shown in Exhibit 4.5, the assumed 60 percent probability of the base value of $200 results in a risk adjusted NPV of $120. In Exhibit 4.7, the final NPV tabulated, $120, was assumed and used to determine the corresponding RAHR resulting in the shown value of 16.28 percent. So, had we analyzed this opportunity using the conventional DCF method with a RAHR, only a relatively low value (16.28 percent) would have led us to the conclusion of an NPV of $120. This result is because, inherent to the use of a RAHR approach, *every* year is discounted by the same value. For projects with a long duration, such as 10 years, or shorter projects with substantial cash inflow toward the end-of-the-period, the RAHR approach combining the effects of risk of return and rental of money tends to under

**EXHIBIT 4.7** Illustration of $200 NPV Base Value Using 10-Year (Plus Terminal Value) Projections Discounted at Various Rates

| | Start | _____ Year _____ | | | | | | | | | | Terminal Value | Total |
|---|---|---|---|---|---|---|---|---|---|---|---|---|---|
| | | 1 | 2 | 3 | 4 | 5 | 6 | 7 | 8 | 9 | 10 | | |
| **Revenues** CAGR = 8.0% | | $0.00 | $25.00 | $125.00 | $200.00 | $216.00 | $233.28 | $251.94 | $272.10 | $293.87 | $317.37 | $952.12 | $2,886.69 |
| **Costs** C/R = 82% | | $65.00 | $20.50 | $102.50 | $164.00 | $177.12 | $191.29 | $206.59 | $223.12 | $240.97 | $260.25 | $780.74 | $2,432.08 |
| **EBIT** | | –$65.00 | $4.50 | $22.50 | $36.00 | $38.88 | $41.99 | $45.35 | $48.98 | $52.90 | $57.13 | $171.38 | $454.60 |
| **DCF** | NPV | | | | | | | | | | | | |
| *Discount Rates* | | | | | | | | | | | | | |
| MHR 12.50% | $163 | –$61.28 | $3.77 | $16.76 | $23.84 | $22.88 | $21.97 | $21.09 | $20.25 | $19.44 | $18.66 | $55.98 | |
| WHR 10.00% | $200 | –$61.98 | $3.90 | $17.73 | $25.79 | $25.32 | $24.86 | $24.41 | $23.96 | $23.53 | $23.10 | $69.30 | |
| CHR 15.00% | $133 | –$60.61 | $3.65 | $15.86 | $22.07 | $20.73 | $19.47 | $18.28 | $17.17 | $16.12 | $15.14 | $45.43 | |
| RAHR 16.28% | $120 | –$60.28 | $3.59 | $15.43 | $21.23 | $19.72 | $18.31 | $17.01 | $15.80 | $14.67 | $13.63 | $40.88 | |

*Notes:* Terminal Value is assumed to equal three times the Year 10 value, discounted to the midpoint of the 10th year. MHR is the hurdle rate at the marginal cost of capital. WHR is the hurdle rate based on the company's weighted average cost of capital (WACC). CHR is the company's designated hurdle rate, normally set based on its WACC; in this example, five points above WHR was chosen. The RAHR value shown is derived from the chosen NPV value of $120. Underlined values are discrete assumptions; italicized values are assumed inputs that calculated corresponding projected values.

predict NPV as might be estimated by the use of a probability tree. Exhibit 4.8 depicts the RAHR value corresponding to various NPV values determined by multiplying the base NPV value ($200) by the respective probability.

Two lines are shown in Exhibit 4.8. The straight line labeled Probability Applied to Base NPV = $200 is simply the probability percentage that is used to multiply the calculated base NPV determined in Exhibit 4.7 for WHR of 10 percent; so, a 50 percent probability corresponds to $100, and so forth. The other line labeled RAHR Corresponding to NPV Probability plots the calculated value of NPV using RAHR that corresponds to the NPV probability value; so, the 50 percent probability NPV ($100) corresponds to an RAHR calculation using 18.5 percent, or 8.5 points above the base WHR value of 10 percent, and the 5 percent probability (NPV $10) corresponds to an RAHR of 37.8 percent (27.8 points above the WHR), and so forth. Thus, using values of RAHR in the range of 30 percent to 35 percent, which are not uncommon for high-risk project investments, corresponds to a probability of success of approximately 10 percent, which is a relatively low likelihood event. Although the specific values given in this example are restricted to the financial model of Exhibit 4.7, they are illustrative of the important effect that high values of RAHR have when applied to typical financial assessments extending out to more than about 5 years.

Exhibit 4.9 depicts a general relationship between present value of $100 projected to be received in any future year for a range of RAHR rates from 10 to 50 percent. On a semilog graph, the shown relationships are approximately

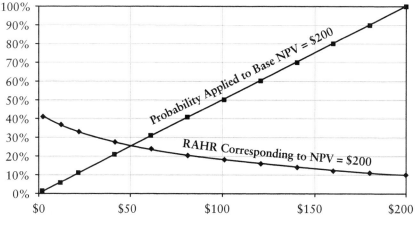

**NPV as Determined by Probability**

**EXHIBIT 4.8**   RAHR Corresponding to Scenario Probability NPV Values

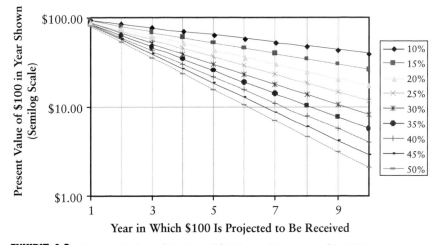

**EXHIBIT 4.9** Present Value of Projected $100 as a Function of RAHR

straight lines. As can be seen, discount values such as 10 percent to 15 percent, for short periods, such as 3 to 5 years, have only modest discounting effect on a projected cash flow, from approximately 20 percent discounting of NPV value using a 10 percent discount rate and 3 years, to 50 percent discounting in NPV at a 15 percent discount rate and 5 years. For situations more typical of company investments, the expected horizon is likely to be 10 years or more of important cash flows and an appropriate project RAHR could be 20 percent or more. For a 10-year horizon, at an RAHR of 20 percent to 50 percent causes discounting of 10th year cash flows of approximately 80 percent to 98 percent. So, even a massive, projected year cash inflow in the 10th year would have small or even negligible present value at high RAHR values. Such severe discounting of distant (even substantial) cash flows is one of the limitations of the RAHR approach and one of the attractions of the scenario method using probabilities applied to NPV calculations and models based on WHR, MHR, or CHR, as appropriate.

The difficulty, however, as discussed earlier, is establishing probabilities for each scenario that can be estimated on a rational basis. Although the RAHR method has its own difficulties in determining an appropriate value for RAHR, there exists substantial experience with the method and ranges of RAHR values for various perceived risk categories. Exhibit 4.10 shows various values of RAHR for different categories of projects.[6]

In summary, although application of DCF methods is powerful and useful even with the limitations associated with long durations and high RAHR values, it can be combined with a scenario analysis to address different possible outcomes and overcome the risk-adjusted heavy discounting of future,

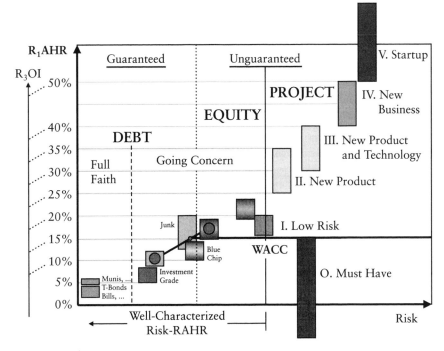

**EXHIBIT 4.10** RAHR Versus Risk: Types and Values

risky cash flows. However, the calculations quickly get complex and are subject to difficulties of deciding what relative probabilities to ascribe to each set of scenario assumptions. Although the amazing power afforded by spreadsheets such as Excel can easily support essentially any level of analysis to which one is inclined to subject oneself, what happens is the results are obscured by the complexity and very little insight is available to negotiation planning and decision making. Further, self-, or other, delusion is all too easy with these methods because significant changes in estimated value can be made by small changes in RAHR or scenario probability.

Making financial complexity easier to both analyze and grasp is exactly what the Monte Carlo method addresses, which is our next subject.

Before considering how Monte Carlo and other Real Options afford a new way of looking at value and risk and, thereby, dealmaking negotiations, let us think first about how we organize our perceptions. It is in our nature to adopt frameworks by which we make more comprehensible (to us) what is too complex to be easily characterized. Since antiquity, the night's stars have been organized into constellations such as Orion the Hunter or the Big Dipper. But there are no constellations or groupings up there because the stars in

Orion and the Big Dipper are not proximate or related to one another[7]; the constellations exist only in our minds but nonetheless govern how we see things. In an analogous way, using any method by which we grasp how something prospective, complex, and uncertain may be valued and negotiated both illumes and constricts our perceptions. The motivation for considering Monte Carlo (and Real Options) is that they provide an alternative perspective on value and, more importantly, as we shall see, a means of portraying a deeper insight into the substance of what's being valued. These other methods are still representational tools; but as we will see provide a new perspective, and in many cases, a better perspective both in terms of the quality of understanding and as a tool for negotiations.

## MONTE CARLO METHOD: AN INTRODUCTION

One powerful analytical tool that emerged from science and engineering analysis is commonly known as Monte Carlo. Its traditional uses have been in domains for which the algebraic complexities are effectively unsolvable. In business applications, the complexity is usually not the algebra but the otherwise incomprehensible spectrum of possible future outcomes as they affect a present decision. Monte Carlo does not produce a single-valued answer. As we have seen earlier with the DCF/NPV method, once a set of assumptions is imposed, a single-value answer results. However, what happens in practice is an extensive investigation of "what if's" that look at the effect of certain assumptions, the creation of alternative scenarios, the sensitivity of alternative discount rates, or other changing factors. So, in practice, the DCF/NPV rarely is used solely for a single-valued answer. In a somewhat similar, but more powerful, way, the result from a Monte Carlo analysis is a distribution of the present value of many possible future outcomes. By analyzing such distributions one can reach judgments as to the present value of the overall opportunity even though one does not, and generally cannot, know which outcome will occur. So the uncertainty we observed in the previously considered DCF/NPV method concerning future outcomes does not get solved by the use of Monte Carlo. Rather, Monte Carlo provides a more powerful means of characterizing such possible future outcomes and interpreting the present value of all such possible outcomes.

    The essence of the method can be illustrated in Exhibit 4.11 by returning to the initial example we considered in the DCF analysis in Exhibit 4.2. There are four, single-valued projected values that define this spreadsheet, namely, the investment required in Year 1 ($8), the magnitude of sales in Year 2 ($10), and the CAGR (15 percent) and C/R (80 percent) factors applied against all the respective cell values. In addition, there are two data values that have been assumed: That the investment required is completed in Year 1, and

**EXHIBIT 4.11** DCF Example of Exhibit 4.2 Illustrating Effect of Uncertainty in Assumed Uniform Distribution CAGR

| | | | | Year | | | | |
|---|---|---|---|---|---|---|---|---|
| | Start | 1 | 2 | 3 | 4 | 5 | Total |
| Revenues *CAGR = 15%* | | $0.00 | <u>$10.00</u> | $11.50 | $13.23 | $15.21 | $49.93 |
| Costs     *C/R  = 80%* | | <u>$8.00</u> | $8.00 | $9.20 | $10.58 | $12.17 | $47.95 |
| EBIT | | –$8.00 | $2.00 | $2.30 | $2.65 | $3.04 | $1.99 |
| | NPV | | | | | | |
| DCF     *RAHR = 5.00%* | $0.76 | –$7.81 | $1.86 | $2.04 | $2.23 | $2.44 | |
| Revenues *CAGR = 10%* | | $0.00 | <u>$10.00</u> | $11.00 | $12.10 | $13.31 | $46.41 |
| Costs     *C/R  = 80%* | | <u>$8.00</u> | $8.00 | $8.80 | $9.68 | $10.65 | $45.13 |
| EBIT | | –$8.00 | $2.00 | $2.20 | $2.42 | $2.66 | $1.28 |
| | NPV | | | | | | |
| DCF     *RAHR = 5.00%* | $0.18 | –$7.81 | $1.86 | $1.95 | $2.04 | $2.14 | |
| Revenues *CAGR = 20%* | | $0.00 | <u>$10.00</u> | $12.00 | $14.40 | $17.28 | $53.68 |
| Costs     *C/R  = 80%* | | <u>$8.00</u> | $8.00 | $9.60 | 11.52 | $13.82 | $50.94 |
| EBIT | | –$8.00 | $2.00 | $2.40 | $2.88 | $3.46 | $2.74 |
| | NPV | | | | | | |
| DCF     *RAHR = 5.00%* | $1.38 | –$7.81 | $1.86 | $2.12 | $2.43 | $2.77 | |

that sales begin in Year 2. In DCF analysis using the power and flexibility of spreadsheets, we can change each of these values to our heart's delight. The four numerical values can be changed simply, the two dates require restructuring the spreadsheet, all of which can be done for the scenario analysis described earlier. But Monte Carlo gives us a powerful alternative. We can prescribe a function (i.e., a recipe) for any of these values and the software will show us the statistical effect on DCF and NPV.

This use of a recipe instead of a single value can best be understood by example. Let us consider first how we might obtain a better understanding of the impact of the CAGR assumption. Instead of just assuming a single value of 15 percent, let us assume that such 15 percent value was a midpoint of our reasoned belief that the actual value would be between 10 percent and 20 percent. In other words, we think it is equally probable that the CAGR will have any value between 10 percent and 20 percent. Such a prescription is known as a uniform distribution, because we are saying there is a uniform (equal) probability of any value between 10 percent and 20 percent; such a prescription reflects a low level of confidence as to the future value of CAGR, because apart from the boundaries of 10 percent and 20 percent, namely, the CAGR cannot (in our reasoned judgment) be less than 10 percent nor more than 20 percent, we are not able to be more specific as to what we think the most-likely value will be.

One brute force method of doing this would be to consider a range of CAGR values in Exhibit 4.11 and to compute the NPV for each. We can create our own Monte Carlo analysis by using our DCF spreadsheet by making multiple iterations for the value used in the CAGR cell. By our assumed uniform distribution, we know that we need to repeat the NPV calculation using successive assumptions of CAGR that approximate the uniform distribution we have assumed. Suppose we start with one NPV calculation at the lower end of our range, namely, CAGR = 10 percent.

We shall for a moment consider only a RAHR of 5 percent as shown. We can see that for CAGR of 10 percent, the predicted NPV is $0.18, compared to the $0.76 we obtained for a CAGR of 20 percent in Exhibit 4.11, the direction of the result makes sense because a lower CAGR should correspond to a less favorable business outcome and value. Now, if we calculate the NPV using a CAGR at the upper end of our range (e.g., 20 percent), we see in Exhibit 4.11, that the result is $1.38. So using the minimum, maximum, and midpoint of our CAGR distribution, we have: $0.18, $1.38, and $0.76. Since we are assuming a uniform CAGR distribution between the bounds of 10 percent and 20 percent, we could just take the average of these three values as a first approximation, namely: $0.7715, which is not quite the same as the NPV of $0.76 corresponding to the midpoint (15 percent) of our CAGR range because the model, typical of such models, is nonlinear. We could improve our characterization by repeating the calculation at CAGRs of 11 percent, 12 percent, and so forth.

Using the three (or more) calculated values of NPV, we can use the Trend function in Excel to develop a least-squares fit to these calculations as shown in Exhibit 4.12.

Monte Carlo software can automate this process for us and produce a much fuller representation of the effect of CAGR uncertainty on NPV distributions. Throughout this book I use the Monte Carlo software product Crystal Ball® by Decisioneering.[8] What such Monte Carlo software can do is to define this CAGR Excel cell as an assumption cell and then load in the assumed uniform distribution for CAGR between the chosen range of 10 percent and 20 percent. The software then performs the earlier-described parallel-universe calculation: The first time it calculates the DCF and NPV values it looks to this CAGR cell and conducts a table lookup using the recipe that the value must be equally probable between 10 percent and 20 percent, selects one value that meets this criterion, uses that value, and calculates all the DCFs and the NPV. Then, it creates a second parallel universe, by assuming that we could rerun our business opportunity and so it goes back to the CAGR cell and conducts a second table lookup but does so cognizant of the uniform probability recipe such

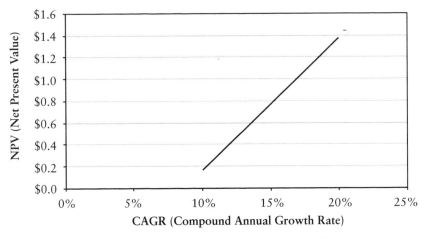

*Note:* Relationship calculated using the TREND function based on
   the calculations of Exhibit 4.11.

**EXHIBIT 4.12**   Least Squares Relationship Between CAGR and NPV

that when this is repeated many times, say 1,000, it will in fact exhibit a uniform distribution of CAGR values between 10 percent and 20 percent, as shown in Exhibit 4.13, which comes from a screen shot in Crystal Ball.

In Exhibit 4.13 and this immediate discussion, we are using 0 percent in contrast to a value of 5 percent used in Exhibit 4.12 because we will highlight the effect of risk by the use of a Monte Carlo determined probability. Now the Monte Carlo software automates the application of the earlier assumed variable and calculates the corresponding NPV value. Exhibit 4.14 depicts the first three iterations calculated in Crystal Ball. As can be seen, the Monte Carlo software in this case selected for the first iteration a value of CAGR equal to 13.5 percent. This selection was random between the chosen bounds of 10 percent and 20 percent. For this value, the software found the NPV to be $1.78. This result can be thought of as a present view of one possible future universe where the actual CAGR for the future project turned out to be 13.5 percent for the 5-year period modeled, with the result of a positive NPV of $1.78. However, given our assumption that the CAGR could be anywhere between 10 percent and 20 percent, this initial solution is just one possible future universe.

In the second iteration, the software again selects a value in accordance with the assumed distribution. In this case, the selected value was 18.5 percent, again a random value (because the assumed distribution is uniform), between the bounds of 10 percent and 20 percent. In the third iteration, a CAGR of 10.8 percent was selected.

The software repeats this process until some termination condition is reached, usually specified as a total number of trials (parallel universes). Generally, 500 such trials are adequate, although as we shall see in Chapter 5 the

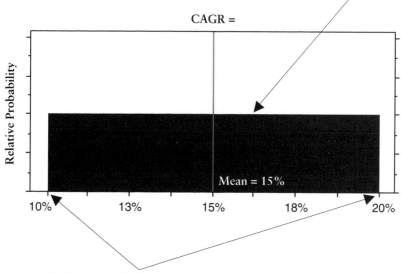

**EXHIBIT 4.13**   Assumed CAGR Uniform Distribution

results are more smoothly determined by using a higher number such as 1,000 or even 5,000. Given the amazing processing speed of modern PCs, and assuming one has not created an inordinately complex financial model, the computational time difference between 500 and 5,000 iterations is inconsequential so there is no reason not to use the larger number of iterations. It is a good practice to perform the first several iterations one at a time so that you can see how the assumed values are being determined, entered into the appropriate cells, and the results (typically NPV) calculated. Once you are assured that the model is working properly at least at the single iteration level, then the remainder of the iterations are completed and the results viewed and interpreted.

The results of the Monte Carlo financial model of Exhibit 4.14 are shown in Exhibit 4.15. This exhibit shows 3 Monte Carlo results of the model Exhibit 4.13 and Exhibit 4.14. In the top two graphs are shown the frequency distributions (charts) of NPV for 1,000 and 5,000 iterations. The X axis gives the NPV result for each of the iterations (trials); for this example, the Crystal Ball software has suggested the range of NPV values will be substantially encompassed by the values $1.28 and $2.73 and by $1.28 and $2.74 for the respective charts. In the upper right of each graph are shown the number of trials that resulted in NPV values outside the proposed range; for this example there are not such outliers, though later we show examples where outliers do occur. Because these two top graphs differ only by the number of iterations,

**EXHIBIT 4.14**   First Three Interations in Monte Carlo for the Distribution of Exhibit 4.12

| Initial Universe (Run #1) | | Year | | | | | |
|---|---|---|---|---|---|---|---|
| | Start | 1 | 2 | 3 | 4 | 5 | Total |
| Revenues *CAGR = 13.5%* | | $0.00 | $10.00 | $11.35 | $12.89 | $14.64 | $48.88 |
| Costs *C/R = 80%* | | $8.00 | $8.00 | $9.08 | $10.31 | $11.71 | $47.11 |
| EBIT | | −$8.00 | $2.00 | $2.27 | $2.58 | $2.93 | $1.78 |
| NPV | $1.78 | | | | | | |

| Next Universe (Run #2) | | Year | | | | | |
|---|---|---|---|---|---|---|---|
| | Start | 1 | 2 | 3 | 4 | 5 | Total |
| Revenues *CAGR = 18.5%* | | $0.00 | $10.00 | $11.85 | $14.03 | $16.63 | $52.51 |
| Costs *C/R = 80%* | | $8.00 | $8.00 | $9.48 | $11.23 | $13.30 | $50.01 |
| EBIT | | −$8.00 | $2.00 | $2.37 | $2.81 | $3.33 | $2.50 |
| NPV | $2.50 | | | | | | |

| Next Universe (Run #3) | | Year | | | | | |
|---|---|---|---|---|---|---|---|
| | Start | 1 | 2 | 3 | 4 | 5 | Total |
| Revenues *CAGR = 10.8%* | | $0.00 | $10.00 | $11.08 | $12.28 | $13.61 | $46.97 |
| Costs *C/R = 80%* | | $8.00 | $8.00 | $8.87 | $9.82 | $10.89 | $45.58 |
| EBIT | | −$8.00 | $2.00 | $2.22 | $2.46 | $2.72 | $1.39 |
| NPV | $1.39 | | | | | | |

they reflect the same outcome. The 5,000-iteration example in the middle shows a smoother distribution by virtue of the larger number of trials. In both cases what is graphed is the number of iterations that exhibited the corresponding NPV values given on the X axis. The Crystal Ball software automatically creates discrete intervals of NPV values and then determines the number of iterations that resulted in NPV values within each such interval. If the relationship between CAGR and NPV were precisely linear, then we would expect that the frequency distribution exhibited in both of these graphs to approximate a horizontal line, reflecting an equal frequency of occurrences at the high end of the NPV range as at the low end. For 1,000 trials the result is so jagged that it is impossible to visually reach a determination. For the 5,000-trial graphs on the top right, it does appear that the result is nonlinear as there is a higher frequency, by a small amount, at the lower end of the NPV range than at the higher end of the range. This behavior is because the NPV is

Probability Frequency (probability of any single value of NPV)

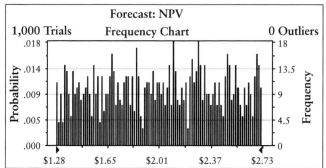

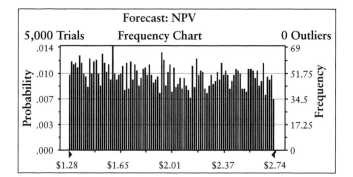

Cumulative NPV Probability

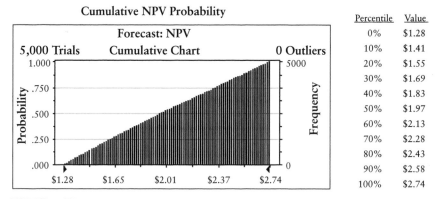

| Percentile | Value |
|---|---|
| 0% | $1.28 |
| 10% | $1.41 |
| 20% | $1.55 |
| 30% | $1.69 |
| 40% | $1.83 |
| 50% | $1.97 |
| 60% | $2.13 |
| 70% | $2.28 |
| 80% | $2.43 |
| 90% | $2.58 |
| 100% | $2.74 |

**EXHIBIT 4.15**   Monte Carlo Results of the Financial Model of Exhibit 4.13 for a Uniform CAGR Distribution

in fact nonlinearly dependent on CAGR. Because we have assumed that the revenues of each succeeding year increase by a factor of (1 + CAGR), there is a compounding, nonlinear increase in NPV as the value of the CAGR increases. Although the effect for this small range is small, it is interesting that the Monte Carlo model reveals it.

The bottom graph of Exhibit 4.15 shows the same result as the middle graph but displayed on a cumulative-probability basis against the NPV values on the X axis. Normally, such cumulative probability is the most useful portrayal of the results of a simulation. The table on the bottom shows these same data but in tabulated form for each decade (i.e., each 10 point interval) of cumulative probability. This result shows that the 50 percent probable value of NPV is $1.97, the 0 percent value is $1.28, and the 100 percent value is $2.74, which means that of the 5,000 trials (iterations, or parallel universes), the lowest NPV realized was $1.28, the highest was $2.74, and half the time it was at $1.97 or less, and half the time at $1.97 or more.

Because this simple example was chosen to illustrate the Monte Carlo method, we could have obtained approximately the same result using the DCF approach of Exhibit 4.11 by simply using RAHR = 0 percent in the three examples of CAGR shown (10 percent, 15 percent, and 20 percent). The minimum and maximum NPV values ($1.28 and $1.97) are identically determined by both methods. However, selecting a CAGR of 15 percent and RAHR of 0 percent in Exhibit 4.11 calculates an NPV of $1.99, which is slightly different than the 50 percent value determined in Exhibit 4.15 of $1.97, because of the previously described effect of nonlinearity. In the more realistic examples we consider in Chapter 5 there is no practical way to compute comparable results using a DCF approach because of complex nonlinearities and the massive number of calculations that would be required.

In closing this introduction to the Monte Carlo Method, we want to consider one other effect. In the example given in Exhibits 4.14 and 4.15, we did not account for any discounting of future cash flows, which corresponds to an assumed value of RAHR of 0 percent. An important issue to consider is what value of discounting, if any, is appropriate to a Monte Carlo analysis. To answer this question, first consider how we might actually use the Monte Carlo result. If we were negotiating around the opportunity of Exhibit 4.15, the relative perceptions of value of the buyer and seller of the opportunity will be dependent on the range of risk that is appropriate. If, for instance, the seller of the opportunity of Exhibit 4.15 insists on a fully paid transaction at closing and suggests a valuation corresponding to the 50 percent probability, then (assuming the financial model is valid), half the time the buyer paid more than the opportunity will be worth, because half the time the resulting NPV is less than the $1.97 at the 50 percent level, and half the time the buyer will have paid less than it will be worth. In Chapter 5 we address the issue of the appropriate probability of a negotiation. For now we want to recognize that even if the parties agreed on such a standard of fairness, the $1.97 overestimates the value of the opportunity because there is a time value of money involved that is not accounted for in the presently constructed Monte Carlo model because we have used zero discounting.

So, what discounting should be used? Well if we use an RAHR value such as might be selected from Exhibit 4.10, and then use some standard such as 50 percent probability for a value we will have double-counted for risk. If the use of RAHR over discounts the value, what discount rate should be used? A generally reasonable selection is the WHR (WACC hurdle rate), or possibly the MHR (marginal cost of capital hurdle rate), of the prospective buyer of the opportunity because this represents the bare cost of capital required or the value of capital paid back to investors. Such a discount rate then imbeds all the cost of capital, but only the cost of capital in the discounting, and all the risk, and only the risk in the Monte Carlo determined probability. The result is shown in Exhibit 4.16.

To show the effect of increased smoothing that results from additional iterations, the calculation is shown for 5,000 iterations. The nonlinearity of the frequency distribution is now more clearly evident. The format of Exhibit 4.16 is a standard report format available in Crystal Ball. The NPV forecast values at 0, 50, and 100 percent probability are, respectively, −$0.69, −$0.21, and $0.31. These values are significantly reduced from the previous case where zero discounting was used. In fact, at a WACC of 10 percent, there is a 70 percent probability that the buyer will lose money on the alternative even if it paid nothing to acquire it, and only a 30 percent probability that there is any positive value in the opportunity.

The powerful Monte Carlo method can easily create any number of "what if" analyses by adjusting the distribution functions and values for the key input parameters, including an appropriate cost of capital, and then interpret the result based on a willingness to undertake a level of outcome risk. These Monte Carlo features of separating the cost of capital from the risk, the ability to consider the impact of almost any type of uncertainty, and portraying results in a way that enables a judgment to be reached as to the appropriate level of risk for the prospective reward make it extremely powerful and useful and surprisingly easy to implement.

## CLOSURE AND APPLICATION TO NEGOTIATION

In this chapter, we considered three related but distinct financial modeling tools: (1) DCF calculating a NPV using an RAHR; (2) probability trees for various scenarios, such as high, low, and base, using discount rates that reflect only the buyer's cost of capital; and (3) Monte Carlo probabilistic analysis

**Summary:**
Display Range is from ($0.69) to $0.31
Entire Range is from ($0.69) to $0.31
After 5,000 Trials, the Standard Error of the Mean is $0.00

| Statistics: | Value |
|---|---|
| Trials | 5000 |
| Mean | ($0.20) |
| Median | ($0.21) |
| Mode | — |
| Standard Deviation | $0.29 |
| Variance | $0.08 |
| Skewness | 0.04 |
| Kurtosis | 1.80 |
| Coefficient of Variability | −1.43 |
| Range Minimum | ($0.69) |
| Range Maximum | $0.31 |
| Range Width | $1.00 |
| Mean Standard Error | $0.00 |

| Percentile | Value |
|---|---|
| 0% | ($0.69) |
| 10% | ($0.59) |
| 20% | ($0.50) |
| 30% | ($0.40) |
| 40% | ($0.31) |
| 50% | ($0.21) |
| 60% | ($0.10) |
| 70% | ($0.00) |
| 80% | $0.09 |
| 90% | $0.20 |
| 100% | $0.31 |

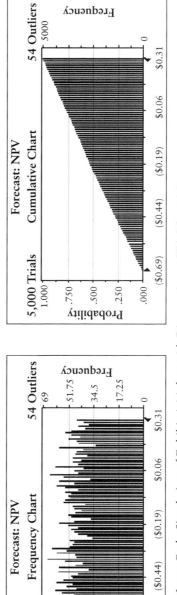

**EXHIBIT 4.16** Monte Carlo Simulation of Exhibit 4.14, but with Discounting at WACC = 10 Percent

73

that can easily handle almost any type of uncertainty and scenario. In Chapter 5, we consider the Monte Carlo method in further detail.

However, at this point it is useful to review our ¹Dealmaking objective in developing these tools and methods expressed by the 4C acronym. Conceiving a deal, Box, Wheelbarrow, terms, value, structure, parties, should all be empowered by such tools as we have considered in Chapters 4 through 7. Further, the application of such tools and methods provides the content and vehicle for communication both internally and to, and with, the other side of the prospective deal. They also provide the means of doing "what if" analyses to comprise either the Box or Wheelbarrow, or the spine of the deal, in some alternative way. Finally, they provide a way of identifying, prioritizing, and ultimately determining mandatory points of any agreement in the activities of deal consummation.

The key elements of this process are thinking about possible futures in terms of their effect on present value in a way that enables me to develop a negotiation plan, to communicate my interests and perspectives to others whose agreement I need, to adjust my interests and possibly my beliefs about the future and present value based on the real-time experience of listening to other perspectives and gaining new information, and finally to come to closure on the subject negotiation. These key elements can all be done "by gosh and by golly," but not consistently well, at least for us normal mortals.

What is needed is a flexible, powerful, and meaningful way of looking at the future potential of a given opportunity expressible in monetary, present terms. NPV calculations are the gold standard of such present value consideration because, by definition, they determine the NPV. NPV determined by the DCF method using the tool of RAHR gives us the simplest, easiest way of performing this determination. Using the scenario method, we can expand our perspective of how multiple future outcomes can affect our present perception (and confidence) in an NPV calculation. Finally, Monte Carlo method enables us to consider the effect of many parallel assumptions or uncertainties and create an unbounded number of future outcomes to aid in a reasoned judgment of a present value.

## NOTES

1. This midyear correction is only a useful approximation. If cash inflows are uniform throughout the year, then simply taking the total of the inflows for the year and ascribing them to a single point at midyear will result in a slightly higher present value than would have resulted from the more accurate approach of discounting each such inflow by the very hour in the year it was projected to occur. However, in most circumstances the corrective effect of timing each individual cash inflow and outflow is not warranted, given the other uncertainties and assumptions involved in developing a financial model of the opportunity.

2. This result can be determined in Microsoft Excel by the use of the Goal Seek function available under the Tools header. By setting the cell corresponding to NPV to zero and identifying the RAHR variable as the cell to be adjusted, Excel iteratively solves for the corresponding value of RAHR.

3. The idea being that one starts a philosophical, or here a valuation, analysis from some belief about a normative situation and then considers the significance of other situations. For a valuation, such significance is the combination of the value associated with the assumed non-normative condition and the corresponding probability of occurrence. In valuation contexts we are not making moral judgments concerning the validity of non-normative conditions, only judgments as to their value and likelihood.

4. Such bond rates and ratings are published by Moody's Investor Service, and are available on the Web site of the Federal Reserve Bank of St. Louis. A "Baa" bond is defined as: "**Baa** Bonds which are rated Baa are considered as medium-grade obligations (i.e., they are neither highly protected nor poorly secured). Interest payments and principal security appear adequate for the present but certain protective elements may be lacking or may be characteristically unreliable over any great length of time. Such bonds lack outstanding investment characteristics and in fact have speculative characteristics as well." (Source: http://www.lon.com/moodys.html).

5. Although for illustrative purposes, the Exhibit 4.7 uses the same template as was used for Exhibit 4.5, other assumed values were changed, for instance, to show a lower, more typical CAGR value (8 percent) applicable to the 10-year period, a higher average C/R ratio, and a higher initial investment.

6. A detailed discussion of RAHR as given in this exhibit is provided in *Valuation and Pricing of Technology-Based Intellectual Property*, Richard Razgaitis, John Wiley & Sons, 2003.

7. There are a few genuine star clusters such as the Pleiades, but they are exceptions.

8. Decisioneering, Inc., whose product is Crystal Ball®.

# CHAPTER 5

# Monte Carlo Method

In Chapter 4, we introduced the Monte Carlo method. We saw with simple examples how we can transform fixed simple assumptions into distributions, or functions, and use available software tools such as Crystal Ball to create reports that show and give weight to many possible future outcomes.

In this chapter we consider many more assumptions and distributions associated with such assumptions. Also we use the power of the software to gain a deeper understanding of the results being forecast. Finally, we consider how the results can be used, interpreted, and applied to negotiation contexts.

Until recently, the limited power of personal computers and the unavailability of packaged software confined the use of Monte Carlo techniques to graduate-level finance studies and before that to engineering analysis. Accordingly, the method is just emerging into wider audiences. One example of Monte Carlo's increasing use is in personal financial planning, particularly retirement planning. Financial Engines of Palo Alto, CA, supplies such a Monte Carlo simulation tool based on 15 types of investments ("asset classes") including 20,000 stocks and mutual funds coupled with data and models on the range of expected returns. This simulation tool is provided to 20 financial institutions such as Vanguard, which in turn make it freely available to their investors, and 800 companies such as McDonald's and Occidental Petroleum that provide it for employees to use in planning their retirement. Morningstar and Fidelity Investments also provide Monte Carlo modeling tools for financial planning. So, in addition to the common use of Monte Carlo methods in MBA programs, ordinary souls, trying to discern their economic future in high-uncertainty times, are finding it comprehensible and useful.

Two main companies make general purpose Monte Carlo software for personal computers:

1. Decisioneering, Inc., whose product is Crystal Ball® (www.decisioneering.com)
2. Palisade Corporation, whose product is @Risk® (www.palisade.com)

Both products operate on Microsoft's Excel software. Financial modeling is performed in a standard spreadsheet form as illustrated in Exhibits 4.1 through 4.11 in Chapter 4. As in Chapter 4, all the Monte Carlo examples shown in this chapter use Crystal Ball 2000 Professional.

## A MODEL CASH FLOW TEMPLATE

In the examples of Chapter 4 we considered 5- and 10-year projections from a simple perspective of annual revenues less all annual costs, leading to net gross annual EBIT, which for simplicity purposes we took as being equal to cash flow realized from the subject opportunity. Before embarking on the Monte Carlo method we want to standardize on a more realistic financial model of cash flows. Our challenge in developing such a model template for didactic purposes, as is the challenge for negotiation purposes, is to hit the right level of complexity. The world is an extremely complicated place that is made all the more complicated by any consideration of all the things that could happen in the future. We actually do not want to attempt to consider all possibilities because we would leave ourselves with an insoluble problem, which even were it solvable would be unintelligible and impotent to help our negotiation process.[1] Such a situation would be akin to our listening to a fool asking a question that seven wise men cannot answer. However, we can simplify a model, or a question, so that the answer easily achieved lacks bearing because of how we have trivialized the context. This situation would be like gaining an understanding of a simple answer for which no one is asking the underlying question. With the exception of very simple problems that can be solved exactly even considering all factors, we are normally faced with this challenge of choosing an effective level of analysis that incorporates a reasonable, important level of complexity without weighing ourselves down with details that add little meaningful information or encumber our finite ability to grasp reality or projections of reality.

There is no single right place to locate our analysis on this simplicity–complexity space. Further, it is often difficult to make good judgments at the beginning of an analysis of what to include and what can be safely ignored or greatly simplified. This predicament is akin to the paradoxical aphorism of "you can't read a book once" (meaning you have to read it and see the whole picture before you can really "read it" and grasp how it all fits together); to some extent this point also applies to financial analysis—through experience it becomes ever easier to know what to include and what can be ignored. Later in this chapter we show how the tools associated with the Monte Carlo method can aid us in ignoring those variables whose impact on net present value (NPV) are inconsequential.

This modeling design problem is not unique to financial analysis. As discussed in Chapter 6, even "exact" equations do not directly apprehend reality, but only certain idealized representations of reality. (There is a genuine philosophical question as to whether we would know reality if we saw it, because we are always dealing with representations.[2]) The explanatory power of models depends on whether such representation is adequate for control, prediction, and decision making. This axiom is true in physics, combustion, biological systems, psychology, economic policy, and virtually every human endeavor involving complex behaviors. Albert Einstein (1879–1955), known for many pithy quotes had one that is applicable here: "Every problem should be made as simple as possible, but not simpler." This is the guidance we seek to follow in the examples considered throughout this book.

## INCOME AND CASH FLOW STATEMENTS: 3M EXAMPLE

Developing cash flow projections requires solving several problems. One of the inherent complexities of financial analysis is dealing with a single-year cost having a longer-term benefit. Accounting and tax systems are established to apportion such cost over the period of years in which the benefit is expected to be realized. This apportionment is known as *capitalizing* an asset and is distinguished from *expensing* for which all the cost is assigned to the year of purchase. Such capitalized asset is then "written down" by some principle of *depreciation* (for tangible assets, such as plant and equipment) and *amortization* (for intangible assets, such as patents, know-how, and goodwill). Depreciation and amortization are dependent on the specific assets involved and allowed periods of such write down, all of which tends to be industry specific; these accounting treatments and tax matters are beyond the scope of this book.

Our accounting practices have evolved into certain ways to account for such value-beyond-cost factors, the tax code, and a host of other factors. To make this as simple and concrete as possible, we consider actual values from a well-known company, shown in Exhibit 5.1 for 3M (Minnesota Mining and Manufacturing, symbol MMM), an interesting company that celebrated its centennial of formation in 2002. It is generally classed as a "diversified chemical company" in SIC code 2813,[3] though it manufactures and sells 60,000 products, making it a remarkably diversified company. These data summarized in Exhibit 5.1 are 3-year averages for 3M's annual filings with the U.S. Securities and Exchange Commission (SEC) from a standard financial report known formally as a 10-K, or simply 3M's annual financial report. The values reported by 3M for their fiscal years 1999, 2000, and 2001 have been averaged to show the results in Exhibit 5.1 (all dollars are in thousands). The upper box represents 3M's *income statement*, after some category simplifications have been made. The first line is the revenues (also known as sales). Subtracting from such sales are a series of cost categories that are shown in italics. The first cost is generally called COGS for cost of goods sold, or sometimes COS for cost of sales. This cost represents the direct cost in labor, materials, and equipment (expensed and capitalized) incurred during the period that produces the revenues that 3M receives. The net of revenues and COGS is commonly known as the gross margin, and is a measure of the innate profitability of the products sold. For 3M, averaged over 3 years over all their revenues, we see that their gross margin, weighted over all their 60,000 prod-

**EXHIBIT 5.1**    Summary Income and Cash Flow Statement Information from 3M

**Income Statement 3-year Avg (1999–2001)**

|  | **$ thousands** | **Revenue Ratios** |
|---|---|---|
| Revenues | $16,184 | 100.0% |
| *COGS* | ($8,554) | 52.9% |
| Gross Margin | $7,630 | 47.1% |
|  |  |  |
| *SG&A* | ($3,912) | 24.2% |
| *R&D* | ($1,080) | 6.7% |
| *Total Overhead* | ($4,992) | 30.8% |
|  |  |  |
| EBIT | $2,637 | 16.3% |
|  |  |  |
| *Interest* | ($82) |  |
| EBT | $2,555 | 15.8% |
|  |  |  |
| *Provision for Tax* | ($877) | 34.3% |
| EAT | $1,678 | 10.4% |
|  |  |  |
| **Operations Adjustments to Income** |  |  |
| Dep & Amor | $1,005 | 6.2% |
| All Other Adjust. | $165 | 1.0% |
| Purchases PPE | ($1,048) | 6.5% |
| Net Adjustments | $122 | 0.8% |
| Cash Flow | $1,800 | 11.1% |

*Notes:* COGS = Cost of goods sold; SG&A = Sales general and administrative; R&D = Research and development; EBIT = Earnings before interest and tax; EBT = Earnings before tax; Dep & Amor = Depreciation and amortization; PPE = Plant, property, and equipment (new investments). Because of rounding not all numbers add and subtract exactly as shown.

ucts, was just over 47 percent of their total revenue. The other costs are often called *overhead* because they are necessary costs to manage the business but they are not directly associated with the products and services sold that produced the revenues. Two common components of such overhead cost are sales, general, and administrative (SG&A) and research and development (R&D). These costs are sometimes lumped together as overhead. For 3M, together these costs are 30.8 percent of revenues. When such overhead costs are subtracted from the gross margin the result, shown in Exhibit 5.1 as $2.6 billion (16.3 percent), is termed EBIT for earnings before interest and taxes, and sometimes called *operating profit*, though different companies ascribe the term operating profit to different places in their income statements. For 3M there is a small net interest expense that reduces their income to the shown EBT, earning before tax, value. The provision for tax is based on 3M's tax return that, for a large company operating in many states and countries, is determined from a very complicated calculation. Shown is the provision of 34.3 percent of EBT (not revenues) based on the average of their three most recent years. Finally we have EAT, earnings after tax, which is often called the *bottom line*. Such earnings are then available to pay dividends to shareholders or to retain by 3M for future investment or some combination of both. Such earnings are a new resource to the company—the reward from its customers for the capital and human assets deployed in their service.

In the lower box of Exhibit 5.1 we have the operations adjustments to the income statement to determine the actual cash flow that occurs.[4] As discussed earlier, when capital investments made have multiyear benefit they are depreciated or amortized over time. When 3M determined their COGS and other costs that are contained within this income statement, such costs included depreciation and amortization expenses ascribed to each year based on investments made in some earlier year. So, in the income statement such depreciation and amortization reduced the calculated revenues received from 3M's customers by an amount that was not a literal cash expense in that year. In order to determine the actual cash flows we must then add back to the EAT number bottom line of the income statement the amount that had been deducted for such noncash costs. For 3M, and for many other companies, the adjustment is dominated by the depreciation and amortization costs as shown in Exhibit 5.1. All the other adjustments, including increases in accounts receivable and changes in inventory levels, are in 3M's case relatively small as shown.

To sustain its revenues and margins, 3M has to make new investments. For a completely static situation, one can conceive of a company's new investments each year exactly offsetting its depreciation and amortization amounts, sustaining the same total value of plant, property, and equipment. In practice, even for a mature company, the new investment differs from such depreciation and amortization either because the company is planning to grow, it is becoming more capital intensive, it is exiting certain businesses (and revenues), or it is becoming less capital intensive. In the 3M example, the investment in new plant, property, and equipment (PPE) of $1.048 billion almost exactly offsets the depreciation and amortization amount of $1.005 billion (within ca. 4 percent). The net effect of all such adjustments determines that the average cash inflow to 3M was $1.8 billion or 11 percent of revenues (averaged over the 3 years 1999–2001).[5] If 3M's revenues and costs all arrived and left in small unmarked bills, a scary thought in these trust-challenged times, we should see in the company shoebox on the 365th day of their fiscal year that $1.8 billion cash inflow (having started the year with the shoebox empty).

In order to apply cash flow models we need to make estimates of just such adjustment to income factors. (Recall that in Chapter 4 we, for simplicity, simply did our cash flow analysis by subtracting all cash costs from each year's revenues in one single entry.)

The values for the categories shown in Exhibit 5.1 vary widely depending on the industry in which the company operates and the individual company itself. Some industries, such as software and pharmaceuticals, characteristically have very low values of COGS and very high values of SG&A and especially R&D, although there can be significant company-to-company variation within any given industry segment. Other industries, such as commodity chemicals or consumer electronics, tend to have very high values of COGS and lower values of SG&A and especially R&D, again with company-to-company variation. Likewise, companies with high capital investments, such as are associated with a multibillion dollar semiconductor chip manufacturing facility or large polymer factory, have significant depreciation expenses as those large capital investments are written down over their useful lives. Intangible investments under recently adopted accounting rules can also, in certain industries and companies, represent significant annual deductions to income.

The specific opportunity being valued in the context of a negotiation can itself differ substantially from the norms of the selling or buying company. In the 3M example we have been considering, COGS, and appropriately allocated SG&A and R&D overheads for each of 3M's products no doubt varies widely because its products span so many industries and product applications from stationery to automotive, from electrical to medical, for business, government, and consumer customer categories. In theory, a company with a product line having a gross margin greater than zero provides some economic benefit to the company because it makes an overhead contribution; in practice, every product requires some overhead, if only the distraction of thinking about it and reporting on it, such that once a product's gross margin erodes to low values it is likely to be killed. 3M's objective for its R&D and business-acquisition groups is obviously to create new products with very high gross margins. So we should not assume that a new opportunity being considered by 3M as a buyer will be characterized by the average gross margin, EBIT, and cash flow values shown in Exhibit 5.1; except for certain unusual circumstances, buyers are seeking to acquire opportunities with substantially higher financial ratios than their current average.

Accordingly, the financial model for any given opportunity needs to be specific to that opportunity. No universally applicable set of financial parameters exists. For purposes of the examples in this chapter, we refer to the 3M ratios because they are reasonably illustrative of a broad range of valuation opportunities. However, even if the buyer (or seller) was 3M itself, the appropriate parameters should be analyzed so that they are specific to the opportunity and as accurate as possible.

There are an increasing number of products and resources available to assist in the development of sophisticated, individual financial models. A bibliography is provided at the end of this book.

Now, we turn our attention to how, using 3M data as a benchmark, we can construct financial models. Following our principle of making our model as simple as possible, but not simpler, we consider two primary issues that affect the value of an opportunity during the transition from dealmaking until operations at the 3M benchmark are expected. In contrast to purchasing of equities in the stock market, in most dealmaking contexts such transition period involves additional investment by the buyer and a delay to the realization of the anticipated financial performance anticipated by the 3M benchmark we are using. This need for subsequent investment is the distinction between taking ownership of, or having proportional rights to, the fruits of a going concern, such as would be the case in purchasing all or some of the shares of, say, 3M versus buying from (or selling to) 3M a technology or nascent product line that has the potential of exceeding the 3M financial benchmarks but is presently only in the lab, or beginning manufacturing operations, or having initial "beta" sales.

For the purchase of a going concern, we can make first-order estimates of the value of an enterprise by assuming that the cash flows now being generated will continue in perpetuity. It turns out the formula for present value $A$, of an annual cash stream $B$ in perpetuity is simply:

$$A = B/(RAHR - CAGR) \tag{5.1}$$

where RAHR is again the risk-adjusted hurdle rate, and CAGR is the compound annual growth rate (where such CAGR must not be too close in value to RAHR for the equation to be valid).[6] For a going concern, especially a 100-year old going concern with 60,000 products, such RAHR is a relatively low number. For simplicity, using an RAHR of 9 percent and a CAGR of 5.3 percent based on 3M's historic, 10-year growth rate in earnings per share, means that the present value of 3M, in accordance with the simplifying assumptions described above, would be 27 times the $1.8 billion cash flow calculated in Exhibit 5.1, or $49 billion. At this writing, 3M's market capitalization (total value of outstanding equity shares) is $44 billion, and its outstanding debt is approximately $2 billion, so its enterprise value is $46 billion, which is essentially identical to the simple calculation based on an RAHR of 9 percent.

What makes this calculation simple is the going-concern assumption of a large, many-product entity such as 3M because its present financial performance can be reasonably understood and reasonably projected to continue in the future. In many negotiations, however, even of a going concern, what is being sold and bought is something that has the prospect of performance substantially greater than evidenced today and requires investment and nurturing by the buyer. It is this combination of (1) prospect, (2) nurturing, and (3) investment that makes calculating contingent value so much more complicated, and interesting, and negotiating agreements so much more challenging.

First, let us consider the investment that is estimated to be required of the buyer, and the time period of that investment, in order to create a business that can be thenceforth sustained from the overhead investments (a total of 30.8 percent of annual revenues based on the 3M data); such investment is sometimes called the "CapEx" cost, for capital expenditures for depreciable assets (PPE) in addition to other expenses and labor that will be required during a startup period. Thus, during the startup years of our financial model, there normally needs to be included such CapEx and additional overhead investment to complete R&D, prototype manufacturing, test the market, develop sales channels and customers, scale up production, and fully staff the then-going concern.

Secondly, we need to consider the time to initial revenues from sales, and the growth profile of those revenues during a (it is hoped rapidly growing sales) period before we can make reasonable approximations for future revenues using CAGR estimates. The growth of revenues from new product introduction has been widely studied. The profile of revenue growth is generally modeled by an S-curve, also known as a sigmoid shape, as shown in Exhibit 5.2.

Shown in Exhibit 5.2 is the Fisher-Pry equation from which the shown curves were derived, all for an assumed 50 percent penetration at the 5th year, and for the five different market shape factors, $s$. As shown, for low values of $s$, the market response is slow to start but grows rapidly to maturity near to the $t_{50}$ year (in this case, the 5th year). For high values of $s$, the market response is early to start, but grows slowly to maturity.

Other S-shaped adoption curves are shown in Exhibit 5.3. Shown here are two closely related relationships known as Pearl-Reed and Gompertz. Instead of prescribing a year of 50 percent penetration, these relationships use a factor $a$, termed a *location coefficient* in addition to $s$, a market response (shape) factor. Unlike Fisher-Pry, these curves do not cross over each other,

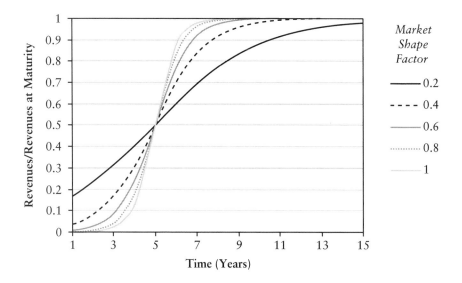

Based on the Fisher-Pry Model, with 50 percent penetration at the 5th year

$$\frac{\textit{Revenues for year t}}{\textit{Revenues at Maturity}} = 1 + tanh \; [(s(t - t_{50})]$$

Where $t_{50}$ is the year for 50 percent penetration, and $s$ is the market shape factor

**EXHIBIT 5.2**   *S*-Curve Revenue Growth Model: Fisher-Pry

meaning that a curve corresponding to a particular market response factor
will always reflect sales above the curve corresponding to a smaller value of *s*.

These (or other) new product introduction models can be used to project
the rate of market penetration and revenue growth for a new product opportunity. They are more important to a financial model when the startup phase
of an opportunity is anticipated to be long (say 10 years or more). For short
startup phase opportunities, however, manual, annual estimates, or even
straight-line estimates, can work reasonably well for valuation purposes.
Again, we favor simplicity when it does not cost us an important degree of
understanding.

For our purposes, we use as the baseline template for our Monte Carlo
demonstrations the financial model as shown in Exhibit 5.4. For the reader's
convenience, an Excel downloadable version of this exhibit is available at
"Dealmaking Resources" at the author's web site, www.razgaitis.com.
The exhibit reflects a 10-year projection divided into two segments: the first
five *startup* years, and the last five *mature* years. The distinction between the
startup and mature periods is that during the mature period we assume

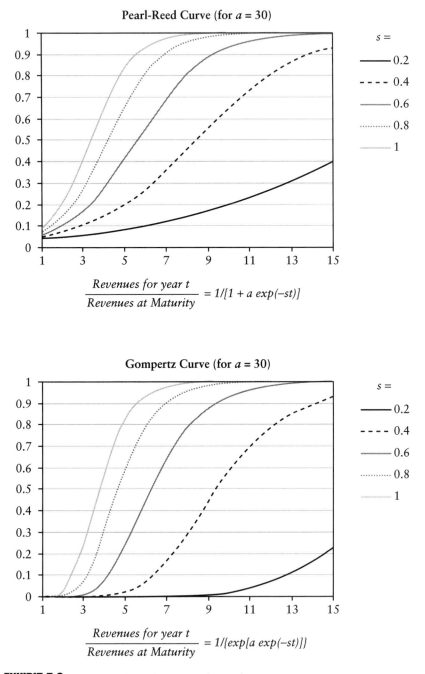

**EXHIBIT 5.3**   Other S-Shaped New Product Adoption Curves

# EXHIBIT 5.4  Baseline Template for Monte Carlo Demonstrations

| | A | B | C | D | E | F | G | H | I | J | K | L | M | N | O | P | Q | R | S |
|---|---|---|---|---|---|---|---|---|---|---|---|---|---|---|---|---|---|---|---|
| 1 | | | Year | 1 | 2 | 3 | 4 | 5 | | | | | 6 | 7 | 8 | 9 | 10 | | |
| 2 | | | | | | Startup Period | | | Startup Total | | Assumed Ratios | | | | Mature Period | | | Mature Total | 10-Year TOTAL |
| 4 | Revenues | | | 0.00 | 2.00 | 15.00 | 70.00 | 180.00 | 267.00 | Revenues | 100.0% | | 201.60 | 225.79 | 252.89 | 283.23 | 317.22 | 1280.73 | 1547.73 |
| 5 | CAGR | | | – | – | 650% | 367% | 157% | | CAGR | 12.0% | | 12.0% | 12.0% | 12.0% | 12.0% | 12.0% | | |
| 6 | | Costs | | | | | | | | | Costs | | | | | | | | |
| 7 | Dep-Amor(1) | 10 | | 0.20 | 1.20 | 4.20 | 8.20 | 10.00 | | Dep-Amor(1) | 10 | | 11.11 | 12.34 | 13.71 | 15.23 | 16.92 | | |
| 8 | All Other(2) | 1.80 | | 1.80 | 10.20 | 6.30 | 40.80 | 116.00 | | All Other(2) | | | 130.01 | 145.71 | 163.31 | 183.03 | 205.14 | 827.20 | 827.20 |
| 9 | Total Costs | 70.0% | | 2.00 | 11.40 | 10.50 | 49.00 | 126.00 | 198.90 | Total Costs | 70.0% | | 141.12 | 158.05 | 177.02 | 198.26 | 222.06 | 896.51 | 1095.41 |
| 11 | EBIT | | | (2.00) | (9.40) | 4.50 | 21.00 | 54.00 | 68.10 | EBIT | 30.0% | | 60.48 | 67.74 | 75.87 | 84.97 | 95.17 | 384.22 | 452.32 |
| 12 | PFT (of EBIT) | 34.0% | | 0.00 | 0.00 | 0.00 | 4.79 | 18.36 | | PFT (of EBIT) | 34.0% | | 20.56 | 23.03 | 25.79 | 28.89 | 32.36 | | |
| 13 | EAT | | | (2.00) | (9.40) | 4.50 | 16.21 | 35.64 | 44.95 | EAT | 19.8% | | 39.92 | 44.71 | 50.07 | 56.08 | 62.81 | 253.59 | 298.53 |
| 14 | Carry forward loss | | | (2.00) | (11.40) | (6.90) | 9.31 | 44.95 | | | | | | | | | | | |
| 15 | Adjustments | | | | | | | | | | Adjustments | | | | | | | | |
| 16 | Dep-Amor(1) | 10 | | 0.20 | 1.20 | 4.20 | 8.20 | 10.00 | | Dep-Amor(1) | 10 | | 11.1 | 12.3 | 13.7 | 15.2 | 16.9 | 69.31 | 69.31 |
| 17 | Incr WC(3) | 10% | | 0.20 | 1.30 | 5.50 | 11.00 | 2.16 | | Incr WC | 10% | | 2.42 | 2.71 | 3.03 | 3.40 | 3.40 | | |
| 18 | CapEx | | | 2.00 | 10.00 | 30.00 | 40.00 | 18.00 | 100.00 | CapEx | | | 11.1 | 12.3 | 13.7 | 15.2 | 16.9 | 69.20 | 169.20 |
| 19 | GCF | | | (4.00) | (19.50) | (26.80) | (26.59) | 25.48 | (51.41) | | | | 37.51 | 42.04 | 47.05 | 52.71 | 59.43 | 238.73 | 187.32 |
| 20 | | RAHR | | | | | | | | | | | | | | | | | |
| 21 | DCF | 15.00% | | (3.73) | (15.81) | (18.90) | (16.31) | 13.58 | | | | | 17.39 | 16.95 | 16.49 | 16.07 | 15.75 | | |
| 22 | NPV | 41.49 | | | | | | | | | | | | | | | | | |

Notes

1 Depreciation/Amortization assumed (a) 10 years, straight line, (b) 50% of startup investment (balance is non-PPE investment)

2 "All other expenses" for the Years 1 and 2 is calculated using the 70% Cost Ratio plus an expense equal to the CapEx for the corresponding year.

3 Increase in Working Capital (WC), to fund receivables, inventory, and other purposes is assumed to be the shown percentage of the increase in Revenues year over year

revenue growth is determined by a constant value of CAGR, all the other parameters are determined as fixed ratios as shown, and the CapEx investment is exactly equal to the current year depreciation and amortization, maintaining a constant total asset value. During the startup period, we are creating the transition financial model between the initial time at which it is assumed that no revenues exist and that additional CapEx and overhead investment is necessary to complete R&D and manufacturing, as well as market development to launch the product. Other important aspects of this template are:

- CapEx is estimated to be a total of $100 million that will be expended as shown during the startup period and depreciated on a straight-line basis over 10 years from investment.

- The tax rate is 34 percent (of EBT). Note there is a calculation of the carry-forward losses during the first 3 years that is credited against taxes due in Year 4.

- The combined COGS and overhead cost ratio is assumed to be 70 percent, which is approximately 14 points less than the 3M 3-year average, leading to an EBIT value of 30 percent. This assumption is made because it is assumed that the opportunity under investigation will cause the buyer (3M or some other company) to improve its average current economic performance.

- The CAGR is assumed to be 12 percent and applicable after the 5th year.

- No account has been presently made for any terminal value. Accordingly, the analysis cuts off at the 10th year with no additional value ascribed.

- The increase in working capital requirements is assumed to be 10 percent of the growth of subsequent year's revenues (to fund receivables and inventory and all other purposes).

- The entries for overhead costs in Years 1 and 2 are assumed to be the costs as would be determined by the 70 percent cost ratio plus an additional cost equal to the corresponding CapEx investment for that year. Accordingly, in Year 1, there are no revenues, so the cost ratio calculation leads to zero cost, and the overhead cost is simply equal to $2 million determined from the estimated CapEx investment required that year. In Year 2, the cost ratio calculation plus the $10 million is used. Starting in the Year 3, only the 70 percent cost ratio is used.

- An NPV calculation is listed for the RAHR of 15 percent, showing that the modeled opportunity has a large positive NPV of more than $41 million for this discount rate. Using a conventional discounted cash flow (DCF) approach and the Excel Goal Seek function one can determine that the RAHR corresponding to an NPV of zero is 30.21 percent. Thus, for perceived RAHR below this threshold value there will be a positive NPV and the project will be deemed worth doing, and vice versa for values above 30.21 percent. As is discussed later, when using Monte Carlo the appropriate value for discounting future cash flows is some direct measure of the cost of capital such as WACC hurdle rate (WHR), marginal hurdle rate (MHR), or company hurdle rate (CHR) as discussed in Chapter 4.

■ The revenue projection is based on the assumption that zero revenues will be achieved during the first project year, and modest market-testing revenues in Year 2. Revenues in Year 3 are still assumed to be small and correspond to production from prototype (semiworks scale) manufacturing equipment. Based on the assumed revenue growth, significant CapEx investments are made in Years 3 and 4 to support the large projected revenue increases in Years 4 and 5.

The revenue projection shown in Exhibit 5.4 can be compared with the three *s*-curve production adoption models previously depicted in Exhibits 5.2 and 5.3. The comparison with the assumed revenue projection of Exhibit 5.4 is shown in Exhibit 5.5.

In the table at the top of Exhibit 5.5 are the previous Monte Carlo template revenues for the first 6 years. Below such assumed revenues are the Fisher-Pry, Pearl-Reed, and Gompertz models in table format. Below the tables is a graph depicting all four revenue models, with the Monte Carlo assumed revenue of Exhibit 5.4 shown by the thickest line. As can be seen, all three of these models can be adjusted to follow closely the assumed revenue growth rate during the startup period, although the Gompertz model underpredicts the revenues during the initial 3 years. With research and experience, it may be possible to establish an independently developed model with corresponding coefficients to derive startup revenue projections. Comparing the total projected revenues for the 6-year period, the Pearl-Reed fit is essentially identical to the Monte Carlo template assumption, the Fisher-Pry fit is only 1 percent below the template, and the Gompertz fit is 5 percent below the template. Using the Goal Seek function in Excel one can iterate on the twin parameters of each model to reduce the difference to zero.

Revenue projections are commonly made from either a *top-down* or *bottom-up* basis. The top-down approach starts with some perception of the size and growth of the total market either based on experience or market studies or research. From this perception, estimates are made as the capture (or "penetration") that the subject opportunity will evidence as some percentage of such "addressable" market. A bottom-up approach starts with an analysis of how many customers exist of each type, the corresponding sales channel model that will reach such customers (number of salespeople, the

| | | | | | | 12.0% | | |
| Year | 1 | 2 | 3 | 4 | 5 | 6 | Total | Difference |
|---|---|---|---|---|---|---|---|---|
| Monte Carlo Model | 0 | 2 | 15 | 70 | 180 | 202 | 469 | 0% |
| Fisher-Pry  $t_{50} = 4.2$  $s = 1.4$ | 0 | 0 | 7 | 73 | 182 | 200 | 463 | –1% |
| Pearl-Reed $a = 15,000$  $s = 2.3$ | 0 | 1 | 13 | 80 | 175 | 199 | 468 | 0% |
| Gompertz $a = 11,000$  $s = 2.3$ | 0 | 0 | 0 | 66 | 179 | 198 | 443 | –5% |

**Startup Revenues of Monte Carlo Template
Compared with 3 S-Curve Models**

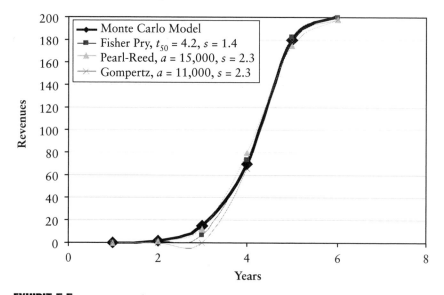

**EXHIBIT 5.5**   Monte Carlo Revenue Projection Compared with S-Curve Models

sales cycle, and so forth), the units of the product that can be sold as a function of unit pricing. This model then builds up from individual accounts to an overall total revenue projection. Revenue projections are often made from both a top-down and bottom-up perspective and then compared as a test of reasonableness. An initial bottom-up analysis, for example, may lead to a revenue projection in excess of a reasonable projection of market share based on a top-down analysis of the overall market. Or an initial top-down model may have missed the effect of significant revenue potential available from certain large customer segments. The three s-curve models discussed above and shown in Exhibit 5.5, provide another means of testing for reasonableness. By tracking actual results and correlating such results to solve for the pair of factors required in any of the three s-curve models considered (such as *a* and *s* for Pearl-Reed and Gompertz), one can develop a database of examples that can be used to develop new opportunity revenue models or test for reasonableness such models developed by a top-down or bottom-up approach.

The opportunity model of Exhibit 5.4 is now applied in multiple examples to gain an understanding as to how Monte Carlo techniques can be used in negotiation and dealmaking.

## MONTE CARLO ASSUMPTION TOOLS

In Chapter 4 we introduced the underlying concept of the Monte Carlo method, namely, the use of distributions (or functions) instead of single-value assumptions. We illustrated this concept by the use of the uniform distribution as shown in Exhibit 4.12 that we used to model CAGR between the lower limit of 10 percent and the upper limit of 20 percent. In this section we examine other distributions that can be used.

Crystal Ball (and @Risk) provide with the Monte Carlo software a variety of preestablished distribution functions that can be used as tools from what is essentially a pull-down menu. The various available distribution functions are made specific to the opportunity, as we did with the CAGR distribution assumed in Chapter 4, by choosing specific parameters to specifically define the distribution.

### Uniform Distribution: Highest Uncertainty Between Certain Bounds

The uniform distribution, as depicted in Exhibit 4.12, applied to a particular assumption cell in a Monte Carlo model assumes that there is no possibility of values below or above the lower and upper bounds (i.e., perfect certainty with respect to such bounds), but between such bounds there is no basis from experience or reason to give higher weight (probability) to any value within the range. This assumption tool is easy to use because of the only requirement of specifying the upper and lower bounds. Also, in many circumstances it is possible, by experience or reason, to choose and defend such bound selections. However, as one makes the bounds further and further apart, which is easy to do in the software and perhaps comforting to the modeler because it is inclusive of possibilities, the predicted result becomes proportionately more diffused and less useful.

Let us now apply the uniform distribution again to the CAGR assumption but now on the Monte Carlo template of Exhibit 5.4. For this purpose and throughout this chapter we use a discount rate of 15 percent, a value that we will assume reflects a company's internally imposed cost of capital (CHR), which is typically somewhat higher than its weighted average cost of capital (WACC; WHR). Exhibit 5.6 depicts the results of a Monte Carlo distribution on NPV, based on the template of Exhibit 5.4, for the two uniform CAGR distributions shown, the top one being relatively wide (plus and minus five percentage points about the mean of 12 percent), and the bottom one being comparatively narrow (plus and minus 2.5 percentage points).

There are several things we should note about the results on the right-hand side of this figure. The shown NPV result is the cumulative NPV distribution based on 10,000 iterations. The shape of the distribution is almost, but not quite, a straight line. Over the range of CAGR values considered, the value of NPV is almost linear because changes in CAGR cause approximately proportionate changes in cash flow and DCF. The "tails" of the NPV distribution refer to the values at the extreme range of possible outcomes, say, below 10 percent probability and above 90 percent probability. For a near-linear distribution as shown, the tails are considered "fat," meaning there is a comparatively significant change in NPV for small increases in probability. Later we see how other distributions have the effect of creating "thin" tails.

The mean NPV is as shown, $41.58 and $41.52 million, respectively. This result suggests that if the seller and buyer of the subject opportunity were willing to negotiate a single-payment transaction at the mean-weighted average of all the possible range of outcomes (considering just this uncertainty in CAGR), the value of the transaction would be approximately $41.5 million. Such mean value is essentially unaffected by the uncertainty in CAGR because, by definition, it is the mean value of NPV. So, as long as the uncertainty in CAGR is symmetrical about the mean value of 12 percent and changes in NPV are approximately linear with changes in CAGR over the range of consideration, the mean NPV is almost unaffected by the degree of uncertainty in the input variable (here, CAGR). However, in the broad CAGR-distribution assumption, the maximum NPV experienced was $50.15 million versus just $45.72 million for the narrow CAGR distribution. This difference is because the upper bound on CAGR for the top example was 5 points above the mean (i.e., 17 percent), whereas in the bottom case it was just 2.5 points (i.e., 14.5 percent). Accordingly, for the very best outcomes, the NPV will be higher in the upper example because of the possibility, however remote, that the opportunity will experience a higher growth rate in revenues during the mature period. Correspondingly, the worse case NPV is proportionately lower in the upper example because the worst-case CAGR is lower (7 percent).

What value would reasonable buyers be willing to pay for the opportunity shown in Exhibit 5.5? The buyer certainly should be willing to pay $33.60 million because even in the more uncertain CAGR, 9,999 out of 10,000 the NPV experienced will exceed this figure. On average it exceeds $33.6 million by approximately $8 million (providing the buyer finds reasonable these

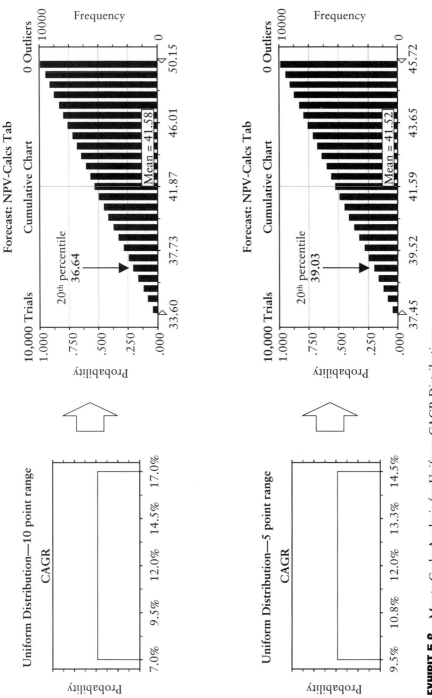

**EXHIBIT 5.6** Monte Carlo Analysis for Uniform CAGR Distributions

underling assumptions). In the very best case, it exceeds it by approximately $17 million (in the upper example) or by $13 million (in the lower example).

A seller could take the reciprocal extreme position and say, "This opportunity has the potential to be worth $50 million, so that's what I want." However, $50 million only occurs once in 10,000 parallel universes, and only for the highest uncertainty CAGR. This rare occurrence is not likely to be persuasive to a prospective buyer.

If the compromise between the seller and buyer is taking the median value, then in either the broad or narrow CAGR examples the deal price would be approximately $41.5 million. For that price, and under these assumptions, the buyer would then understand that it could lose as much as $12 million (for the worst case, broad CAGR distribution) or make as much as $9 million (for the best case, broad CAGR distribution). For reasons discussed later in this book, it is unlikely that a reasonable buyer will accept such median value as fair value. A buyer is more likely to require that the odds of meeting or exceeding the purchase price are substantially greater than 50:50.[7]

For the moment, let us consider the NPV value at the 20th percentile: $36.64 million and $39.03 million for the broad and narrow CAGR distributions, respectively. Here the buyer would be willing to pay approximately $2.4 million more for the less uncertain result (the narrow CAGR distribution). And, 80 percent of the time, the buyer will experience a return in excess of what it paid for the opportunity.

The uniform distribution has a logical incongruity. Under most circumstances, there is no physical reason why CAGR or other assumed variables are so certainly bounded as to be greater and less than prescribed values. Further, one would expect that by reason or experience there is a central value of CAGR that is more likely, and the further from such central value the less likely we would be to experience the corresponding CAGRs. In other words, if we really believe the mean value of CAGR is 12 percent, it is not likely that we would accept that CAGRs above and below 12 percent are all equally likely regardless of the deviation from such 12 percent right up to the precipice where, under the uniform distribution tool, the probability drops to zero. In most physical situations, it is more logical to expect the probability of occurrence to decline in some proportion to the deviation from the *best* estimate value, which leads us to the triangular distribution.

## Triangular Distribution

The triangular distribution is the next simplest form of uncertainty. The highest probability occurs at the value of CAGR perceived to be most likely. Then one specifies the lowest and highest values of CAGR that are believed to be reasonably conceivable. The triangular distribution then creates a straight line for the relative probability from the maximum at the most-likely value decreasing to zero at the upper and lower limits. If the upper and lower limits are symmetrical about the best estimate, then such estimate is also the mean value. However, the triangular distribution does not require such symmetrical assumption. Exhibit 5.7 illustrates the NPV results for a broad and narrow CAGR distribution using symmetrical triangular distributions.

The effect of such assumed triangular distributions can be readily seen on the shape of the resulting cumulative NPV distributions. Instead of being nearly a straight line as in Exhibit 5.6, the center-weighting of the triangular distribution causes "thinner" tails at the lower and upper extremes of NPV probability. This result makes sense because there are comparatively fewer occurrences of CAGR values distant from the mean value of 12 percent so we should expect the NPV values to be more weighted about their mean as shown. Interestingly, the mean value in both the narrow and broad CAGR distributions is identical ($41.53 million) and the same as for the uniform distribution case. This result is because all four of the uniform and triangular distributions were symmetrical about the chosen mean value for CAGR (12 percent) and, as discussed earlier, small changes in CAGR cause corresponding small and nearly linear changes in NPV. Likewise the extreme NPV values are essentially identical to the uniform distribution examples. This result is because, in the least favorable case in both the uniform and triangular cases, the minimum CAGR values were the same. What was different was how often CAGR was experienced near the extremes. Accordingly, when one examines the 20th percentile, in both of the triangular distributions, the value is higher than the corresponding values for the uniform distribution: $38.55 million versus $36.64 million (approximately $1.9 million greater) for the wider distribution, and $40.02 million versus $39.03 million (approximately $1 million greater) for the narrower distribution. Is it logical that a buyer would pay more for the opportunity if it accepted the assumption of the triangular distribution? The answer is yes, because even paying more it still has the prospect of meeting or beating the purchase price 80 percent of the time.

Using 20th percentile as a one-time payment valuation point, the effect of a triangular distribution leads to reduced uncertainty and higher perceived value. One unrealistic feature of such a distribution is the impossibility of values below and above the selected bounds. In the real world we would expect that however low the probability there would not be a prohibition against the possibility of extremely low and high values of CAGR. Another feature of the triangular distribution is the linearity in probability variation for deviations from the best estimate. If one really believes that the best estimate is a good estimate, then it is also reasonable to believe that the probability of CAGR values declines more rapidly than a linear relation as one deviates from such best estimate, which leads us to the normal distribution.

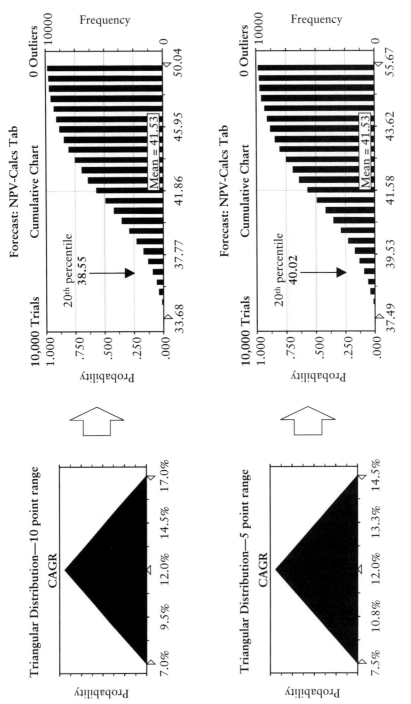

**EXHIBIT 5.7** Monte Carlo Analysis for Triangular CAGR Distributions

## The Normal Distribution

In many physical circumstances, there is a famous distribution that characterizes the probability of occurrences away from a mean. This distribution is known as the "*normal*," because it is common, or more formally a *Gaussian* distribution or more colloquially as the *bell curve* because it looks like a bell in profile. One of the settings in which normal distributions tend to arise is manufacturing. 3M's factories are designed to make their 60,000 products exactly the same every time. However, because we are only human and our machines express and may even compound our limitations, we never experience exactly and only the idealized properties of what we produce. Each part manufactured varies in weight and length by (it is hoped for 3M and their customers) small amounts about the designed mean value. If we collected all the thousands of parts of a particular product manufactured during, say, a day or week, and measured each one and plotted a distribution of such measured values, we would likely find a bell-like distribution where the peak of the bell corresponds to the design mean but exhibiting values that are scattered about that mean. It has been found in many circumstances such as manufacturing, or the heights of humans, or IQ scores (about which there is substantial controversy), and many other examples, that the distribution of observed results can be very well correlated by this particular function known as a normal distribution. The relative width of the bell is measured by a parameter known as the standard deviation (or sigma). Although the mathematics is more cumbersome than we want to deal with here, approximately 68 percent of the occurrences take place within one standard deviation on either side of the mean, and approximately 99 percent within three standard deviations. Exhibit 5.8 illustrates the use of a narrow and broad normal[8] distribution on the resulting NPV distribution.

The upper CAGR distribution assumed a standard deviation of two percentage points about the mean of 12 percent, so approximately 68 percent of all the occurrences of CAGR will occur within the range of 10 percent and 12 percent. According to the equation of the normal distribution, this value of standard deviation also means that 90 percent of the occurrences of CAGR will be between 8.7 percent and 15.3 percent. In the lower case, a narrower CAGR distribution is assumed with a standard deviation of one percentage point about the mean of 12 percent as shown. Even though the normal distribution packs more of the CAGR values near to the mean, it should be noted that there is literally no imposed upper or lower bound. That is, the assumed CAGR distribution itself has very thin tails going out to plus and minus infinity. Such thin CAGR tails in turn causes the calculated NPV distributions to also have thinner tails than was the case with the triangular CAGR calculations, which in turn were thinner than those associated with the uniform distribution.

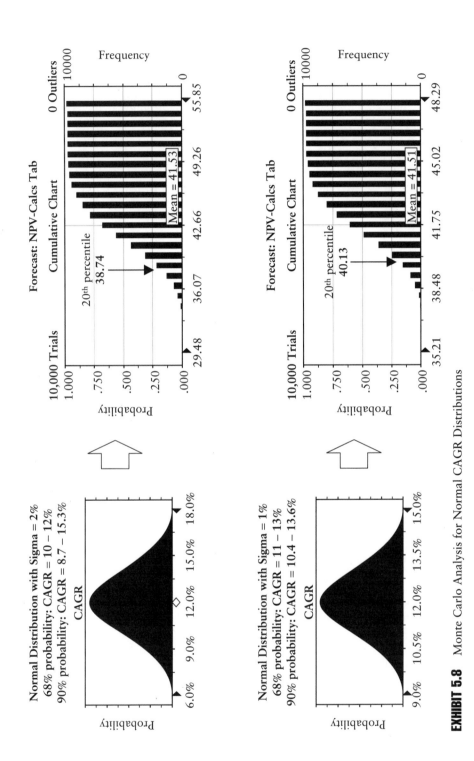

**EXHIBIT 5.8** Monte Carlo Analysis for Normal CAGR Distributions

As shown in Exhibit 5.8, the mean values are essentially unchanged from the uniform and triangular examples in Exhibits 5.6 and 5.7 for the reasons stated previously, namely, the symmetry of the assumed distributions about the mean and the near linearity of NPV within the range of the CAGR values considered. Notice, however, that the maximum and minimum NPV values experienced in 10,000 trials are more extreme than the previous two distributions. This is because in both the uniform and triangular distributions there were abrupt cutoffs below and above which no value of CAGR was permitted, whereas in the case of the normal distribution such extreme values are rare but possible. For most circumstances, therefore, the use of a normal distribution is a more realistic assumption because it admits the possibility of a continuum of values.

The 20th percentile values shown are approximately the same as was found for the triangular distribution. The 20th percentile results for all three distributions can be seen in Exhibit 5.9.

The lower curve shows the NPV at the 20th percentile for the broader distribution for each of the uniform, triangular, and normal distribution examples just considered. The upper curve corresponds to the result for the corresponding narrower distributions.

Three general principles can be espoused based on this result:

1. The 20th percentile NPV values are higher when the range of uncertainty in the assumed value (in our present case, of CAGR) is diminished. This result is because values of CAGR closer to the mean will occur more often and, correspondingly, values of NPV closer to the mean will occur more often. Since the mean NPV is always higher than the 20th percentile NPV, such narrowing in the range of the CAGR assumption results in a higher NPV value of the 20th percentile.

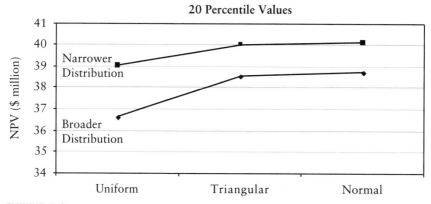

**EXHIBIT 5.9** Effect of CAGR Assumed Distribution Type and Broadness on NPV Value

2.  The 20th percentile NPV values resulting from triangular distribution assumptions will be higher than uniform distributions because the range of CAGR values are concentrated toward the mean and, accordingly, there are more NPV outcomes near the mean value than in the case of the uniform distribution.

3.  The 20th percentile NPV value for the normal distribution will (almost always) be higher than the uniform distribution for the same reasons as the triangular distribution exhibits higher values. Only in the unusual case in which the assumed normal distribution was very wide could the 20th percentile be lower than the uniform distribution. However, 20th percentile NPV may be higher or lower for the normal distribution when compared to a triangular distribution. This result is because there are two balancing effects occurring. The normal distribution normally has a more peaked shape than the triangular distribution, causing more NPV values near the mean and thereby higher 20th percentile values, but it admits to the possibility of infinitely low and high values, which tends to cause more extreme NPV values and thereby lower 20th percentile values. Depending on the specifics of the respective triangular and normal distributions, one effect will outweigh the other, causing the 20th percentile associated with the normal distribution to be higher or lower. In the examples reflected in Exhibit 5.9 such competing effects were chosen to give slightly larger NPV values for the normal distribution than the triangular. However, by assuming larger values of standard deviation, making the bell more squat shaped than peaked, the reverse would be true.

## Other Distribution Functions

In addition to the three commonly used distribution functions considered previously, there are numerous other functions available as modeling tools in Crystal Ball (and in @Risk). Exhibit 5.10 depicts the 17 functions available in Crystal Ball as tools to implement Monte Carlo models.

Following is a brief description of the possible application to negotiation of the more commonly used tools:

■   The log-normal distribution is closely related, as the name suggests, to the normal distribution. It is based on the natural logarithm of a normally distributed variable, not the variable itself. This distribution has a very useful property in that negative values are precluded and the resulting log-normal distribution is skewed toward positive values above the mean. Such a distribution would make more sense than a normal distribution for, say, a direct revenue projection because projected revenues can be zero but not negative, whereas CAGR factors can be both positive and negative, with negative values causing a decrease in revenues year over year. Log-normal distributions are observed in many physical cir-

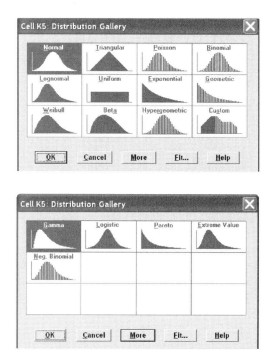

**EXHIBIT 5.10** Screen Shots of 17 Crystal Ball® Assumption Distribution Tools

cumstances when the mean value is sufficiently close to zero and negative values cannot exist. So if we were measuring the distribution of weights of large objects, a normal distribution could be acceptable because in practice the probability of having such distribution compute a negative weight is negligible. If, however, we are measuring the distribution of weights of very light objects, then using a log-normal distribution is likely to lead to a better physical model because of the inadmissibility of negative weights.

■ The binomial distribution like the normal distribution is widely observed to occur in any number of physical processes. It is however a discrete probability distribution, as distinct from all the previous ones, which were continuous distributions. This distinction means that for this distribution and all of the other distributions shown in Exhibit 5.10 by vertical bars instead of continuous fill, only discrete values are permitted. So, for example, suppose our revenue model had been developed on a bottom-up basis assuming sales calls on, say, 100 large potential customers. Each such customer would either purchase the product or not. So the range of possibilities is 1 customer, 2 customers, 3, and so forth up to the maximum possible number of 100 customers. We could not have 2.7 customers. Such a discrete possibility distribution can be modeled by the binomial function.

■   The custom distribution enables one to create any perceived relationship of probabilities. This relationship can be based on data obtained in previous experience or through reasoned judgment or some market testing. An example of such a custom distribution will be shown later.

Any statistical distribution can in principle be modeled in Monte Carlo. In practice, extensive modeling may not aid in improving the value of the projection because, as the saying goes, the chain is only as strong as the weakest link. In any opportunity model, there are numerous assumptions that could be made. Invariably, some of these can be made on a more well-grounded basis because of market research, extensive experience, or some other reason. However, there invariably are other variables for which the assumptions are more speculative. Depending on the relative importance of each of the assumed variables, it can be of little value to refine any one distribution function beyond some initial point of reasonableness. As will be shown later, there are tools available within Monte Carlo software to assist in this very judgment of determining which distributions are the more important and, correspondingly, where one should work on refining the opportunity model.

## MONTE CARLO MODEL OF THE DCF TEMPLATE

In this section, we consider the more realistic case of multiple, parallel assumptions of our Monte Carlo template given in Exhibit 5.4 for the purpose of illustrating how the method can be used in negotiation.

### Combined CAGR and Cost Ratio Uncertainty Distributions

First we consider including an uncertainty distribution for the total cost ratio. If we have some basis intrinsic to our analysis of the opportunity to conclude that a 70 percent cost ratio (therefore, 30 percent EBIT) is reasonable, then it is also reasonable to use a center-weighted distribution such as the normal distribution. (If our confidence level concerning the 70 percent figure was less, we might assume a triangular distribution with a broad range for minimum and maximum values, or even a uniform distribution.) Further, our consideration of our assumed best estimate for 70 percent cost ratio may lead us to conclude that it is more likely that deviations from 70 percent will be toward higher costs rather than lower costs. The basis of such reasoning could simply be the recognition of how difficult it is to find business opportunities that evidence 40 percent, or even 35 percent, EBITs. To provide such upward bias, we can choose a log-normal distribution with the mean value set at 70 percent. Although such a distribution includes some small probability that the cost ratio could exceed 100 percent, there is nothing physically impossible about such an outcome, no matter how unappealing it would be for a buyer. However, cost ratios below 50 percent are unlikely and are impossible below 0 percent. The specific distribution parameter assumptions made for CAGR and cost ratio and the resulting NPV distribution is shown in Exhibit 5.11.

The effect of these twin uncertainty distributions clearly creates a very pronounced *s*-shape NPV distribution with long, thin tails. This result is reflected in the very large value of the maximum ($114) and the very negative value of the minimum (–$36.84). Because this simulation was done using 10,000 iterations, the extreme values occur only 0.01 percent of the time (once each out of a 10,000 parallel universes). Because our assumptions are both compounded, given that there are two simultaneous ones working here, each with long tails, the maximum and minimum values are substantially more extreme than in our previous examples. The median value, however, has changed very little, namely, $41.59 in Exhibit 5.11, which is only slightly higher than the mean values in Exhibits 5.6 through 5.8. Although the lognormal distribution assumed for the cost ratio is biased upward, it has only a small effect on the mean value because the mean value of the cost ratio distribution was still assumed to be 70 percent.

There is an important change at the 20th percentile. In Exhibit 5.11 for the combined CAGR and cost ratio assumptions, the 20th percentile is $24.44, which compares with the 20th percentile values graphed in Exhibit 5.9 where all the values were above $36. This decrease in 20th percentile value is caused by the combined adverse probabilities of reduced CAGR (compared with the mean of 12 percent) and increased cost ratio (compared to 70 percent).

Thus, for our envisioned negotiation (for a one-time payment for the opportunity), if the parties are operating on a median NPV, the effect of the more realistic model is negligible, which seems, and is, counter to common sense. The higher perceived uncertainty should diminish the buyer's willingness to pay. If the parties are operating on the extreme values, the seller seeking values near the maximum and the buyer near the minimum, the model clearly shows that no agreement will be possible; not only are the extreme values farther apart, the negative value for the minimum would cause any rational buyer fixated on the worst-case outcome to walk away from the opportunity at any price. However, for a negotiation based on, say, the 20th percentile value, we have a comprehensible result: The opportunity is still perceived to have substantial value, because of the mean value and the high maximum, but the higher associated uncertainties and the possibility of substantial losses cause a reasonable buyer to be willing to pay less than it would have under reduced uncertainty conditions such as considered earlier.

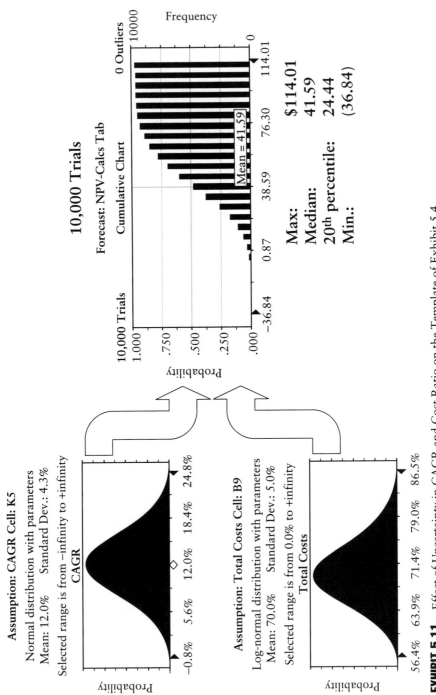

**EXHIBIT 5.11**    Effect of Uncertainty in CAGR and Cost Ratio on the Template of Exhibit 5.4

## Correlating Assumptions

Introducing two simultaneous assumptions as just above introduces a new consideration: To what extent are these assumption distributions correlated? In other words, how does the Monte Carlo method choose values for cost ratio once it has chosen (for the particular trial) the value of CAGR? Is there any relationship between the two choices? Should there be?

This question is one of the presence (or absence) of a correlation between these two assumption distributions. The default condition for Monte Carlo is zero (0.0) correlation between the assumption variables, which means that it is equally probable for a high CAGR trial that the software will choose a high cost ratio as choose a low cost ratio. One of the tools of the method is the ability to create a correlation between any variables, which we now illustrate. Let us consider the following line of reasoning. One way to grow unit sales more rapidly is to decrease prices, which is a fundamental tenet of economics. In our model, we can assume that we can grow revenues more rapidly by increasing the cost ratio, which at first may seem counterintuitive. However, recall that the cost ratio is a percentage of the total revenues, and not a total cost. So for fixed costs, if we were to reduce our prices, such an action would have the effect of increasing the cost ratio. Assuming this is a legitimate perspective, we can now create a correlation between the CAGR and cost ratio values.

In Crystal Ball the correlation is established between the limits of –1.0 to +1.0, with 0.0 being the baseline, uncorrelated condition. Positive correlations mean that for CAGR being larger than the mean, there is a bias to make the cost ratio larger than its mean, which is the direction our earlier analysis has concluded. If we choose +1.0 as the correlation, the software will always have higher-than-mean cost ratio values whenever there is a higher-than-mean CAGR, and vice versa. If we choose 0.5, then there will be a significant positive-to-positive correlation, but that correlation will not occur in all circumstances. Exhibit 5.12 depicts the results of such +0.5 correlation.

This exhibit shows some interesting results: For the correlated case, the range narrowed, meaning the maximum value was reduced and the minimum value was larger, while the 20th percentile value increased; as before, the mean value is relatively unchanged. In this case a positive correlation means that when higher values of CAGR are chosen, which would tend to drive NPV upward, then higher values of cost ratio are also likely (but not always, because the correlation coefficient chosen was +0.5) and higher cost ratio values drive the NPV lower. So this positive correlation results in lower highs and higher lows. Shown at the bottom of Exhibit 5.12 are these same data but in frequency form, which is the origin of the term *bell curve*. The statistics below these bell curves are measures of the shape of the NPV distribution.

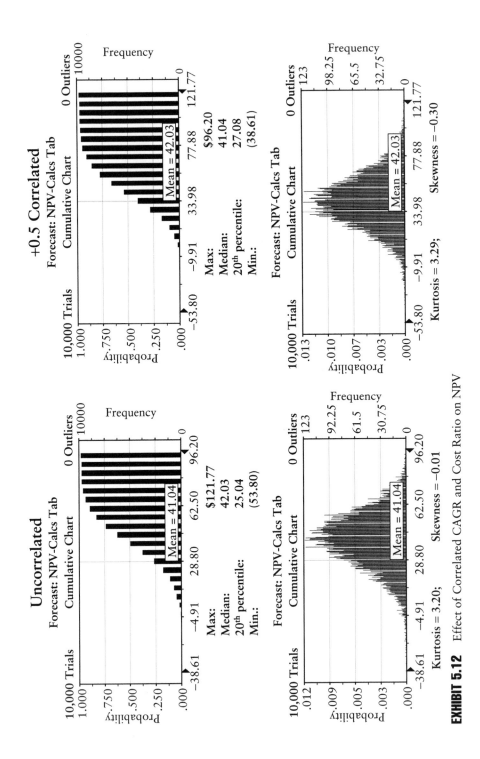

**EXHIBIT 5.12** Effect of Correlated CAGR and Cost Ratio on NPV

The kurtosis is a measure of its peakedness. For a normal distribution, the kurtosis is exactly 3.0. So both these outcomes exhibit a more peaked distribution than the normal distribution of the assumptions, with the correlated case being more peaked for the reason given above. The skewness is a measure of the symmetry of the distribution around the mean value. For a normal distribution the skewness is exactly 0.0. Here, both distributions have a slight skewness toward the negative values of NPV, because the log-normal distribution chosen for the cost ratio assumption is skewed toward higher cost that causes lower NPV. The skewness for the correlated case is slightly higher and this result is reflected in the difference in the minimum and maximum values between the two cases: The maximum value is approximately $26 less in the correlated case ($96 versus $122), but the minimum value is only approximately $15 less negative (negative $39 versus negative $54). So the maximum value decreased more than the minimum value increased.

The metric of the 20th percentile value increased from $25 to $27. Again, this is a reflection of the distribution being more concentrated toward the mean value because the uncertainty has been reduced. In the correlated case there is a presumed relationship between the two uncertainties.

## Additional Assumption Distributions

We now consider two more assumptions, again using our template of Exhibit 5.4. So far we have considered assumed distributions for CAGR and cost ratio. The two other primary assumptions in Exhibit 5.4 are the CapEx investments during each of the first 5 years (the startup period), and the revenues in years 2 through 5 (prior to when the CAGR calculation is used).

The assumptions and results are shown in a Monte Carlo report that is given in Appendix 5A. As can be seen, the CAGR and cost ratio assumptions are as before, normal and log normal, respectively with the shown parameters, and correlated by a +0.5. Now, in addition, assumptions have been made for each of the five CapEx values as given by the distributions for Cells 18D through 18H (corresponding to Years 1 through 5). The Year 1 CapEx has been characterized by a normal distribution under the reasoning that these costs should be comparatively well known. For Year 2 the distribution chosen is the triangular one, reflecting increased uncertainty. Likewise, the triangular distribution has been used for Year 3, but with a wider base (greater range of uncertainty), reflecting the common belief that the further in time one is projecting costs the less certain one is likely to be. Then in Years 4 and 5 an even more uncertain distribution is chosen, namely, that of the uniform distribution, with Year 5's range larger than Year 4's. The distributions have not been correlated with each other under the reasoning that there would not necessarily be a cause-and-effect relationship between higher (or lower) costs in one year and the costs for the succeeding year.

Finally, Appendix 5A also shows assumed distributions for the revenue projections in Years 2 through 4 for Cells 4E through 4H. Here we assume an uncertain uniform distribution for Years 2 and 3 and a somewhat less uncertain triangular distribution for Years 4 and 5. The underlying reasoning in this example is that the magnitude of the early revenues is more uncertain because of technology and market-development timing. As we go out further in the forecast period, it is assumed here that it is actually somewhat more likely to meet our revenue forecasts. Here the revenue forecasts are in fact correlated. The logic is that if a previous year had higher than mean revenues, then it is highly likely that the subsequent year will also have higher than mean revenues because annual revenues are likely to build up from a base of existing revenues. Accordingly, all these revenues are correlated at +1.0 with the preceding year.

The results for 10,000 trials of this complete model are:

- Maximum NPV = $139
- Mean NPV = $41
- 20th percentile NPV = $22
- Minimum NPV = –$46

These results are compared with the three earlier cases we considered as shown in Exhibit 5.13. As can be seen, all three s-curves can be made to closely approximate one another with the result that the mean NPV value changes very little across all these cases and varying assumptions; the standard deviation around the mean of the means is only $0.45, or about 1 percent of the mean. However, there is an enormous variation in the minimum and maximum values with a standard deviation of $28 and $22 as shown. As might be expected, the 20th percentile value shows more variability than the mean, but much less than the minimum and maximum; its standard deviation is just under $4.

Up until now we have been considering the 20th percentile as a to-be-noted benchmark value under the reasoning that for two sides to agree on value the other alternatives considered, namely, the minimum, maximum, and mean, are unlikely to be acceptable. Now, let us consider other possible dealmaking reference points.

### Twentieth (and Other) Percentile Valuations

If we accept the principle that the bounds of 0th and 50th percentile values will likely be unacceptable to one side of a negotiation, where might a reasonable middle, negotiating ground be? We should not expect there to be a concrete answer, such as the value of pi, because the answer will be influ-

| Year | | | 1 | 2 | 3 | 4 | 5 | 6 | Total | Difference |
|---|---|---|---|---|---|---|---|---|---|---|
| | | | | | | | | *12.0%* | | |
| Monte Carlo Model | | | 0 | 2 | 15 | 70 | 180 | 202 | 469 | 0% |
| Fisher-Pry | $t_{50} = 4.2$ | $s = 1.4$ | 0 | 0 | 7 | 73 | 182 | 200 | 463 | −1% |
| Pearl-Reed | $a = 15,000$ | $s = 2.3$ | 0 | 1 | 13 | 80 | 175 | 199 | 468 | 0% |
| Gompertz | $a = 11,000$ | $s = 2.3$ | 0 | 0 | 0 | 66 | 179 | 198 | 443 | −5% |

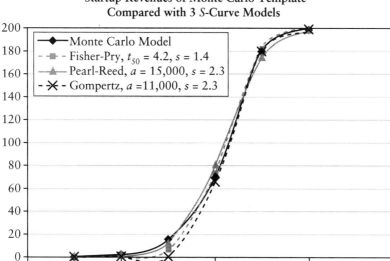

**Startup Revenues of Monte Carlo Template Compared with 3 *S*-Curve Models**

|  | Case 1 | Exhibit 5.12 Case 2 | Exhibit 5.12 Case 3 | Appendix 5A Case 4 Revs. Y2-5 CapEx Y1-5 | Mean | Standard Deviation |
|---|---|---|---|---|---|---|
|  | CAGR | Uncorrelated Cost Ratio CAGR | Correlated Cost Ratio CAGR | Cost Ratio CAGR | | |
| NPV Maximum | $ 75.31 | $ 121.77 | $ 96.20 | $ 139.12 | $ 108.10 | $ 24.32 |
| NPV Mean | $ 41.73 | $ 42.03 | $ 41.04 | $ 40.99 | $ 41.45 | $ 0.45 |
| NPV 20th Percentile | $ 35.64 | $ 25.04 | $ 27.08 | $ 28.57 | $ 29.08 | $ 3.99 |
| NPV Minimum | $ 17.69 | $ (53.80) | $ (38.61) | $ (46.29) | $ (30.25) | $ 28.20 |

**EXHIBIT 5.13** Comparison of NPV Results for Four Cases Studied

enced by the particular negotiating context. What are the seller's alternatives? If they are poor and few, or if the seller has put this on the "just get a deal done by X" list, then the seller's willingness to accept fair value will diffuse down to lower percentiles. What are the buyer's alternatives? If this opportunity is strategic to its future, or fits with other products and present customers and channels, and the alternatives to a deal are speculative and distant, its reasoning will permit it to conclude fair value at higher percentiles. There is no universal percentile answer, but there is a reasonable negotiating range.

Exhibit 5.14 is the NPV distribution for various percentiles from the minimum NPV to the median value (50 percentile) based on the Monte Carlo model presented in Appendix 5A.

Buyers seek to buy low and sell high. (Naturalists like to characterize the survival pressure on animals as life on the "margins" of ecostructures; business people think of life on and by the "spread" between the low and the high.) Additionally, buyers, like most normal people, prefer risk-free opportunities. Accordingly, they will seek to negotiate NPV values that are as nearly certain to be exceeded in practice as can be negotiated. This desire is shown in Exhibit 5.14 by the leftward arrow. As might be expected, sellers see things in an opposite way, because they are now trying to experience the "sell high" moment, and perhaps because they see the significant upside potential as being not all that risky.

Buyers fear project failure that can occur even with a successful technology and market by the buyer having overpaid for the opportunity. Sellers who are forgoing the opportunity by selling it fear seeing a buyer gain huge financial benefits for something they acquired on the cheap. Negotiators on both

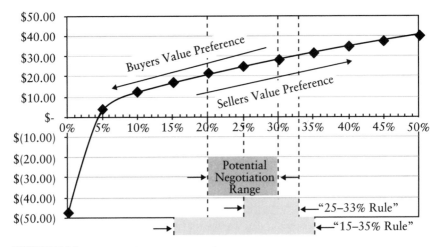

**EXHIBIT 5.14**   NPV Valuation Percentiles

sides want the deal value to be such that it is unlikely they will find themselves wearing a lifelong *de*-merit badge as the one who did the deal that is held out as the poster child of what never should be done again.

Thus, even assuming both the seller and buyer agree on the financial model, including all the relevant assumptions, there remains the issue of where along the spectrum of probabilities should a fair trade occur? The answer lies in the alternative to the agreement, sometimes called "Plan B." If prospective Buyer #1 offers to pay no more than the 10th percentile (which here is approximately $12 million) or will walk away (really), what would a reasonable seller do? In other words, the seller is negotiating with a buyer who insists that 9 times out of 10 it must experience more in value than it paid for the opportunity, recognizing that although there is a 10 percent chance that even at such valuation the buyer will lose money, there is an equal 10 percent of possibilities at the top end that projects it will make $70 million up to even more than $130 million. Further, Buyer #1 in this hypothetical would also have recognized that the mean value of $41 million represents a gain of $29 million over its proposed purchase price of $12 million, a gain of approximately 250 percent of investment. (Any buyer who could acquire a statistically significant number of similar opportunities at the 10th percentile would be *assured* of making approximately 2.5 times its investment ($29 million return versus $12 million invested), recalling that all the cash flows have been discounted at a CHR of 15 percent).

From a seller's perspective, Buyer #1 looks to be (a) too greedy, (b) too risk averse, (c) operating within a different universe of assumptions, or (d) all of the above. Although Buyer #1 can point out that if the seller thinks this investment is such a great opportunity, then why doesn't the seller keep it and realize the mean value (on average) of $41 million? (To which the appropriate answer should be that the seller has higher-valued alternative opportunities.) Under these circumstances, it is likely that the seller will vigorously seek out prospective Buyer #2 (and #3 and so forth) under the belief that there will be a reasonable buyer willing to value the opportunity closer to the mean than the 10th percentile offer it now has. The seller may propose to such Buyer #2 a valuation at the 40th percentile, namely, $35 million, under the reasoning that if it pursues a statistically significant number of such opportunities it can be assured an average return of $6 million (subtracting $35 from the mean value of $41), which represents an approximate 20 percent return on the seller's investment on an NPV basis, again based on a 15 percent CHR. However, for this percentile, Buyer #2 would understand that there is a 40 percent likelihood on this specific opportunity that it will realize less than it paid. Further, any buyer is likely to view as hollow the argument that if it pursues a statistically significant number of such opportunities, it will make money on the spread between the 40th percentile and the mean.[9] The reason this argument is unlikely to persuade is that the buyer is represented by a core group of humans who are not likely to live long enough to experience a mean. If a significant upfront payment for a purchased opportunity "tanks," just the first one, they could "tank" with it. For this reason, buyers as humans tend to be risk averse, and are unlikely to be persuaded by the seller's argument on behalf of the 40th percentile value. However, there can be exceptions, not always well-advised exceptions. One exception example is the strategic-fit category. The buyer is in some way in the business of keeping its present customers happy and finding new, more, and even better customers. Such a buyer can face a situation in which there is a product "hole" in its present family of offerings that is inhibiting satisfying fully its customers and/or gaining new customers. A buyer in such a situation may be willing to pay the 50th percentile, or even more, because of other significant benefits it will enjoy as a result of the opportunity.[10] Another example, which is a seller's dream, is Buyer A who is terrified of the implications of Buyer B acquiring the opportunity, believing that Buyer B might be willing to pay any price to do so (either out of fit or folly).

Another example, for which there are too many dead bodies to count, has been the "dot.com" (also known as "dot con" and "dot bomb") craze and the somewhat related telecom startup explosion. During the height of the recent startup and dealmaking frenzy, there was a suspension of restraint by opportunity buyers perhaps in part because they performed no analysis but also because they viewed many such opportunities as "must haves." During the short term, the marketplace rewarded such buyers under the doctrine of "get big fast," "the new gold rush," "being the central switchboard of the grand thought matrix,"[11] and so forth. So, there can be both legitimate justification and crazed speculation for a buyer's willingness to value at the mean or above, but normally sellers should not count on this occurring.

If 10th and 40th percentiles are too safe and too risky for buyers (in many circumstances), what is the right level of risk? When managers are asked to project revenues for their operating businesses, there is a common expectation that such projections will be met or exceeded essentially without fail. Sometimes such expectations are made overt ("your job depends on meeting these numbers"), sometimes it is simply reflected by the culture of the company that is intolerant of negative surprises. Though no projection is ever certain in the sense of 100 percent certainty, such risk-averse contexts of projecting on existing businesses are likely using some standard such as 90 percent to 95 percent certainty, which is equivalent to saying that 18 to 19 years out of 20, I will meet or exceed my projection.[12] However, if a researcher within a company is proposing a new R&D project and is asked as to the likelihood of success, the normal expectation is that success probability is something much lower than, perhaps in some cases, at the 50 percent level, but others at the 80 percent level. For R&D projects that have very high potential payoffs, or for interesting ones that require very little investment, it is conceivable that a project advocate could accept only a 20 percent, or even a 1 percent, chance of success because of the high potential payoff and, after all, that is why they call it "research." Such 20 percent chance of success is sometimes called the "commando project," because in military settings elite commando units are sometimes committed to high-stakes missions whose projected likelihood of success is only about 20 percent.

Exhibit 5.14 also includes three possible negotiating ranges. The top one, between the 20th and 30th percentiles, reflects the perspective that the 10th percentile, preferred by the buyer, is too conservative and likely to be unacceptable to a seller with other options, and the 40th percentile, preferred by the seller, is too close to the mean and thereby near a normally unattractive 50:50 result. Why might this be reasonably acceptable to both sides? Well, one perspective would be to recognize the 25th percentile as representing a 50:50 split, in terms of probability, of the mean value. In this instance the seller would argue that if you made enough investments, you would realize the mean value but we recognize that what is on the table is one investment and, accordingly, we are agreeing to discount the probability used for computing the value to recognize the risk associated with buying just one opportunity.[13] So, the 25th percentile is analogous to the parties meeting halfway to the mean. (Note that this "meeting halfway" is not splitting the difference between the value at the minimum and the mean as that would be: –$47 + $40 = –$7, dividing by 2 = –$3.5.) Another "meeting halfway" perspective would also lead to the 25th percentile: Following the reasoning given earlier whereby the seller would seek the 40th percentile and the buyer the 10th, the midpoint would be the 25th percentile.

The following perspective could lead to a 20th percentile conclusion. There is a widely quoted aphorism attributed to Paretto known as the 80:20 Rule. It is widely cited in many different contexts in business books: 20 percent of one's customers are the source of 80 percent of one's profits, 20 percent of one's "to-do" list affects 80 percent of one's success, 20 percent of the employees cause 80 percent of the grief, and many other applications. The 20th percentile value has this same kind of appeal, namely, a buyer can conceive of an opportunity being fairly valued if 80 percent of the time it will receive in benefit more than it paid to acquire the rights to the opportunity.

Also shown in Exhibit 5.14 are two "rule" ranges. In licensing contexts, there is a common rule of thumb (heuristic) known as the 25-Percent Rule. This rule works as follows: In a licensing situation, the parties will tend to negotiate agreements that split the EBIT, revenues minus appropriately allocated costs but before interest and taxes, 75:25 in which the buyer receives the 75 percent and the seller the 25. I have written another book that has an extensive discussion of the context and application of this rule: *Early Stage Technologies: Valuation and Pricing* (John Wiley & Sons, 1999); and *Valuation and Pricing of Technology-Based Intellectual Property* (John Wiley &

Sons, 2003). This rule is predicated on the R&D of the subject opportunity being substantially completed but manufacturing engineering and creating and satisfying the market being left to the buyer. Because the buyer takes on those tasks and the full risk, it receives the greater reward. In practice, the 25-Percent Rule is often stated as the 25-Percent to 33-Percent Rule or even the 15-Percent to 35-Percent Rule in recognition that specific circumstances can warrant a higher or lower sharing of profits with the seller. See the previously cited sources for a fuller discussion of this subject.

Although Exhibit 5.14 shows both the 25–33-percent and 15–35-percent rule, it is important to note that the context is not the same as the origin of such rule. The 25-Percent Rule is applied to running EBIT values, not to percentiles associated with probabilistic outcomes. Here, if we were to apply the 25-Percent Rule to the mean value of $41 million, it would lead to valuing the opportunity at approximately $10 million, which corresponds to the 7th percentile. However, the root of the 25-Percent Rule is based on recognizing equity between a seller and buyer, given what each party brings to the negotiation. The same forces and inclinations at work in a Monte Carlo context may well conclude as reasonable a 25-Percent Rule but be interpreted on a percentile basis as shown in Exhibit 5.14. As more experience is gained in the use of Monte Carlo methods in negotiation, it may be that a new form of the 25-Percent Rule will be recognized as was done in conventional licensing of single-valued financial models.

## Comparison of Monte Carlo Results with DCF (RAHR) Method

In Chapter 4 we presented ways by which a DCF model coupled with RAHRs can forecast an NPV value. It is interesting to note how the DCF method compares to the earlier Monte Carlo results.

Using the Monte Carlo template in Exhibit 5.4 with the shown mean values for each of the assumption variables, we can determine the NPV value for any prescribed value of RAHR. From the results of Appendix 5A, we can then map each such NPV value against the percentile probability of occurrence as determined by the Monte Carlo method using the distribution functions described earlier for each of the assumptions of this same Exhibit 5.14. The result is shown in Exhibit 5.15.

If we were to evaluate this opportunity from an RAHR perspective and saw it as having a risk warranting a 15 percent RAHR value, Exhibit 15.15 shows that we would conclude the value to be approximately $41 million, which corresponds in this specific instance to the median. However, notice the dramatic changes in opportunity value for relatively small changes in RAHR. At an RAHR of 20 percent, this graph shows the value at the 20th percentile (again a coincidence) that is approximately $22 million; there is a reduction

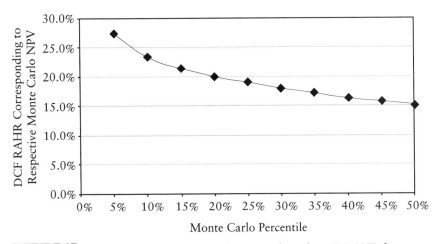

**EXHIBIT 5.15** Comparison of Monte Carlo Percentile with DCF RAHR for Identical NPV Values

in perceived value from a DCF perspective for just a five-point increase in RAHR. At an RAHR of 25 percent, corresponding to approximately the 7th percentile, the value would be only $9 million. And for an RAHR of 30 percent, a DCF model would suggest a value of just $0.3 million, corresponding to less than the 5th percentile. This dramatic decrease in perceived value for relatively small incremental increases in RAHR is a consequence of the hurdle rate diminishing all future cash flows in a compounded way so that even significant future cash flows have very little present value. The power of Monte Carlo is that it can show, through the use of assumption distributions and a CHR of, say, 15 percent, that such high values of RAHR and low values of NPV are overly pessimistic. From a perspective of 20th to 30th percentile negotiation, as discussed earlier, this suggests that an equivalent DCF RAHR would be 18 percent and 20 percent (20 percent RAHR corresponding to the 20th percentile, and 18 percent RAHR to the 30th percentile).

## Scenario Modeling in Monte Carlo

In Chapter 4 we considered how scenario analysis has several levels of appeal. One is simply the ability to see "what happens if" certain future worlds are realized. The difficulty is developing rational probabilities for each such future world envisioned. In Monte Carlo there are elegant ways of incorporating scenario modeling.

Consider again our template of Exhibit 5.4. We can now consider how to incorporate scenarios in some of the assumptions. To illustrate the effect dramatically, we consider the only uncertainty in the cost ratio distribution.

Crystal Ball allows one to "freeze" any (or all) assumptions though a pull-down menu. This tool is particularly useful when trying to assess the effect of each individual assumed distribution or certain combinations of assumptions. So, for this example, we freeze all the assumption distributions shown in Appendix 5A except the one for cost ratio.

One of the ways to create a scenario distribution in Crystal Ball is to use the "custom" distribution function and select the option of "fit" to data. Then, by specifying the range of cells in the worksheet, the software accepts such data as the distribution. Exhibit 5.16 illustrates two adjoining normal distributions that were created in Excel using the NORMDIST function. Shown is a "camel-humped" (double normal) distribution for a cost ratio whose overall mean value is 70 percent as before, but with the high cost ratio scenario (the adverse outcome) having its own normal distribution with a mean value of 80 percent, and the low cost ratio scenario (the favorable outcome) having its normal distribution with a mean at 60 percent. Such a situation could be conceived if there were two technologies being investigated in parallel during the first year of the project. If the high-efficiency technology can be made to work, then we expect a very low cost ratio and highly favorable NPV returns. However, we have a backup technology we are investigating that is expected to be workable but it will cause a significant increase in costs. So, we are projecting the possibility of either technology *A*, or technology *B* becoming available, and at this point we conceive them as being equally probable (so the camel humps are the same height). We recognize that there is some range of uncertainty regarding the operating parameters of each technology, which is why there is a distribution of outcomes for each rather than just a single value at the respective means of 80 percent and 60 percent.

Exhibit 5.16 was created in Excel by creating first in Column A the *x* variables corresponding to the cost ratio ranging from 0.50 to 0.90 in 0.01 increments corresponding to the overall range of variability of the cost ratio. Then, in Column B, we insert the NORMDIST function with the arguments set as follows:

- The first argument is simply the corresponding cell in Column A (the particular cost ratio of interest, say, 0.55).

- Next is the mean value of the normal distribution, which for the rows in Column A corresponding to cost ratios of 0.50 to 0.70 (the first "hump"), is set to 0.60, the mean value for this first range.

- Next is the standard deviation to be used to establish the relative peakedness of the distribution. The value 0.03 (as a decimal) was chosen for both "humps" of Exhibit 5.16.

- Finally, the word "false" is entered to inform the software that we want to see the frequency distribution and not the cumulative distribution.

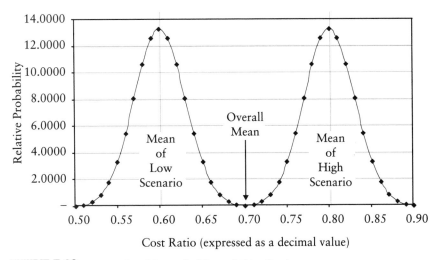

**EXHIBIT 5.16**   Example of Scenario Normal Distribution

■ Then we repeat the above steps for the second range in Column A, from cost ratio values of 0.71 to 0.90, only now the mean value is 0.80 for all these cells.

Then, using the graph function in Excel for Columns A and B, and selecting the scatter graph, we obtain the result shown in Exhibit 5.16.

In Crystal Ball, when the "custom distribution" is selected for the cost ratio followed by choosing the "fit" option, we can then enter the entire data range developed earlier, namely, A1:B41 (A1 is the cost ratio value of 0.50, and B41 is the normal distribution value calculated by the NORMDIST function for the final cost ratio value of 0.90). This data range results in a mirror double-humped camel distribution in Crystal Ball with 41 discrete values of cost ratio (0.50, 0.51, . . . , 0.89, 0.90). Finally, the software enables by a single click to set the entire double-humped probability to 1.00 so that each corresponding cost ratio has its appropriate individual probability. The assumption screen in Crystal Ball now looks as shown in Exhibit 5.17.

Now, with all the assumptions but the cost ratio frozen, and with our two-scenario model of such cost ratio as shown earlier, we can simply allow the software to perform the simulation. The results are shown in Exhibit 5.18. The top left graph repeats the distribution assumption for the cost ratio that was shown in Exhibit 5.17; recall that for this initial scenario example we are only considering the effect of such cost ratio distribution. The upper right graph shows the NPV distribution in frequency form, and the bottom graph in cumulative form. Clearly, the frequency NPV distribution mirrors

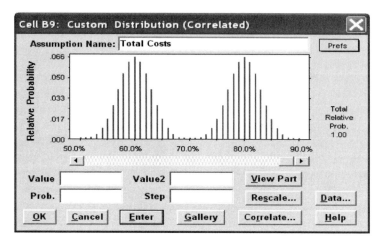

**EXHIBIT 5.17**    Crystal Ball® Cost Ratio Scenario

the cost ratio assumption by exhibiting a double-humped shape. The corresponding cumulative distribution shows a wide, flat zone in the middle of the graph that is caused by there being essentially no NPV outcomes in the area around a cost ratio of 0.70 because the twin input cost ratio distributions are centered about their respective means of 0.6 and 0.8 with a combined distribution minimum at 0.7.

The table of statistics in Exhibit 5.18 gives the corresponding effects in digital form. Note that the 20th percentile benchmark that we have been using leads to the conclusion that the opportunity would not be worth pursuing. This result anticipates the value and power of Real Options that will be discussed in Chapters 6 and 7. The limitation in the previous Monte Carlo model is that in accordance with the assumed reasons for the two-humped cost ratio distribution we would know which outcome occurred at the end of the first year, or by the second at the latest. Accordingly, the opportunity would likely only be pursued if the more favorable technology was successfully demonstrated. This example is an ideal context for the use of Real Options.

Finally, let us consider what happens if we now unfreeze all our other assumptions with the double-humped cost ratio distribution. The result in report form is given in Appendix 5B. The NPV frequency distribution relationship clearly shows a broadening effect caused by the combination of assumption distributions. However, the overall result is still dominated by the very important cost ratio factor, especially because of the significant difference between the favorable and adverse scenarios considered. The effect on cash flow for a mean cost ratio of 0.8 is dramatic in comparison to a mean cost ratio of 0.6. Again, these results suggest the value of another method that will

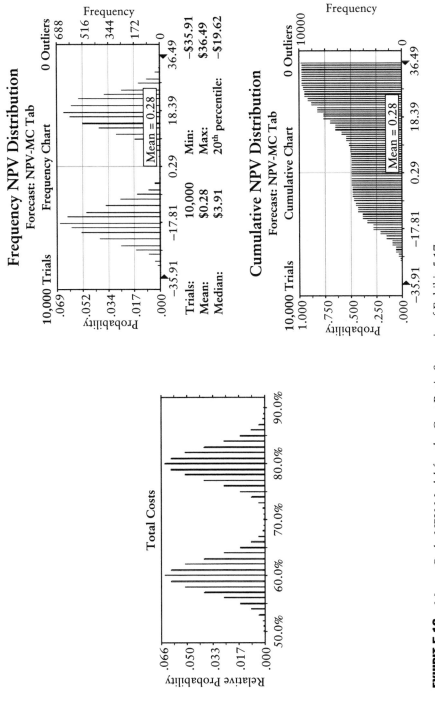

**EXHIBIT 5.18**  Monte Carlo NPV Model for the Cost Ratio Scenario of Exhibit 5.17

permit an initial payment for the right to determine which technology wins and a second payment if the favorable technology proves workable and efficient (and likely abandonment by the buyer if it does not).

## Monte Carlo Tools for Determining Variable Significance

In most models we find that some of the variables have an important effect on the outcome and others have a relatively small effect and still others have essentially no effect. Another Einstein quotation bookends this chapter's discussion on portraying reality: "Not everything that can be counted counts."[14]

It would be useful to be able to rank the relative importance of all the variables to enable us to focus our energies on making more realistic (if possible) the assumptions that really matter.

In Monte Carlo software there is an output generally known as a Tornado Diagram that shows the relative contribution of each of the assumptions on the resulting NPV prediction.

Exhibit 5.19 illustrates the effect of all the assumption distributions on the NPV result ranked from the largest contribution to NPV uncertainty (variance) to the least. As anticipated, the cost ratio distribution is by far the most important uncertainty, followed by the CAGR distribution, then the 5th-year revenue, and so forth. The relative contribution to the overall NPV uncertainty is shown in the variance column next to each assumption. (The Crystal Ball chart only shows the right half of the effect of uncertainty; when the Monte Carlo software shows both halves, then it has the appearance of a tornado in profile; hence, the common name.)

Such tornado charts can be extremely valuable. In the Appendix 5B result reflected in Exhibit 5.19, for example, very little improvement would result from further refining our estimates for CapEx expenditures. This fact would not necessarily be obvious without the portrayal of Exhibit 5.19. If some refinement of CapEx estimates is possible, this chart suggests that the focus should be on Year 4 because it contributes about 5 percent of the NPV uncertainty. The projected revenues during Years 2 through 5 are also relatively unimportant, though somewhat more important than the effect of CapEx. Again if we were to prioritize our energies, the assumption to work on would be revenues in Year 5 followed by Year 4. However, our primary energies should be in developing the best models we possibly can for the cost ratio and then, far less importantly, the CAGR distribution. Exhibit 5.20 is an example of how such a tornado chart might be used in practice.

The left columns merely repeat the results of the tornado chart but also included is the cumulative contribution to uncertainty (variance). Then a judgment is made as to importance, as shown in the next column; this particular judgment by example shows that all assumptions that contribute less than

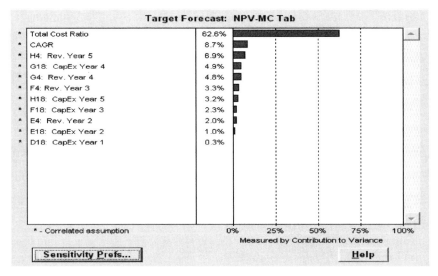

**EXHIBIT 5.19**   Tornado Diagram for Results of Appendix 5B

5 percent of the uncertainty can be ignored. (In ancient days, one would then remove such assumptions from the model because it often required a day or more to run each case; now with lighting fast PCs, there is very little to be gained by stripping out assumptions that are loaded into the model.) In the rightmost three rows are shown by the respective boxes with note references as hypothetical examples the perceptions of the level of confidence in the assumption distribution that has been used. Once such a chart is filled out, the place to begin work is where the contribution to uncertainty is high (the topmost rows) and the confidence level in the respective assumption is low (the rightmost columns). Where the confidence level is high, even for high-importance assumptions, it may be that nothing more can or should be done to refine the assumption.

## FINAL POINTS ON THE MONTE CARLO MODEL

The examples in this chapter are not intended to be directly used because, as stated in the opening paragraphs, opportunities are by definition specific. There is usually an industry norm within which the opportunity will reside that can guide some of the analysis but, in addition, it is best, and usually necessary, to perform a specific analysis on the costs and benefits and timing of same associated with the opportunity. It is helpful to create and use a template such as Exhibit 5.4 that can be applied to many kinds of opportunities by adjusting the assumptions and their distributions. When this template is

**EXHIBIT 5.20**  Prioritizing Assumption Refining

| Assumption | Variance | C-Variance | Importance | Confidence Level in Present Assumption Distribution | | |
| --- | --- | --- | --- | --- | --- | --- |
| | | | | High | Medium | Low |
| Cost Ratio | 62.60% | 62.60% | Very High | | Note 1 | |
| CAGR | 8.70% | 71.30% | Low | Note 2 | | |
| Rev. Year 5 | 6.90% | 78.20% | Low | | | |
| CapEx Year 4 | 4.90% | 83.10% | Negligible | | Note 3 | |
| Rev. Year 4 | 4.80% | 87.90% | Negligible | | Note 4 | |
| Rev. Year 3 | 3.30% | 91.20% | Negligible | | | |
| CapEx Year 5 | 3.20% | 94.40% | Negligible | | | Note 5 |
| CapEx Year 3 | 2.30% | 96.70% | Negligible | | | Note 5 |
| Rev. Year 2 | 2.00% | 98.70% | Negligible | | | |
| CapEx Year 2 | 1.00% | 99.70% | Negligible | | | |
| CapEx Year 1 | 0.30% | 100.00% | Negligible | | | |

Example of 5% Significance Threshold

*Notes:* 1. Highest priority for refinement. 2. No further refinement is warranted. 3. Some effort at refinement could be warranted. 4. Refinement is probably not warranted. 5. Together, these two account for 8.1 percent of the uncertainty and, so, some effort at refinement of revenue projects could be warranted.

created, then even very complex financial models can be adjusted quickly and used to prepare for negotiations or respond to the back and forth of active negotiations and to determine walk-away and Plan B triggers.

As noted previously, the model of Exhibit 5.4 did not consider the effect of terminal value. Depending on the circumstances of the transaction, this could have a very significant effect on value. When making projections beyond 10 years, a common technique is to treat all future value as a lump sum at the conclusion of the 10th year. Such a lump sum would be dependent on the number of years and associated cash flows for all the years beyond the 10th year that value is attributable to the opportunity seller. If the value of the opportunity is sustained only by patent protection, then the expiry of value can be tied to the associated patent life. In other cases, it may be more reasonable to assume a finite life to the opportunity for either market or competitive technology reasons. In any case, terminal value considerations are important and can be easily included in a Monte Carlo model.

The tax rate shown in all the examples was 34 percent of the EBIT, based on the 3M example. The effective tax rate of a company is a complicated and geography specific subject and has an important effect on opportunity value because it has just the same kind of effect as an increase in cost ratio. Some parties simply standardize on 40 percent for the tax rate, a value that appears to be more typical than the 3M example.

All the cash flows were discounted at a CHR of 15 percent as shown in Exhibit 5.4. It is important that such discount value not be made large to account for risk because by the technique of Monte Carlo we are separately judging the effect of risk by valuation at selected percentile values. The use of the buyer's WACC (i.e., WHR) is a logical choice for such a discount factor. However, many companies impose a discount rate somewhat higher than their WACC, with continuous changes depending on market conditions and financing operations, to standardize all their analyses on a common basis. Monte Carlo is particularly effective for this purpose as the effect of risk is accounted for independently of the discount rate used.

One approach to the Monte Carlo method is simply to adjust, tweak, goose, and otherwise fold, spindle, and mutilate the assumption distributions, the model template, the baseline values, and anything else one can think of to get "the answer" one wants. This corruption of purpose abuses the wonderful power of Monte Carlo to give credibility to what is in effect a made-up answer. If that is your purpose, may you get only the blue screen of death on a locked-up box. For those seeking wisdom, the power contained in Monte Carlo modeling is incredible. It enables you to gain the best thinking of the best thinkers and develop a coherent understanding of not only what you think something should be worth but the basis of such belief and a tool that can create changes in your belief on the emergence of better data and assumptions. For you pure in heart, may your wisdom flow like the course of a crystal river through your fingers into the appropriate Monte Carlo cells and may it lead to confidence in what you can know and humility for what you cannot, and may you earn the respect of your colleagues on both sides of the negotiating table by your leadership in fact based reasoning and valuation.

## NOTES

1. Consider the simple everyday situation of a falling leaf, a much more complex question than Newton's falling apple. What would it be like to develop the system of equations that would accurately model a particular leaf falling from any particular branch under any condition of wind, sleet, snow, or hail? All the kings horses and all the kings men, and every Intel processor made in history harnessed by the world's smartest scientists, cannot solve that simple problem at an exact level. However, a child with a $10 digital watch, a tape measure, a glass of lemonade, and several summer afternoons of observation lying on the warm grass can get an understanding of the answer that is reasonably, and surprisingly, accurate.

2. See Arthur Schopenauer's classic work entitled *The World as Will [or Idea] and Representation*, trans. E. F. J. Payne (Mineola, NY: Dover Publications, 1969).

3. SIC, Standard Industrial Classification, designates a code number developed by the U.S. government as a shorthand means of categorizing a company's products or services. SIC codes are being replaced by NAICS: North American Industry Classification System (www.census.gov/epcd/www/naics.html).

4. There are also adjustments for other business functions such as financing operations that are not relevant to our purposes here.

5. In addition to the shown investment in new PPE, 3M also invested in the purchase of new businesses, which is not shown; also it realized modest gains on the sale of previously acquired PPE and businesses. For simplicity, I have not shown these or other investing and financing activities that also had an effect on cash flow. The entries shown are the ones that correspond most closely to cash flow from operations, which is the focus of our interest.

6. For CAGR values 2 percentage points less than RAHR, the perpetuity equation calculation of 5.1 results in an error of only ca. 2 percent. For example for a CAGR of 13 percent and an RAHR of 15 percent, the perpetuity calculation over-predicts the true NPV by ca. 1.2 percent. As the difference between CAGR and RAHR increases, such over-prediction reduces to zero.

7. For this discussion we are presuming the most challenging valuation (wheelbarrow) framework of a single payment from the buyer to the seller. Alternatively, if we adopted some form of pay-as-you-go conditional payments, the valuation process can be made simpler because of a reduced reliance on a single, upfront value.

8. The use of the word *normal* can be confusing. It is not meant to indicate "commonly observed" as in the sense that normal basketballs are round. In these examples, normal is simply a noun for a particular, well-studied statistical relationship.

9. In this Monte Carlo example, the mean and median are essentially the same value, namely $40.99 and $40.24, respectively. In other highly skewed outcomes there could be a significant difference between the two. For our purposes I have used mean and median interchangeably.

10. A more comprehensive analysis would include the economic effect of the opportunity being considered on all a buyer's lines of business.

11. Said by someone on behalf of a company known as Critical Path, which went public in March of 1999, reached $150/share, and is presently selling for 82 cents a share.

12. And I really, really hope that my 1 out of 20 failures does not occur my first year on the job but after I have a track record of successful projections.

13. Splitting differences is a common standard of fairness that goes back at least to King Solomon's famous judgment of "splitting the baby" (see 1 Kings 3:25). Even in the extraordinary context of Solomon's proposal, it was acceptable to one of the parties!

14. I am indebted for this quote to a web site of interesting quotes collected by Dr. Gabriel Robins at www.cs.virginia.edu/~robins/quotes.html.

## APPENDIX 5A: CRYSTAL BALL REPORT CORRESPONDING TO THE RESULTS PRESENTED IN EXHIBIT 5.15 FOR A UNIFORM COST DISTRIBUTION ASSUMPTION

Simulation started on 10/15/02 at 21:34:49
Simulation stopped on 10/15/02 at 21:37:45

**Forecast: NPV-Calcs Tab**                                        **Cell: B22**

Summary:

Display Range is from –46.29 to 139.12
Entire Range is from –46.29 to 139.12
"After 10,000 Trials, the Std. Error of the Mean is 0.23"

Statistics:

|                       | *Value* |
|-----------------------|---------|
| Trials                | 100.00  |
| Mean                  | 40.99   |
| Median                | 40.24   |
| Mode                  | —       |
| Standard Deviation    | 22.70   |
| Variance              | 515.40  |
| Skewness              | 0.16    |
| Kurtosis              | 3.12    |
| Coeff. of Variability | 0.55    |
| Range Minimum         | –46.29  |
| Range Maximum         | 139.12  |
| Range Width           | 185.40  |
| Mean Std. Error       | 0.23    |

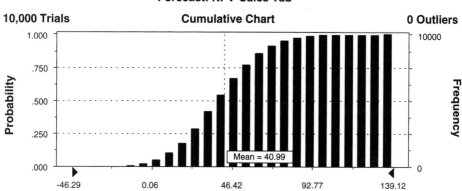

Percentiles:

| Percentile | Value |
|---|---|
| 100% | −46.29 |
| 90% | 12.36 |
| 80% | 22.07 |
| 70% | 28.57 |
| 60% | 34.40 |
| 50% | 40.24 |
| 40% | 46.20 |
| 30% | 52.32 |
| 20% | 59.82 |
| 10% | 70.66 |
| 0% | 139.12 |

End of Forecast

<u>**Assumptions**</u>

**Assumption: CAGR**                                                    **Cell: K5**

Normal distribution with parameters:

Mean                              12.0%
Standard Dev.                     4.3%

Selected range is from –Infinity to +Infinity

Correlated with:

Total Costs (B9)                  0.50

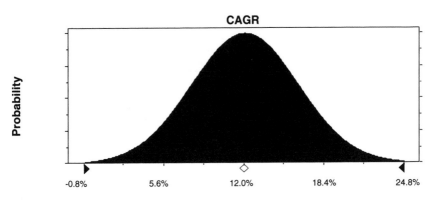

## Assumption: Total Costs                                          Cell: B9

Lognormal distribution with parameters:

Mean                          70.0%
Standard Dev.                  5.0%

Selected range is from 0.0% to +Infinity

Correlated with:

CAGR (K5)                     0.50

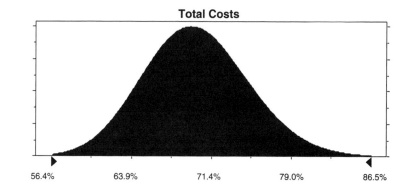

## Assumption: D18: CapEx Year 1                                    Cell: D18

Triangular distribution with parameters:

Minimum                       1.80
Likeliest                     2.00
Maximum                       2.20

Selected range is from 1.80 to 2.20

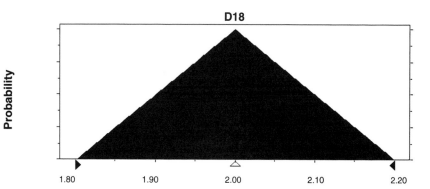

## Assumption: E18: CapEx Year 2                   Cell: E18

Triangular distribution with parameters:

| | |
|---|---|
| Minimum | 8.00 |
| Likeliest | 10.00 |
| Maximum | 12.00 |

Selected range is from 8.00 to 12.00

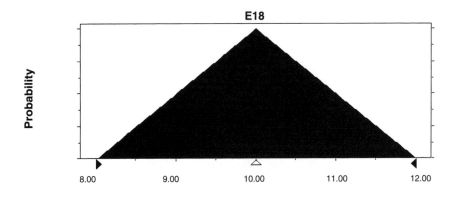

## Assumption: F18: CapEx Year 3                   Cell: F18

Triangular distribution with parameters:

| | |
|---|---|
| Minimum | 24.00 |
| Likeliest | 30.00 |
| Maximum | 36.00 |

Selected range is from 24.00 to 36.00

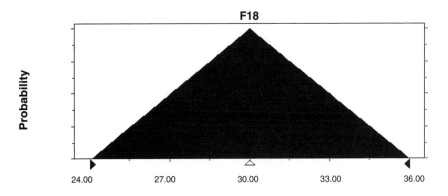

## Assumption: G18: CapEx Year 4　　　　　　　　　Cell: G18

Uniform distribution with parameters:

| | |
|---|---|
| Minimum | 20.00 |
| Maximum | 60.00 |

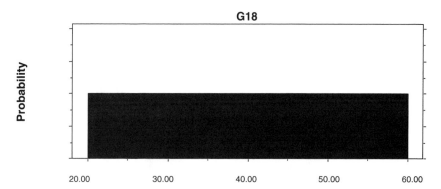

## Assumption: H18: CapEx Year 5　　　　　　　　　Cell: H18

Uniform distribution with parameters:

| | |
|---|---|
| Minimum | 0.00 |
| Maximum | 36.00 |

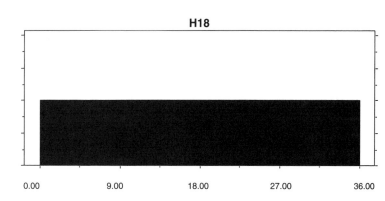

## Assumption: E4: Rev. Year 2                                    Cell: E4

Uniform distribution with parameters:

Minimum                         0.00
Maximum                         4.00

Correlated with:

F4 (F4)                         0.80

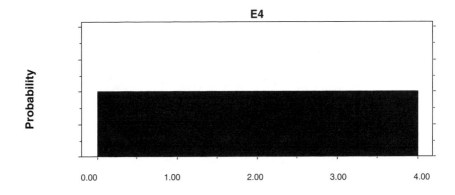

## Assumption: F4: Rev. Year 3                                    Cell: F4

Uniform distribution with parameters:

Minimum                         10.00
Maximum                         20.00

Correlated with:

E4 (E4)                         0.80
G4 (G4)                         0.80

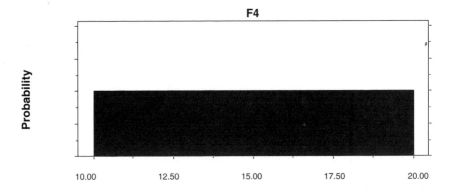

## Assumption: G4: Rev. Year 4        Cell: G4

Triangular distribution with parameters:

Minimum 50.00
Likeliest 70.00
Maximum 90.00

Selected range is from 50.00 to 90.00

Correlated with:

F4 (F4) 0.80
H4 (H4) 0.80

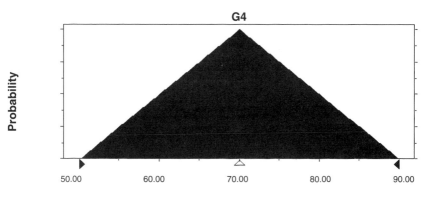

## Assumption: H4: Rev. Year 5                                    Cell: H4

Triangular distribution with parameters:

| | |
|---|---|
| Minimum | 120.00 |
| Likeliest | 180.00 |
| Maximum | 240.00 |

Selected range is from 120.00 to 240.00

**Correlated with:**

G4 (G4)                          0.80

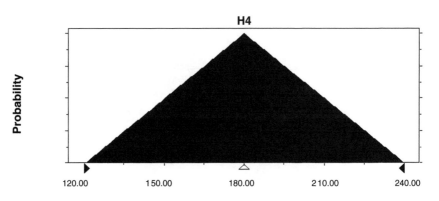

End of Assumptions

## APPENDIX 5B: CRYSTAL BALL REPORT CORRESPONDING TO THE RESULTS PRESENTED IN EXHIBIT 5.16 FOR A DOUBLE-HUMPED COST DISTRIBUTION ASSUMPTION

Simulation started on 10/16/02 at 22:02:16
Simulation stopped on 10/16/02 at 22:06:00

### Forecast: NPV-MC Tab                                      Cell: B22

Summary:

Display Range is from –41.34 to 56.56
Entire Range is from –41.34 to 56.56
"After 10,000 Trials, the Std. Error of the Mean is 0.20"

Statistics:

|                      | *Value* |
| -------------------- | ------- |
| Trials               | 10000   |
| Mean                 | –0.09   |
| Median               | –1.99   |
| Mode                 | —       |
| Standard Deviation   | 19.67   |
| Variance             | 386.81  |
| Skewness             | 0.18    |
| Kurtosis             | 1.85    |
| Coeff. of Variability| –221.49 |
| Range Minimum        | –41.34  |
| Range Maximum        | 56.56   |
| Range Width          | 97.91   |
| Mean Std. Error      | 0.20    |

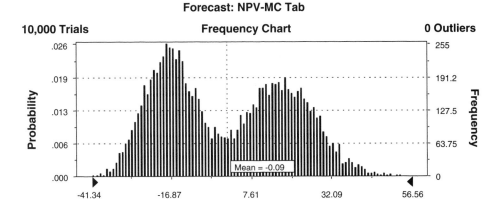

Forecast: NPV-MC Tab

**Forecast: NPV-MC Tab (con'd)**          **Cell: B22**

Percentiles:

| Percentile | Value |
|---|---|
| 100% | −41.34 |
| 95% | −27.72 |
| 90% | −24.27 |
| 85% | −21.71 |
| 80% | −19.42 |
| 75% | −17.43 |
| 70% | −15.49 |
| 65% | −13.35 |
| 60% | −10.58 |
| 55% | −7.43 |
| 50% | −1.99 |
| 45% | 3.96 |
| 40% | 8.16 |
| 35% | 11.35 |
| 30% | 14.13 |
| 25% | 16.90 |
| 20% | 19.66 |
| 15% | 22.82 |
| 10% | 26.18 |
| 5% | 30.71 |
| 0% | 56.56 |

End of Forecast

## Assumptions

### Assumption: CAGR                                           Cell: K5

Normal distribution with parameters:

| | |
|---|---|
| Mean | 12.0% |
| Standard Dev. | 4.3% |

Selected range is from -Infinity to +Infinity

Correlated with:

Total Cost Ratio (B9)        0.50

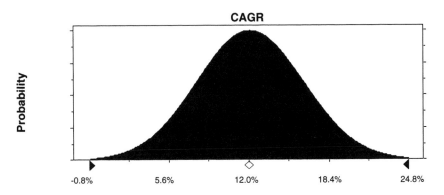

### Assumption: Total Cost Ratio                               Cell: B9

Custom distribution with parameters:

| | | *Relative Prob.* |
|---|---|---|
| Single point | 50.0% | 0.000256 |
| Single point | 51.0% | 0.000004 |
| Single point | 51.0% | 0.000735 |
| Single point | 52.0% | 0.000009 |
| Single point | 52.0% | 0.001891 |
| Single point | 53.0% | 0.000022 |
| Single point | 53.0% | 0.004352 |
| Single point | 54.0% | 0.000045 |
| Single point | 54.0% | 0.008960 |
| Single point | 55.0% | 0.000083 |
| Single point | 55.0% | 0.016508 |
| Single point | 56.0% | 0.000136 |

## Assumption: Total Cost Ratio (con'd)                    Cell: B9

|  |  | *Relative Prob.* |
|---|---|---|
| Single point | 56.0% | 0.027218 |
| Single point | 57.0% | 0.000201 |
| Single point | 57.0% | 0.040156 |
| Single point | 58.0% | 0.000265 |
| Single point | 58.0% | 0.053013 |
| Single point | 59.0% | 0.000313 |
| Single point | 59.0% | 0.062628 |
| Single point | 60.0% | 0.000331 |
| Single point | 60.0% | 0.066205 |
| Single point | 61.0% | 0.000313 |
| Single point | 61.0% | 0.062628 |
| Single point | 62.0% | 0.000265 |
| Single point | 62.0% | 0.053013 |
| Single point | 63.0% | 0.000201 |
| Single point | 63.0% | 0.040156 |
| Single point | 64.0% | 0.000136 |
| Single point | 64.0% | 0.027218 |
| Single point | 65.0% | 0.000083 |
| Single point | 65.0% | 0.016508 |
| Single point | 66.0% | 0.000045 |
| Single point | 66.0% | 0.008960 |
| Single point | 67.0% | 0.000022 |
| Single point | 67.0% | 0.004352 |
| Single point | 68.0% | 0.000009 |
| Single point | 68.0% | 0.001891 |
| Single point | 69.0% | 0.000004 |
| Single point | 69.0% | 0.000735 |
| Single point | 70.0% | 0.000001 |
| Single point | 70.0% | 0.000256 |
| Single point | 71.0% | 0.000004 |
| Single point | 71.0% | 0.000735 |
| Single point | 72.0% | 0.000009 |
| Single point | 72.0% | 0.001891 |

## Assumption: Total Cost Ratio (con'd)          Cell: B9

|  |  | *Relative Prob.* |
| --- | --- | --- |
| Single point | 73.0% | 0.000022 |
| Single point | 73.0% | 0.004352 |
| Single point | 74.0% | 0.000045 |
| Single point | 74.0% | 0.008960 |
| Single point | 75.0% | 0.000083 |
| Single point | 75.0% | 0.016508 |
| Single point | 76.0% | 0.000136 |
| Single point | 76.0% | 0.027218 |
| Single point | 77.0% | 0.000201 |
| Single point | 77.0% | 0.040156 |
| Single point | 78.0% | 0.000265 |
| Single point | 78.0% | 0.053013 |
| Single point | 79.0% | 0.000313 |
| Single point | 79.0% | 0.062628 |
| Single point | 80.0% | 0.000331 |
| Single point | 80.0% | 0.066205 |
| Single point | 81.0% | 0.000313 |
| Single point | 81.0% | 0.062628 |
| Single point | 82.0% | 0.000265 |
| Single point | 82.0% | 0.053013 |
| Single point | 83.0% | 0.000201 |
| Single point | 83.0% | 0.040156 |
| Single point | 84.0% | 0.000136 |
| Single point | 84.0% | 0.027218 |
| Single point | 85.0% | 0.000083 |
| Single point | 85.0% | 0.016508 |
| Single point | 86.0% | 0.000045 |
| Single point | 86.0% | 0.008960 |
| Single point | 87.0% | 0.000022 |
| Single point | 87.0% | 0.004352 |
| Single point | 88.0% | 0.000009 |
| Single point | 88.0% | 0.001891 |
| Single point | 89.0% | 0.000004 |
| Single point | 89.0% | 0.000735 |

## Assumption: Total Cost Ratio (con'd)  Cell: B9

|  | | *Relative Prob.* |
|---|---|---|
| Single point | 90.0% | 0.000001 |
| Single point | 90.0% | 0.000256 |
| Total Relative Probability | | 1.000000 |

Correlated with:

CAGR (K5)          0.50

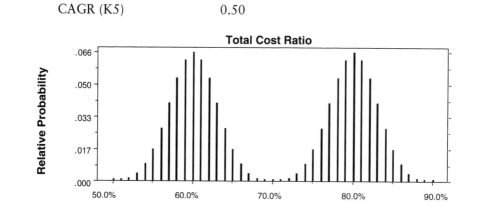

## Assumption: D18: CapEx Year 1  Cell: D18

Triangular distribution with parameters:

| Minimum | 1.80 |
|---|---|
| Likeliest | 2.00 |
| Maximum | 2.20 |

Selected range is from 1.80 to 2.20

Correlated with:

E18: CapEx Year 2 (E18)     0.50

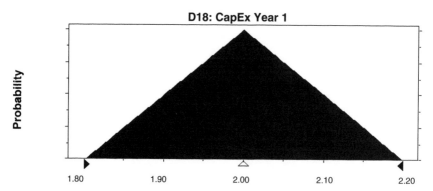

## Assumption: E18: CapEx Year 2          Cell: E18

Triangular distribution with parameters:

Minimum                      8.00
Likeliest                       10.00
Maximum                   12.00

Selected range is from 8.00 to 12.00

Correlated with:

D18: CapEx Year 1 (D18)     0.50
F18: CapEx Year 3 (F18)     0.50

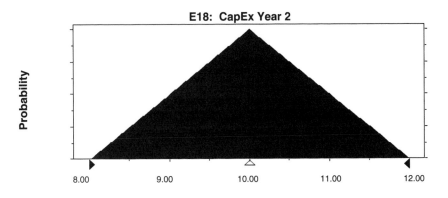

## Assumption: F18: CapEx Year 3                                    Cell: F18

Triangular distribution with parameters:

| | |
|---|---|
| Minimum | 24.00 |
| Likeliest | 30.00 |
| Maximum | 36.00 |

Selected range is from 24.00 to 36.00

Correlated with:

| | |
|---|---|
| E18: CapEx Year 2 (E18) | 0.50 |
| G18: CapEx Year 4 (G18) | 0.50 |

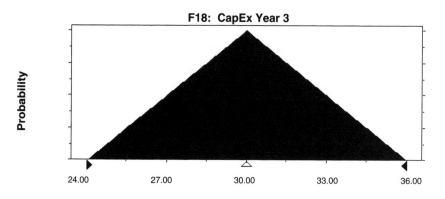

## Assumption: G18: CapEx Year 4                    Cell: G18

Uniform distribution with parameters:

| | |
|---|---|
| Minimum | 20.00 |
| Maximum | 60.00 |

Correlated with:

| | |
|---|---|
| F18: CapEx Year 3 (F18) | 0.50 |
| H18: CapEx Year 5 (H18) | 0.50 |

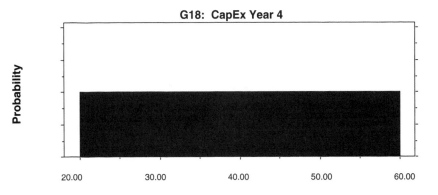

## Assumption: H18: CapEx Year 5                    Cell: H18

Uniform distribution with parameters:

| | |
|---|---|
| Minimum | 0.00 |
| Maximum | 36.00 |

Correlated with:

| | |
|---|---|
| G18: CapEx Year 4 (G18) | 0.50 |

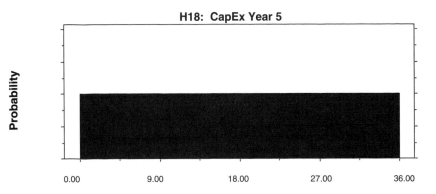

## Assumption: E4: Rev. Year 2          Cell: E4

Uniform distribution with parameters:

| | |
|---|---|
| Minimum | 0.00 |
| Maximum | 4.00 |

Correlated with:

| | |
|---|---|
| F4: Rev. Year 3 (F4) | 0.80 |

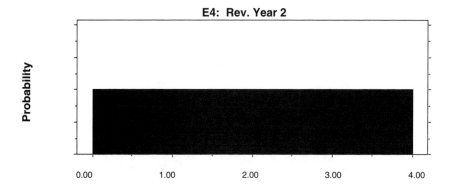

## Assumption: F4: Rev. Year 3          Cell: F4

Uniform distribution with parameters:

| | |
|---|---|
| Minimum | 10.00 |
| Maximum | 20.00 |

Correlated with:

| | |
|---|---|
| E4: Rev. Year 2 (E4) | 0.80 |
| G4: Rev. Year 4 (G4) | 0.80 |

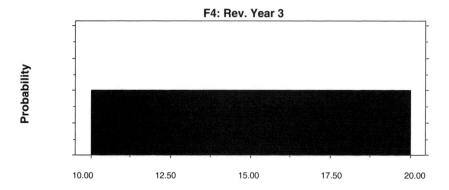

## Assumption: G4: Rev. Year 4                 Cell: G4

### Triangular distribution with parameters:

| | |
|---|---|
| Minimum | 50.00 |
| Likeliest | 70.00 |
| Maximum | 90.00 |

Selected range is from 50.00 to 90.00

### Correlated with:

| | |
|---|---|
| H4: Rev. Year 5 (H4) | 0.80 |
| F4: Rev. Year 3 (F4) | 0.80 |

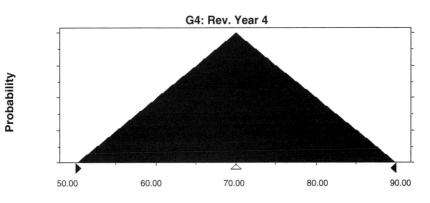

## Assumption: H4: Rev. Year 5                                           Cell: H4

Triangular distribution with parameters:

| | |
|---|---|
| Minimum | 120.00 |
| Likeliest | 180.00 |
| Maximum | 240.00 |

Selected range is from 120.00 to 240.00

**Correlated with:**

G4: Rev. Year 4 (G4)          0.80

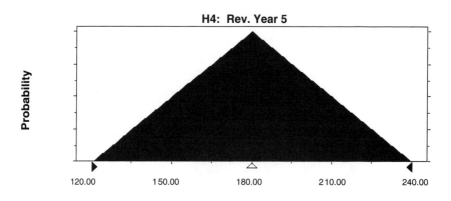

H4:  Rev. Year 5

End of Assumptions

# CHAPTER 6

# Introduction to Real Options

**O**ptions have been a frequent and emotionally charged topic in recent news. The options awarded to employees, principally senior management, have been the subject of accounting-treatment debate as to whether they should be expensed as granted to reflect diminished current earnings. Certain senior management's mismanagement, or more accurately self-management, of the company assets they were entrusted with to create stock valuation spikes that enabled them to cash in huge realizations from the value of their options even when the underlying fundamentals of the company were sick or even at death's door have spearheaded that debate. The significant collapse of Long Term Capital Management brought adverse publicity to the use of options pricing in highly leveraged derivatives investments. The explosion of options markets and options investing even by unsophisticated investors has created concern that the increased volatility of equity investing may have led us, in effect, to Las Vegas online.

All of these options are *financial* options. Such an option is the right, but not the obligation, to acquire financial assets such as 100 shares of Yahoo for $10 a share on June 30, 2003. Here, we are concerned about *real* options, which are the right, but not the obligation, to acquire a *business asset or opportunity* with its associated physical and intellectual capital assets. Financial options and real options are conceptually the same thing: the present value of the future right to make a choice involving the acquisition value of an underlying asset. As discussed in Chapter 5, one can think of the present value of 3M as a company as being the value associated with the right to its future net cash flows. So an option to each share of 3M's equity is related to the idea that such share's ultimate value derives from the stream of cash flow benefits anticipated proportional to the ownership interest of each share. The parallel with a real option is that instead of buying an option to a share of equity in 3M itself, we are considering the value of the option to own a 3M technology or nascent product line. As seen in Chapter 5, the valuation of the latter is at its root the net present value (NPV) of the future cash flows. There is one particularly important difference between financial options and real options: Most financial options have an extant market that enables buyers and sellers of such options to observe a market-based determination of value and the volatility of such value for the option itself and the underlying asset. For real options, the underlying business opportunity is not packaged and available in a public market with trades going back and forth on which such market value and volatility can be established. Further, as was noted in Chapter 5, there is usually very little business history, and perhaps no present earnings or revenues and established financial statements (income, balance sheet, and cash flow) on which to perform a traditional valuation analysis.

Option analysis, even with the attendant uncertainties and complexities, is a powerful method not only for determining value but also for structuring agreements. In the closing Monte Carlo example of Chapter 5, we consider the value of an opportunity whose cost ratio could be very favorable (mean value of 60 percent) or unfavorable (mean value of 80 percent) based on whether or not an advanced technology succeeds. The Monte Carlo method can be used to characterize how this uncertainty of cost ratio distributions will affect NPV. However, as we saw, the result in that instance was unsatisfying because if the low cost technology failed, the entire opportunity was unattractive. So, even using some standard of risk reward fairness such as the 20th percentile, or 30th percentile, or even the mean value, would lead a buyer to decline to pursue the opportunity despite the very significant economic potential. Valuation by the use of Real Options will aid us in negotiating this type of opportunity. As we see later, the use of Real Options is not just a valuation methodology but also a way of preparing for negotiations and reaching ultimate agreement. The key for a Real Options method to be effective is that there must be some future point at which the parties will know an answer that will enable them to make a more economically intelligent decision than they presently can. So in that Monte Carlo example, if, say 12 months after the start of the project, the answer would be known as to which of the cost ratio scenarios considered will in fact occur, we have an alternative available to the parties on how both to structure and to value a deal, namely, consider the transaction as an option to an opportunity whose value will be substantially less uncertain in 12 months' time. Then by considering the range of values as they will be 12 months hence, parties can determine what an appropriate value would be for the option to make that subsequent election.

Let us now consider a simple example from three different perspectives.

## PERSPECTIVE 1: DISCOUNTED CASH FLOW (DCF) VIEW OF THE SIX-SCENARIO OPPORTUNITY

Let us assume that a seller and buyer are attempting to determine a fair value of an opportunity that has two present, crucial valuation uncertainties: the cost of operating the business and the size of the addressable market. With respect to the cost ratio, the parties agree that one of three outcomes will occur: (A) an advanced technology not yet proven will succeed and enable a low-cost structure, or (B) a backup technology also under development will succeed although exhibiting a higher-cost ratio, or (C) a technology will need to be acquired from a third party with the net effect of having an even higher-cost ratio. At the time of the negotiation, the parties agree that the best judgment is that all three cost ratio outcomes are equally probable. This situation is parallel to the Monte Carlo example considered in Chapter 5, because in that case we made the normal bell curve distributions for the two cost ratio scenarios the same size relative to one another, and thereby equal in probability. However, here, for purposes of illustration, we have simplified the problem so that each of the three scenarios has a knowable, single-value cost (instead of a distribution of possible costs).

The range of expected revenues is the second uncertainty. It is believed that there are two possibilities: (X) a small market with correspondingly small revenues, or (Y) a large market. At the time of the negotiation, the parties are able to determine an appropriately discounted present value of both of these outcomes but believe that they are equally probable outcomes.

There are then six equally probable possibilities:

1. AX
2. BX
3. CX
4. AY
5. BY
6. CY

Using the discounted cash flow (DCF) method of Chapter 5, we can create financial models that will allow us to make single-valued estimates for the present value of each of these three costs and two revenues. For our purposes here, we assume that this has been done using the appropriate discount rate with the following present value results, all dollars in millions: costs of A = $40, B = $80, or C = $120; revenues of X = $50, or Y = $130 (all present value dollars in millions).

The parties have calculated, and agreed, that an initial investment by the buyer of $10 million in research and development (R&D) on the two technologies and on market research will be necessary to determine which of the cost ratios and revenue models can be expected to occur.

Finally, the seller informs the buyer that it wants $5 million in a lump-sum payment to transfer all the rights to the buyer at closing.

Now, you are the buyer. How would you analyze the value of the proposed offer?

Well, from this DCF (Perspective 1), we do straightforward math and probability ratios. In addition to the business costs of scenarios A, B, and C (of $40 million, $80 million, and $120 million, respectively), you the buyer will have to invest $10 million in R&D and market research and, according to the seller, pay $5 million now for ownership the opportunity. So the buyer's total costs for scenarios A, B, and C will really be $55 million (A), $95 million (B), and $135 million (C) ($40 + 10 + 5 = $55, etc.). So, we can construct a payoff table as shown in Exhibit 6.1.

Shown are the total costs in the three columns labeled A, B, and C to distinguish them from the base costs of the respective scenarios because such columns include the $10 million R&D and $5 million license fee. Shown in the two rows are the two revenue scenarios, which are unaffected by the additional $15 million in costs. Then, within each of the cells of the three-by-two matrix is the NPV value of that scenario combination of cost and revenue. Because we are assuming that all the values heading the rows and columns have been determined by appropriate discount rates to yield present values we can simply subtract the total costs from the revenues to obtain the NPV value in each cell as shown.

Since, in our best judgment, each of the three cost scenarios and both of the two revenue scenarios are equally probable, each of the six paired outcomes shown in Exhibit 6.1 are also equally probable. So, the NPV of the array of six outcomes is then just the average of the six individual outcomes, or so it seems, as is shown in Equation 6.1.

$$\text{NPV of Opportunity} = (-5 - 45 - 85 + 75 + 35 - 5)/6 = \boxed{-\$5 \text{ million}} \quad (6.1)$$

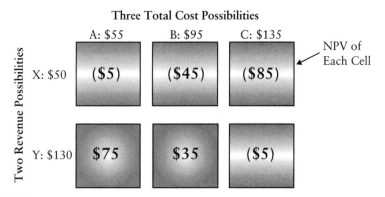

**Three Total Cost Possibilities**

|  | A: $55 | B: $95 | C: $135 |
|---|---|---|---|
| X: $50 | ($5) | ($45) | ($85) |
| Y: $130 | $75 | $35 | ($5) |

*Two Revenue Possibilities*

NPV of Each Cell

**EXHIBIT 6.1**   DCF Analysis of Six-Scenario Example

So, as the prospective buyer, from this Perspective 1, you would conclude that the opportunity was not worth pursuing because the NPV is negative. If the seller then offered to decrease its license fee to induce you, the buyer, to "get to yes," what would it take? From the above analysis it would require the seller to reduce its price to zero! (And, even at a selling price of zero, you as the buyer should be indifferent to pursuing the opportunity because at that "price point" the NPV is exactly zero).

## PERSPECTIVE 2: REAL OPTION VIEW OF THE SIX-SCENARIO OPPORTUNITY

There is something wrong with Perspective 1 considered previously. There are two distinct kinds of costs that were commingled in that analysis. The initial costs associated with the R&D and market development, the $10 million, are certain (within the scope of our assumptions). The $5 million up-front license fee is also fixed, at least provisionally for purposes of the analysis. A buyer can always counterpropose an alternative fee; however, for purposes of the analysis it is legitimate to use the seller's sought for payment as a fixed, certain cost. So, as the buyer, these $15 million are the effective "table stakes" to pursue the opportunity. If agreement is reached, you the buyer will spend the $15 million no matter what.

However, the costs associated with scenarios A, B, and C are not certain because at the end of the initial R&D and market research, you, as the buyer, will have the option to proceed with the opportunity or terminate it. Consider the most-obvious case of the highest cost (C) and the lower revenues (X). The NPV of that cell is $50 million less $120 million or a net loss of $70 million. (Note that we have not included the $15 million as we did in Equation 6.1, because we are now recognizing that $15 million as a fixed, certain cost, whereas the $120 million of scenario C is fixed but not a certain obligation.) The revised NPV outcomes are shown in Exhibit 6.2.

Each of the cell values in Exhibit 6.2 is $15 million larger than the corresponding cell in Exhibit 6.1, because we are going to recognize that that $15 million is an initial, fixed, certain cost of the buyer's option to pursue the opportunity. Those $15 million are "sunk" costs. It is only after such sunk costs that you, the buyer, will have the right, but not the obligation, to pursue whichever scenario is then known to be the outcome as shown in Exhibit 6.2. What is the present value of these six outcomes? Before we just add them together as we did for Perspective 1, consider what choice you would make for outcomes BX and CX? These two outcomes have the two highest-cost outcomes paired with the lower-revenue outcomes, a tough break. (Into every life a little rain must fall.) Both of these cells, and only these cells, reflect a negative NPV value. Accordingly, at the point of knowing that either of these

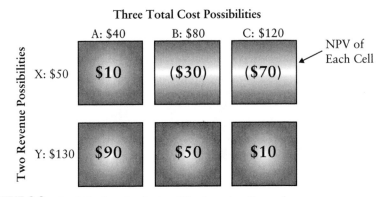

**EXHIBIT 6.2**   Real Option Analysis of Six-Scenairo Example

outcomes has come to be, you, the buyer, would not further pursue the opportunity. The value of these two cells, then, is zero not negative, because no rational buyer would pursue outcomes BX and CX, even having paid for the right to do so, because to do so would only compound the loss on the project investment. At that point the opportunity would be abandoned and no further costs would be incurred. Therefore, the buyer's value situation is as shown in Exhibit 6.3.

Using the previous results, what is the value of the opportunity? The result is determined in Equations 6.2 and 6.3.

$$\text{NPV of Option Right} = -\$5 - \$10 = \boxed{-\$15\text{ million}} \tag{6.2}$$

$$\text{NPV of Option Exercise} = (\$10 + 90 + 50 + 10)/6 = \boxed{\$26.67\text{ million}} \tag{6.3}$$

Thus, the NPV of the opportunity is $26.67 - $15.00 = $11.67 million, compared with the negative $5 million based on the analysis of Perspective 1. The difference in this Perspective 2 analysis is the recognition that this opportunity is an option to a future right, namely, the right without the obligation to pursue any combination of cost and revenue scenarios, and that the costs associated with the license fee and R&D are different in nature from the costs associated with implementing the six scenarios.

A final scenario is depicted in Exhibit 6.4. It shows graphically the difference between the initial DCF analysis and, on the right side of the figure, the Real Option (RO) analysis. Based on this revised analysis, you, the buyer, should conclude that the opportunity conforming to these assumptions and with the seller's terms is worth pursuing.

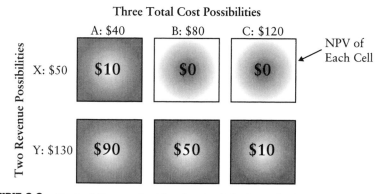

**Three Total Cost Possibilities**

**EXHIBIT 6.3** Revised Perspective Number 2 of Six-Scenario Opportunity

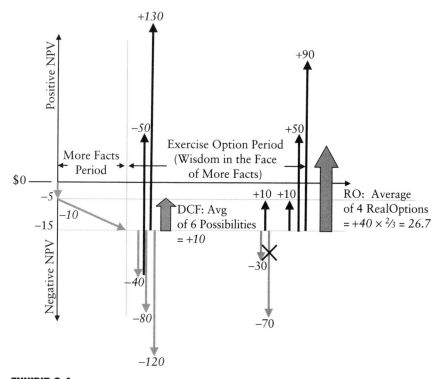

**EXHIBIT 6.4** Distinction Between DCF and Real Option Thinking

## PERSPECTIVE 3: A MODEL FOR A BUYER'S COUNTEROFFER

If we take the $10 million for R&D and market research as immutable, that leaves $16.7 million of value (from the $26.7 million total) than can be apportioned between buyer and seller. The seller's initial proposal of a $5 million license fee payment represents in effect a 30 percent apportionment of the total opportunity value. By the previous analysis, the buyer could accept the seller's proposal concluding that under the circumstances such 30 percent apportionment was fair, or, propose a smaller apportionment of the total value as a license fee, in the traditional spirit of "more for me, less for you."

However, by recognizing the option nature of the opportunity, the buyer can, in a way, propose "more for you, and more for me." Consider the following possibility.

Suppose the buyer counteroffers payment of a $2 million up-front fee, and an additional, say, $4 million if the buyer elects to pursue the opportunity after the initial R&D period during which it will be spending an additional $10 million on R&D. Such a counteroffer has the following result:

$$\text{NPV of the Option Right} = -\$2 - \$10 = -\$12 \text{ million} \qquad (6.4)$$

$$\text{NPV of the Option Exercise} = (\$6 + 86 + 46 + 6)/6 = \$24 \text{ million} \quad (6.5)$$

So, the buyer's net opportunity value by this revised counteroffer is, on a statistical basis, $12 million, up from $11.67 million. The seller's value is $2 + ($4) \times 4/6 = $4.67 million, down from $5 million. The total opportunity value to be apportioned is unchanged by this rearrangement at $16.67 million. However, in the counteroffer, the buyer proposes to pay the seller potentially a total of $6 million, which is $1 million more than the seller proposed; but only $2 million is guaranteed up front. The balance of the $4 million would be paid only if the buyer exercises the option to pursue the opportunity, which will occur the four times out of six times that the option exercise value has a positive NPV. So, six times out of six, the seller receives $2 million up front; then four times out of six, the seller receives a second payment of $4 million, and two times out of six he gets the opportunity returned (along with retaining the initial $2 million). If the option is not exercised, then the buyer is out $12 million for which it gained the knowledge that the opportunity was not worth pursuing. However, four times out of six the buyer will elect to pursue his option. Notice that in two of such four times, the buyer does not earn back its option fee because the value of two of the cells is only $6 million; however, because they are positive NPV values, they are worth pursuing and have the effect of reducing the buyer's loss to $6 million (–$12 million for the cost of the option offset by a plus $6 million from the election of the option). In the remaining two times out of six, the buyer makes a substantial sum, either $86 less the $12 (i.e., $74 million net), or $46 less the $12 (i.e., $34 million net). Note there is no possible outcome (within the confines of our assumptions) by which the seller will make $4.67 million and the buyer $12 million; these are simply the mean values given the probabilities and the scenario values.

One of the primary methodologies used in new product development generally goes under the name "stage gate product development" (or sometimes "phase gate"). With this methodology all the activities needed to go from concept to product completion are classified into distinct stages, usually six. Of interest to us here is that each stage is defined by a "gate" that requires a priori requirements to be met before product development can continue. This gating is intended to sharply define the keys to success and apply metrics to each opportunity during each critical phase. This approach is particularly well suited to Real Options valuation and deal structures. As each gate is reached, there is an opportunity for management intervention (to continue to the next phase, terminate the product because of failure to complete the present stage, redefine the new product goals, etc.). Under an option pricing model, it is possible, in theory, to ascribe a value to passing each gate. A dramatic example of well-defined gates are those associated with obtaining Food and Drug Administration (FDA) approval of a new pharmaceutical drug. Exhibit 6.5 depicts the mortality data for new drugs filed for investigation during the period 1976 through 1978. The study that analyzed what happened to this population showed a significant mortality of such investigations as they coursed through the FDA-defined phases to the New Drug Application (NDA) and approval of NDA. A drug making it through more gates would, apart from any other factor, become more valuable solely because of the decreased likelihood of subsequent failure. For this reason, licensing of new drug opportunities frequently uses *milestone* payments associated with the opportunity passing through these and other gates. Such payments are, in effect, option fees for the buyer-licensee to continue to own the right to commercialize the drug.

The simple financial example considered in Exhibit 6.4 shows how an NPV analysis sequenced around decision points is a useful means of determining rational value. And, it shows how DCF scenario analysis can be used in a brute force way to determine Real Option value if the problem is carefully constructed. We now turn our attention to more elegant methods of calculating Real Option value.

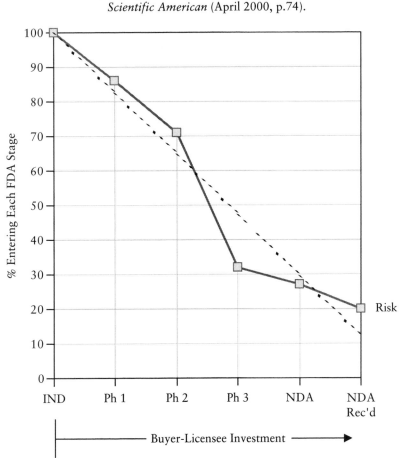

"Food and Drug Administration (FDA) Data for
INDs (Investigations of New Drug) Filed 1976–1978,"
*Scientific American* (April 2000, p.74).

**EXHIBIT 6.5** New Product Development Example Using Pharmaceutical Approval Data

## BLACK-SCHOLES EQUATION FOR OPTION PRICING

It can be said that rational option pricing began with a famous equation named after its discoverers, Fisher Black[1] and Myron Scholes[2] with an assist from Robert Merton[3] in a famous paper published in 1973. At the same time, just a month before the Black-Scholes paper was published, an option market was created at the Chicago Board Options Exchange (CBOE) that created a market not just for options but for the rational pricing of options. The popularity of options and the Black-Scholes equation quickly led to it being incorporated into a financial calculator offered by Texas Instruments (TI). Thus, in a matter of months, the financial world, which had been wrestling with the problem of rationally pricing options for more than 70 years, had an options market, an equation, and a calculator. This combination, something like the perfect storm, made famous, seemingly overnight, Black, Scholes, (Merton was already famous), the equation, the TI calculator, the CBOE, and option pricing of financial securities (derivatives). The fame was appropriately sealed with the Nobel Prize in Economic Sciences in 1997 to Scholes and Merton (Fisher Black died in 1995). A brief biography of this award can be found at a Nobel Prize Web site www.nobel.se/economics/laureates/1997/back.html.

### The Black-Scholes Equation Applied to an Option to a Share of Yahoo!

The simplest form of the Black-Scholes equation (hereafter, BSE1) is for what is known as a European *call option*. First a little background on call options. If you are interested in a particular stock, say, Yahoo! (YHOO), you can simply purchase shares on the open market. Alternatively, you could purchase not a share but an option to purchase (which is a known as a *call*) a share of YHOO. Let us consider a propitious moment in time to illustrate the point. On April 3, 2000, YHOO was selling for $160.13 a share. Say that instead of buying YHOO then you wanted the right to buy YHOO a year from April 3, 2000, namely, April 3, 2001 at its then present price of $160.13, such price being your cost "to call" a share of YHOO on April 3, 2001 (commonly called the *strike price* of the option). Well, at first this seems peculiar. Why would anyone want the right to buy a share of YHOO a year hence for its present share price? Because by having the option, namely, the right to ownership but not the ownership nor the obligation to become an owner, you do not participate in any decline in the value of YHOO because if YHOO is selling for less than the $160.13 strike price you have chosen on April 3, 2001, you will let your option expire.[4]

The important issue here is how would you, buyer of an option, and, say, me an option seller, negotiate a fair price (cost) of your option to my one share of YHOO? What would I the option offerer be giving up? Well, if YHOO decreases in value below the strike price (which in this example is the present price), you the owner of the call right will not exercise your right because to do so would cost you more than you could then buy a share of YHOO on the open market. If, however, the value of a share of YHOO goes above the present April 3, 2000 price, then you as the option holder will exercise your option and pay just the strike price ($160.13 in this example), which would be less than the share is then worth. So I, as the offerer of the option, am effectively giving up the appreciation potential of the stock over the term of the option. What would it be worth to each of us to provide this right to you and this payment to me on April 3, 2000? This simple but elegant question is the one that Black and Scholes sought to answer by an exact equation. Because our purpose here is not to delve into the mathematical model behind their result, we merely jump ahead to their result, which is shown in Exhibit 6.6.

This form of the BSE1 is for what is known as a *European option*, which means that the option can only be exercised on the end date of the option term, which in our example is one year; the so-called American option is much more complicated mathematically because it can be exercised at any time during the year. This equation, although complex, is really amazing in its simplicity. According to BSE1, only five input values are needed to calculate the value of the option:

1. The present price ($S_0$) of the underlying right (YHOO), in this example on April 3, 2000, $160.13.

2. The strike price ($S_1$), namely the price chosen as the cost of exercising the option; here we have arbitrarily selected the April 3, 2000 price, $160.13.

3. The time (t) to expiry of the option (known as the term, or period); here we have arbitrarily selected 1 year corresponding to April 3, 2001.

4. The risk-free interest rate (or risk-free hurdle rate, RFHR), which is a knowable, market-determined value at the time of the option (April 3, 2001).

5. The volatility (V) of the underlying right (YHOO) expressed (and here is the complicated part) as the standardized deviation of the annualized, continuously compounded rate of return of the underlying right. Volatility is a statistical measure of the price swings in the underlying equity over some recent, historic period, often 90 preceding days. Later we show how this can be calculated, but for now we simply note that such volatility is published for any publicly traded equity. For YHOO on April 3, 2000 it

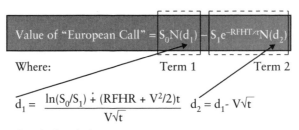

$$\text{Value of "European Call"} = S_0 N(d_1) - S_1 e^{-RFHR \times t} N(d_2)$$

Where:                                          Term 1                    Term 2

$$d_1 = \frac{\ln(S_0/S_1) + (RFHR + V^2/2)t}{V\sqrt{t}} \quad d_2 = d_1 - V\sqrt{t}$$

**EXHIBIT 6.6**    The Black-Scholes Equation (BSE1)

was 80.36 percent (which is a large number corresponding to the significant fluctuations then experienced by Yahoo's stock price).

The two calculated terms in d1 and d2 BSE1 have a physical meaning. The first term is a measure of the expected benefit from purchasing the stock itself; it is not obvious—after all that is why they received the Nobel Prize—but this term is a product of the stock price ($S_0$) and the change in the call premium with respect to changes in the stock price. The second term is the present value of the exercise price that would be paid on the expiry date. The difference between these two values is the measure of the value of the option to a share.

The calculation of the corresponding option value (the call) according to BSE1 is shown in Exhibit 6.7. The two input values shown in plain italics, $S_0$ and $V$, are intrinsic to the underlying asset whose option value is being determined as of the time of sale of the option, subject to the reality that the calculation of volatility ($V$) requires some historic period preceding such sale date. The two bold input values, $S_1$ and $t$, are arbitrary choices of the buyer of the option. The one bold italic value, **RFHR**, is a universal environmental value that measures the risk-free alternative available to any and all investors at the sale of the option. The $N(d)$ values are readily calculated using the NORMDIST(XX) functions available in the Excel spreadsheet. Thus, according to BSE1, the appropriate cost for you to purchase an option right to each share of YHOO from me on April 3, 2000, based on the facts at that time, exercisable on, and only on, April 3, 2001 is $53.43. So it says. (There are now numerous places on the World Wide Web that provide a

**EXHIBIT 6.7**   Calculation of Black-Scholes Option Value (BSE1)

**Five Input Values, for YHOO at 4/3/00**

| $S_0$ | $V$ | $S_1$ | $t$ | *RFHR* |
|-------|-----|-------|-----|--------|
| *$160.13* | *0.8036* | **$ 160.13** | **1.00** | *0.0619* |

**Calculated Terms**

| d1 | d2 | | | |
|----|----|--|--|--|
| 0.4789 | −0.3247 | | | |

| N(d1) | N(d2) | | | |
|-------|-------|--|--|--|
| 0.6840 | 0.3727 | | **Option Value of a Call** | |
| | | | **According to BSE1** | |
| **Term 1** | **Term 2** | | | |
| $109.53 | $56.10 | | $53.43 | |

Black-Scholes calculator; see, for example: www.intrepid.com/~robertl/option-pricer3.html.)

I chose this YHOO example and date because we can see in dramatic fashion what actually transpired. In Exhibit 6.8, we have a graph of the actual Yahoo share price during the 12-month period of the option, starting at $160.13.

Shown at the right portion of the exhibit are four zones defined by $160 + the option value ($53) = $213, and $160 less the option value = $107. Had YHOO's share price exceeded $213 a share (in your dreams), your option would have been "in the money," meaning that after buying your one share of YHOO on April 3, 2001, you would have expended a total of $53 for the option plus the $160 strike price to exercise the option or a total of $213; for any value of YHOO above $213 you would more than pay back the cost of the option. In the next zone, a YHOO share selling for between $160 and $213, you would still exercise your option on April 3, 2001, still paying $160, and to the degree YHOO is above $160 (but less than $213) you recoup some, but not all, of your cost of the option. The next two zones—below $160 but above $107, and below $107—you would not exercise the option because you could buy a share of YHOO on the open market for less than your option entitles you to; so you would lose the entire $53 that you paid for your option. For all three zones above $107 a share, you would have

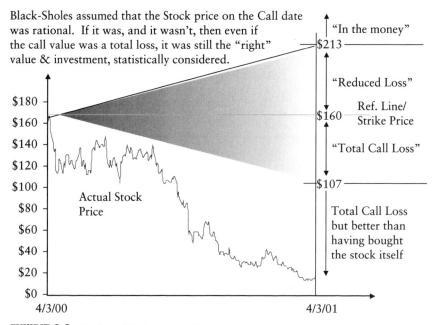

**EXHIBIT 6.8**    Value of Yahoo! (YHOO) from April 3, 2000 to April 3, 2001

been better off having bought YHOO at $160 a share on April 3, 2000 instead of paying $53 for the option to buy it at $160 a share on April 3, 2001. Having paid for the option to a share of YHOO did not enable you to make a greater realization on a share of YHOO than having been a YHOO owner for each of these three zones. If so, what good is an option? The answer lies in the bottommost zone, below $107 a share. Here, you would have been worse off having owned YHOO than owning an option to YHOO. Since, in this specific example, YHOO (alas) "tanked," having an option instead of share ownership turned out to be a great idea because you had rights to an upside in YHOO but lost *only* $53 instead of the more than $140 that a YHOO April 3, 2000 owner lost by holding on until April 3, 2001.

## What Do Equations Represent? "What Is Truth?"

Before turning to our primary interest of real, versus financial, options, let us first consider what equations represent. Are equations true? When we express something as an equation, what does doing so represent? Let us consider first two of the most famous equations of all time:

$$C^2 = A^2 + B^2 \text{ (Pythagorean Theorem, ca. 4th C, BC)} \tag{6.6}$$

$$F = m \times A \text{ (Newton's 2nd Law of Motion, ca. 1686)} \tag{6.7}$$

The Pythagorean Theorem, which is the cornerstone equation of standard (Euclidian) geometry, says that for a right triangle (a triangle with one angle being 90 degrees), the square of the hypotenuse $C$ (the longest side) is equal to the sum of the squares of the other two sides $A$ and $B$.[5] So, for a right triangle with sides 3 and 4, the Pythagorean Theorem asserts (or, predicts) that the hypotenuse is precisely, exactly, and only 5.

Isaac Newton in the seventeenth century generally is credited with being one of the principal founders of modern science and his work was instrumental in precipitating the Enlightenment. In a series of absolutely remarkable discoveries, Newton was able to develop the underlying equations (laws) that govern the motion of bodies (in addition to numerous other discoveries such as calculus and optics). The most famous of these motion equations is that the force accelerating a mass can be determined instantaneously by taking the product of the mass times the acceleration. Or, expressing the equation differently, the acceleration experienced by a body of mass $m$ will be simply the ratio of the force applied ($F$) divided by its mass ($m$).

Now, are these equations true? The answer is: "yes" and "no." How so?

The Pythagorean Theorem is really a corollary that derives from a hypothesized system of analysis that we now call Euclidian Geometry. If one establishes a starting set of hypotheses about a geometrical system, planar (flat) surfaces, lines of zero width and arbitrary length, and so forth, then it can be shown by proof, from such starting assumptions, that $C^2 = A^2 + B^2$. No physical triangle can be drawn exactly conforming to Euclidian assumptions so that were one to try to measure the hypotenuse of a right triangle with sides 3 and 4, it would never be quite 5.0000000 . . . , although we would agree that such hypotenuse must be exactly 5 and it is the limitations of our physical world that makes the representation given by $C^2 = A^2 + B^2$ imperfectly expressed.[6] In addition to our inabilities to perfectly express a Euclidian right triangle in our physical world, there are many non-Euclidian applications. For instance, if we were to attempt to lay out a right triangle on, say, North America, with short sides 3,000 and 4,000 miles long, and even looking from outer space where we might be able to neglect the effects of unevenness of the surface, we would find that the hypotenuse is not 5,000 miles. This deviation from $C^2 = A^2 + B^2$ is not due solely to our physical limitations but that the earth's surface is (roughly) a sphere and the Pythagorean Theorem is restricted to planar geometries. So, is the Pythagorean Theorem *true*? If I live within the geometrical world of a Euclidian geometrician, the answer is an emphatic Yes. If I carefully draw right triangles on approximately flat surfaces, say laying out a baseball infield or a tennis court, the answer is, yes for practical purposes (YFPP). If I am doing geometry on, for example, large curved surfaces, such as surveying a large tract of land, the answer is No.

Considering, now Newton's 2nd Law, $F = m \times A$, we also have the two constrictions considered above with the Pythagorean Theorem, namely: (1) our most-precise measurements will never quite achieve the perfect certainty and precision espoused by the equation, and (2) there is a limited domain for which the equation is applicable, known as an "inertial" (or "Newtonian") coordinate system.[7] If one were to attempt to use $F = m \times A$ on, say, a merry-go-around, whose rotation makes it a strikingly non-Newtonian coordinate system, we would be confounded in our attempts. But there is a further issue with Newton's 2nd Law as modified by Einstein by what is known as Modern Physics. Einstein showed that Newton's 2nd Law is really a special case of motion in which the speeds are small compared to the speed of light and the masses are large compared to individual atoms. At extremely high speeds approaching the speed of light, there are relativistic effects that arise that cause, among other things, for the force required to cause acceleration approaches an infinite value. At extremely small physical dimensions, there are quantum effects that permit only discrete energy levels instead of the continuity of possible speeds suggested by $F = m \times A$. So, with Einstein and the twentieth century, we came to understand that Newton's 2nd Law is a regime-limited simplification of a much richer and much more complicated relationship among forces, masses, and rates of change of speed, even for a Newtonian coordinate system.

So, is $F = m \times A$ true? Within a physics model known as a Newtonian universe, where our coordinate system is fixed or nonaccelerating, and for "ordinary" masses and speeds, YFPP, though only because any calculation incorporating quantum or relativistic effects produces modifications too small to matter. However, when calculating the motion of a long-distance projectile, or the motion of winds and weather, where the rotation of the earth gives rise to real, non-Newtonian effects (so-called Coriolis Forces), then the answer is no.

Now, what about BSE1? Is the Black-Scholes Equation true? Although the details of its derivation are beyond the scope of this book, following is a summary of the assumptions that govern its applicability:

- One uncertainty (volatility)
- Volatility knowable (generally by public trade data) at time of pricing the call value
- One time period
- Constant volatility during such time period
- Volatility characterizable by a continuous-time stochastic process arising from log-normal diffusion (LND). Such LND requires no below-zero values, and an infinitely long tail representing low probability but extraordinary value potential, and causes volatility to increase with the square root of time.
- The "Law of One Price" holds (two assets that have the same future value must have the same current value), or "no arbitrage" condition (known as dynamic tracking)
- European call conditions (option is exercisable only on the expiration date, not before).
- No dividends (or ongoing costs), known as "asset leakage," occur (or if they occur, BSE1 must be modified by the Merton extension).
- "Continuous time finance," meaning that prices change continuously, in infinitesimal increments, without jumps.
- The present share price is rational.

Let us consider first the underlying critical assumption regarding volatility. Volatility ($V$) in BSE1 is a required input variable for the asset in question; for Yahoo on April 3, 2000, we asserted the value of 80.36 percent. This value is determined by an analytical method that is shown later using *historic* share prices for, in this case, Yahoo. This calculation creates an inherent contradiction: How can we expect that the use of a historic input variable (volatility) will enable the prediction of a future result? The answer is: "only if the future replicates the past." So if, for example, we used a Yahoo volatility based on a then-recent history of 90 or 180 days, as is commonly done, to calculate an option value for 1 year hence, how do we know that the past is prelude to the future? We do not, but we need to assume so or we cannot go forward because we have to make a present prediction about tomorrow using only data available to us presently. And studies done of a stock's volatility show that its volatility tends to change less dramatically than its price. Any present data is either an instantaneously available number, such as share price effectively is, or it is based on some mathematical calculation on the past, however recent or distant. Underlying BSE1 is an assumption that an equity's volatility is constant over time such that a recently historic value (such as the past 90 or 180 days) is a reasonable estimate of its future volatility.

Another critical underlying BSE1 assumption is the rationality of the present share price (in the Yahoo! example this was April 3, 2000). Suppose for a moment, that the Nasdaq system processing trading during early April 2000 had some sort of "perfect storm" of Y2K and April Fools' so that there was a maelstrom of inaccurate data on bid-and-ask price of YHOO and other financial information such as Yahoo!'s present and forecasted earnings that caused the share price to be bid as it was in our example at $160.13, whereas without such maelstrom of misinformation it would have been, and should have been, $60.13. Well, in such a case it is garbage in, garbage out. If the then-present price of YHOO was "wrong," then the calculated option value is also going to be "wrong."

Now, from the perspective of 2002, we appear to know that the historic volatility of YHOO as of April 3, 2000, as high as it was at 80.36 percent, was too low compared to the then-impending drama. Further, it appears that we know that $160.13 was not a rational price for the asset but rather some sort of reflection of a "greater fool" effect of an irrational auction fed by generally slanted information about market trends and profitability (not necessarily specific to Yahoo!).

So BSE1 is in ways similar to the Pythagorean Theorem and Newton's 2nd Law in that it is true only in a special universe that enables it to be so, for certain practical purposes.

There are some further issues with regard to option values of equity assets that make their application limited to real assets. First, high volatility (in BSE1) is a good thing. Consider Exhibit 6.9, which shows the option (call) value of YHOO as a function of volatility.

Within a Black-Scholes framework, volatility is good because it increases the odds that there will be a significant future upside to the underlying equity, which an option holder can realize by the exercise of the option; it also increases the likelihood of a significant future downside, but an option holder has the option, not the obligation, so if the equity goes to zero it is not different than the equity selling for a penny less than the call value since in both

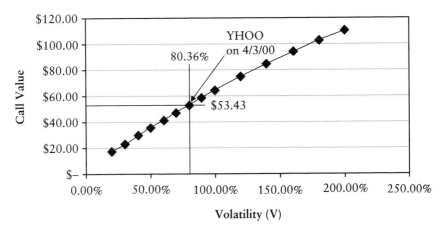

**EXHIBIT 6.9** Yahoo! Call (Option) Value as Function of Volatility

cases the only effect will be the expiration of the option right without its being exercised. Likewise, the longer the option period, the greater the value of an option, all other factors being constant, for the same reason: It increases the likelihood of an upside that can be realized. The RFHR has a small effect on the value of an option. As RFHR rate increases, meaning there are better risk-free returns available as an alternative investment, then the call value increases, and vice versa.

The Black-Scholes equation has also spawned a small industry in creating modifications to BSE1, some proprietary and some published, and alternative option equation theories. Much of this energy is being expended to try to create a statistical advantage on behalf of some over the many who may be buying and selling options with valuations based on an outdated, less market-accurate model.[8] These equations have the power of being "closed form." Closed form is a characterization of mathematical expressions in which all the unknowns can be separated onto one side of the equation with only the unknown sought for, here option (call) value, alone on the other side of the equation. Closed-form equations can generally be solved exactly without the requirement of iteration or other approximation techniques. Accordingly, it would be a delightful outcome if business opportunities, which are real options, could be valued by BSE1 or any of the other option models that have been developed for financial options. However, as we noted at the beginning of this chapter, real options differ from financial options by the absence of market-based present values and a history of such values that enable calculation of innate volatility.

What about the ability to use parallels to extract values in the absence of opportunity-specific data? Returning to the example we considered in

Chapter 4 on DCF analysis, how might we use market parallel data to value an advanced polymer opportunity? Because they make many polymer products, 3M would be a possibility; however, their volatility data is based on 100 years of history, $16 billion of revenues, $1.7 billion of after tax profits, and 60,000 products, all facts that would tend to reflect a much lower volatility than would measure the uncertainty associated with a specific new opportunity. We could examine small, public polymer companies as a proxy for our specific opportunity, or a family of such companies to understand a range of market-based volatilities. Such an approach is often called a "pure play" comparison, meaning that we are seeking to find a publicly traded company whose business is narrowly focused on products and markets close to the subject opportunity. However, such volatilities will be related to the revenues, earnings, inventories, receivables, debt, and other factors comprising the company's financial statements, its management team, its intellectual property position (patents, copyrighted content and software, trademarks, etc.), its market partners and channels, trends and news from its markets and relating to its suppliers and competitors.

There is no simple way of extracting from available volatility data what component of the volatility is traceable to the core question of a technology to make a product or product family to serve a market or several markets. Further, there is often an essential difference between the subject opportunity and the extant market participants. Rarely is an opportunity being analyzed and proposed that has as its value proposition that "this will be just like company X." There is normally something new and special regarding the opportunity's technology and/or manufacturing process and/or business model that allows it (or is asserted to allow it) to make something that is better, faster, cheaper, or more reliable than the incumbents, or it is making a claim to being the first to a market in which case there are no true incumbents.

Finally, the uncertainty associated with the value of a particular opportunity can be thought of as a combination of common and private risk. In the category of common risk would be those issues that any company in a similar business faces. So, all polymer companies face somewhat shared risks about general public favor or anxieties of their use of *plastics* and the environment, the cost and availability of crude oil (the raw material from which polymers are made), the general growth in the economy, cost of capital, and so forth. However, in the private risk category are those factors specific to the subject opportunity: Will it be protected by patents? Will it infringe someone else's patent (3,000 new U.S. patents are issued every Tuesday, any one of which could create a problem for a new entrant)? Will the technology actually work? Can a low-cost manufacturing operation be created? Will there be adverse characteristics of the products made that are not presently understood (long-term durability, toxicity), and so forth? It is these private risks, associated with the unique aspects of the subject technology that can play the dominant role in causing value uncertainty. In such a case, even finding an excellent pure-play market comparable will not enable us to gain a picture of uncertainty about our opportunity. As I look out over my pasture, I wonder whether there is oil under the green grass, which presently consumes oil from my mowing it. If I were to form a drilling company to search for oil there, no analysis of comparables from Exxon or anyone else would provide any rational prospective investor in such a venture what the present value should be for a bore hole somewhere in my tall grass 60 miles west of Newark airport.

## USING BLACK-SCHOLES FOR AN OPPORTUNITY VALUATION

Let us consider how BSE might be used to determine an appropriate option price (call value), based on a perceived present value of the opportunity laden with risk, and a price to exercise the option (the strike price). Reviewing the five factors that the BSE requires to determine such call value, they are:

- $S_0$, the present value of the opportunity. For an equity, such as Yahoo, this is simply the current stock price. For a real option, such as a new business opportunity, the correlate is the estimated present value of the opportunity, considering the future possible outcomes and their respective probabilities.. Such estimate could be made by the use of probability trees, such as those of Exhibits 4.5 and 4.6, by the use of DCF analysis with scenarios, such as Exhibits 5.11 and 5.12 and by Monte Carlo by the use of some percentile standard.

- $S_1$; the strike price, which is the cost to acquire the opportunity in the future. For either an equity or a real option, this is the price of converting the option right to an ownership (or license) right.

- $t$, the time at which such option call right must be exercised or forever lost (in accordance with the terms of a European option, which is exercisable on and only on the expiry date).

- RFHR, the risk free hurdle rate, which is simply the available rate of return for a so-called risk free investment, which is generally taken to be a U.S. Treasury bill of the same period.

- $V$, the volatility, which for equity options is the standard deviation of the historic rate of return of the market price of such equity presuming a long normal distribution. For a real option, as discussed below, there is no direct parallel measure of volatility.

Let us consider a simple situation. A seller possesses an opportunity which by, say, probability tree analysis is believed to have a present value ($S_0$) of $1,000. Let us further assume that such determination of $S_0$ was achieved by an extensive analysis of scenarios that accounted for the extent of significance of patent protection, the conclusions reached about the size of the market and value placed on the associated product compared to competitive alternatives, the technical performance that can be demonstrated at the advance prototype level, and the cost of scale up and manufacture for mass product introduction. Say, each of these 4 uncertainties was considered on a high, medium, and low scenario outcome basis, which could result in 64 possible, independent combinations (assuming that the variables and their outcomes were each independent). Accordingly, it could be hypothesized that it would be known after say, 1 year, which of the 64 possible outcomes occurred, and the value associated with such outcome. At the present time, all that is known, based on a probability tree analysis is that the expected value is simply $1,000. For convenience in illustration, we will establish each of the 64 values in the following way: We will select the worst case outcome (lowest valued outcome at the end of Year 1) at, say $10, with the next higher value higher by a factor of $1 + D$, where D is a value to be determined. Then the next higher value will be $10 times the square of factor $1 + D$, and so forth until we reach the 64th, and best envisioned outcome at the end of Year 1, of $10 times the factor $1 + D$ raised to the 64th power. Then by adding all such end of Year 1 values and dividing by 64 we obtain the average, or expected value, of the opportunity at the beginning of Year 1, assuming, as we will here, that all 64 outcomes are independent and equally probable. (In all cases we are, for convenience, also assuming that the risk free hurdle rate, RFHR, is zero.) Using the goal seek function in Microsoft Excel, we can then set the average value of the 64 possible outcomes at the end of Year 1 at $1,000 by adjusting the value of D as defined in this paragraph. So, for instance, assuming that the worst case outcome is $10, D is determined to be 0.1075, which then determines the 64 outcomes as follows: $10.00, $11.08, $12.27, $13.58, and so forth ending with the highest value of $6,222 (showing the powerful effect of raising a number, here 1.075, to a high exponential power). For this case, the first 46 values are less than the mean value of $1,000, and the final, highest, 19 values exceed $1,000.

We can now calculate a logarithmic rate of return by taking the log ("LN" function in Excel) of the ratio of each of these 64 values divided by the mean value ($1,000 in all cases). Then we can take the variance of this set of 64 values (using the "VAR" function in Excel), and finally by taking the square root of the variance, we have the standard deviation as a proxy for the volatility (V) in BSE1. So, for this example, the resulting volatility is 1.9013 (compared to our previous example for Yahoo in which the calculated volatility 0.8036 as determined by taking the log of each day's closing price divided by the previous day's closing price).

Now, using such volatility value in BSE1, with $S_0$ = \$1,000 (because we predetermined this value), we can calculate the BSE1 determined call value for any chosen value of $S_1$; the strike price. These results the graph of Exhibit 6.10 labeled for Year 1 values ranging from \$10 to \$6,222.

We can now repeat the above example by using different volatilities. This can be easily accomplished by using the same approach of a 1 + D factor multiplied by a different value for the worst case outcome of the 64 envisioned possibilities. Using the value of \$100, and again normalizing the result such that the average value of the opportunity at the end of Year 1, the highest value is determined to be \$6,222. Because this range of outcomes is narrower than in the first example—namely, \$100 to \$3,645 versus \$10 to \$6,222—the volatility will be smaller, namely 1.0628 versus 1.9013.

Finally, we will consider a third set of 64 possibilities, again normalized to yield a mean value of \$1,000, obtained by starting at \$1. Solving for D results in a range of \$1 to \$8,570 and, thereby, exhibiting the highest value of volatility (2.6764).

All three of these examples are shown in Exhibit 6.10. In all cases, we are examining the effect of change the strike price ($S_1$) has upon the call value. Further, we are also showing the net return to the buyer of the opportunity. The buyer experiences a net positive value if the opportunity value at the end of Year 1 exceeds the call price plus the strike price because the buyer paid the call value at the beginning of year 1 and the strike price at the end of Year 1 to own the opportunity. For example, when the worst outcome for end of Year 1 is \$1, for a strike price of either \$100 or \$200, the lowest 49 outcomes exhibit a net loss to the buyer; it is only the highest 15 outcomes that are "in the money" and yield the net average positive value of more than \$600 as shown. For higher selected strike price values, the BSE1 determined call value declines, meaning the buyer pays less at the beginning of Year 1 to secure option rights to the opportunity. Correspondingly, however, the net return to the buyer decreases as shown in these graphs because the line showing the net return declines with increasing strike price. This makes sense because the buyer has taken less risk upfront at the beginning of the year yet participates, through its option right, in acquiring the rights when they turn out to be attractive.

Additional details on this example are available at the author's Web site: www.razgaitis.com, then select "ᶦDealmaking resources."

So, we can see how a closed form equation of option pricing, in this case Black-Scholes, can rationally determine a call price once one has established the range of possible outcomes by some other means. However, the Black-Scholes equation was derived assuming the opportunity's volatility is calcu-

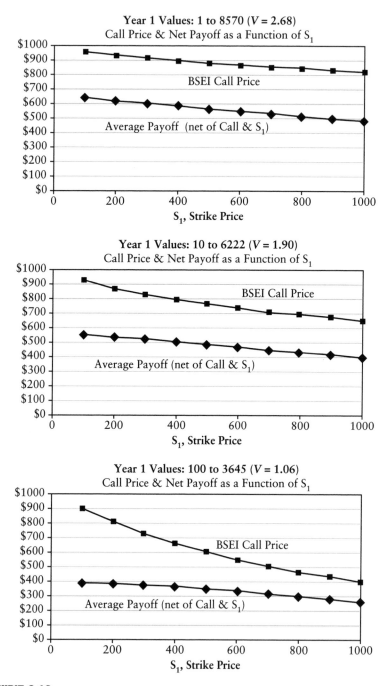

**EXHIBIT 6.10**   BSE1 Calculation on the Example of Exhibit 6.3

lated from a time series of data, such as the closing stock price of an equity, assuming that such variation conforms to a log normal distribution. For a real option, a time series variation of value is not what occurs, nor do we have ready access to any such real-time market data. Suppose that instead of the 64 outcomes we considered just above, the opportunity was a traded equity in which all buyers were evaluating the effect of the same 4 factors (patent rights, market, technology performance, and manufacturability) and based upon different news or perceptions were each day bidding the stock up or down. We could imagine, that in the course of a year with preliminary information about each of these factors becoming available, or simply assumed by investors, that the equity price would exhibit a fluctuation related to some degree as envisioned by 64 fixed outcomes we assumed. However, such calculation of volatility would not be equal (except by a coincidence) to the volatility as was calculated using 64 distinct outcomes compared to the mean outcome of $1,000. So, our use of the Black-Scholes equation does not have the theoretical grounding that it has (in principle, within its assumptions) for a widely traded equity. As a result, we would not expect that the calculated values for call price corresponding to the respective strike price are "right," though the trends appear generally reasonable, because we are operating outside the assumed framework for BSE1.

Negotiations regarding the sale or license of business opportunities, which is the subject of this book, cannot generally be valued by Black-Scholes. They exhibit various possible outcomes and such outcomes are not known until future events unfold. Further, there is not available, as there exists for traded equities, a continuous history of value and volatility of the seller's asset.

## SUMMARY OF REAL OPTION REALITIES VERSUS BLACK-SCHOLES

In considering real—not financial—assets, we have the following four situations and limitations with respect to applications of Black-Scholes:

1. Real assets normally do not have readily known present values because they are not subject to generally useful valuation processes such as open-market bidding, Although a DCF analysis can be used to provide an opinion of present value, based on underlying assumptions, scenarios and probabilities, and RAHR factors, such a result is not normally market tested as it would be (in theory) in a publicly traded equity.

2. There is limited, or no, sequence of historical data on the value of a given real asset and thereby its volatility. Further, high volatility causes the

value of a financial option to *increase* because it increases the probability that the equity will be "in the money" for any given strike price; so volatility is a good thing. For a particular real asset, it is of course a good thing if the potential future value is greatly larger than its present value. However, volatility as calculated measures something more basic: the ups and downs of the value of the underlying asset because, presumably, of changing perceptions of the net present value of the DCF of prospective cash flows.

3.  What we are normally interested in determining is at what value are we willing to sell, or buy, a real asset whose value may transform into any number of possible values, each with a relative probability. Real options are like mathematical hyrdras—they spawn possibilities each distinct from the other. Financial options also have (in theory) an infinite number of possible options but these follow sequentially and continuously from prior values.

4.  Financial options cannot become negative. Real options can. Any time a required investment can exceed the total potential return from any of the possible scenarios, then a real option has, for such condition, an actual negative rate of return. Unfortunately, it does occur with regularity that a technology or product asset turns out, after investment, to be deemed as having zero return potential and a sunk investment cost.

Now, we turn our attention to Real Option tools that can make systematic calculations of option value much as Monte Carlo did in Chapter 5.

## NOTES

1.  Fisher Black was at MIT in 1969 when he began to work with Scholes on mathematical models of pricing options; he was a University of Chicago business school professor at the time of publishing the equation named after him. Sadly, he died of cancer in 1995 prior to the award of the Nobel Prize for the discovery of the Black-Scholes equation and method. Because the Nobel is not awarded posthumously, he was not recognized in the award.

2.  Myron Scholes was a professor at MIT during the period of developing his equation. Subsequently, he was a professor at Stanford University. He later became even more famous for his role in Long Term Capital Management, a derivative investment company for extremely high net worth individuals, whose net worth became substantially smaller through the experience, as discussed later.

3.  Robert Merton, long associated with Harvard University, added an important contribution to the development of Black and Scholes and was recognized, along with Scholes as the recipient of the Nobel Prize for this equation. For Merton, this was his second Nobel, a remarkable achievement.

4.  Another important reason for purchasing such a right—which is not our concern here—it multiplies the possible upside rate of return, so called "increasing leverage."

5. It is reported that on its discovery, Pythagoras was so overtaken with emotion that he immediately went and sacrificed a bull to his god.

6. The deep significance of a simple, one might say, perfect equation able to represent imperfect, real triangles may have been one of the sources of Plato's development of the theory of "forms" and the allegory of the cave where the "truth" (the Pythagorean right triangle) resides in a different, perfect place, but we mortals are confined to the "cave" and its imperfect representation.

7. An inertial coordinate system is generally defined as one that is at rest or in uniform (nonaccelerating) motion with respect to the distant stars, and no such place on the earth meets that requirement because not only is the earth rotating about its own axis, creating a 24-hour day, it is revolving around the sun, creating a 365-day year, and the sun itself is rotating around the center of our Milky Way Galaxy, which center itself is . . . well, you get the idea. We are riding on a multilayered cosmic carousel. No person in human history has stood on Newtonian soil.

8. For those interested in the proliferation of models and equations, many can be found on the World Wide Web using a search engine with terms such as "option equation," "option theory," "Black-Scholes," or "derivatives."

# Real Options Applied to Dealmaking

*Do not turn to mediums or seek out spiritists,*
*for you will be defiled by them.*[1]

In this chapter we seek to integrate the results of Chapters 4 through 6 within a broad framework and method known as "real options." As we will see, real options uses, or can use, all of the methods and tools we have thus far considered: discounted cash flow (DCF) and net present value (NPV), probability (or decision) trees, scenario analysis, Monte Carlo, and, in a way, Black-Scholes, a very special type of options analysis.

The power and flexibility of combining these methods and tools make possible highly sophisticated opportunity analysis applicable to all four of the stages of Dealmaking as we have been considering them: conceiving, communicating, comprising, and consummating—the 4Cs of dealmaking. For example, at the stage of conceiving, real options can open new ways of selling, or buying, opportunities by which risk can be shared, or deferred (in part), value can be ascribed to components or aspects of the overall opportunity, and partnering or other dealmaking constructs can be developed that expand the terrain of conceivable deals by, for example, including the option of expanding (or contracting, or altering) the deal Box at some future point when more is known about present uncertainties. When communicating opportunities internally or externally, real options can create alternatives that are more likely to unveil highly valued and specific interests that might not have been grasped by all or nothing approaches; by using options one can decrease the immediate financial commitment of the deal in exchange for more substantial future payments when they can be better rationalized because of new information. At the point of comprising the deal, these option-based additional dimensions enable both seller and prospective buyers to create customized structures of both the Box and the Wheelbarrow. Finally, at the stage of consummating an agreement, real options can make possible grounds of agreement on both terms and value that would have been more difficult or perhaps not possible (with the ultimately paired parties) and by negotiating around the value of various options can illuminate points of disconnect regarding the present value of future choices.

Dealmaking is normally a particularly appropriate context for the use of real options. As discussed in Chapter 1, when an NPV analysis yields notably large positive or negative values, the decision to go forward or not is usually pretty straightforward. The tough calls are when the NPV is near zero. In negotiating contexts, one expects that near-zero NPV situations are common because sellers naturally want to maximize the payments they receive and so are motivated to price the opportunity to maximize *their* NPV by minimizing the NPV of the buyer; to do otherwise is called "leaving money on the table," meaning there was additional, forgone value that a willing buyer would have paid if asked and persuaded. Likewise, buyers seek to move to their account as much of the NPV of the opportunity as possible. The give and take of dealmaking typically requires compromises on these respective self-interest positions such that at the end of the process each party is motivated to consummate the deal, because it is mutually value-enhancing, but neither party feels like it has emerged with a one-sided victory in the process.

Two cautionary notes are appropriate at this point of introduction. As is soon evident, this additional flexibility is not without cost. Assessing the various possible options that could be incorporated takes time and effort in both creation and communication. Just as was discussed when considering a la carte pricing of a model deal Box, or the possible inclusion of every possible variable in a financial, or the temptation to rerun yet another simulation, every expansion of analysis needs to be measured by the practical value of such effort and complexity. There is the need for judgment in choosing an Aristotelian mean of deal analysis between the extremes of cursory and compulsive that is appropriate to the value of the opportunity and the significance of uncertainties on such opportunity value. For high potential value and significant uncertainties affecting our perception of such value an appropriate mean moves to more complete and complex analysis. Yet even then, there always comes a point when one has to say "enough" and move to the next stage of dealmaking which, as is discussed in Chapter 11, could well be Plan B.

The second caution has to do with the elusive quest of certainty. Having raised the hope, even promise, of the dealmaking power of real options, it is appropriate to remind ourselves of its limits, thus the quotation from the Bible that opens this chapter. Real options do not provide omniscience, nor are they capable of foreknowing the future, and practioners of these methods do not become mediums or spiritists conveying to this mortal world secrets from immortal worlds to tell us now what only God knows and time will unfold.[2]

In *Real Options: A Practitioner's Guide*,[3] Chapter 2 written by John Stonier, Marketing Director, Airbus Industrie, recounts the change process that occurred within Airbus as it sought to improve its ability to negotiate more wisely by using real options. One of the key points of this interesting story is the effort required to communicate simply and actionably within Airbus what can be highly abstract and mathematical in real-options analysis. It is the point of this chapter in this book to present real-options analysis with minimal reference to equations and underlying theory in as user friendly a way as possible. The reader is encouraged to refer to the Copeland and Antikarov book, and to Johnathan Mun's book[4] discussed in more detail later for comprehensive presentations of the theoretical foundations of real options as well as numerous examples from many different business contexts.

## BEYOND BLACK-SCHOLES

In Chapter 6, we introduced the concepts underlying real options by considering two extremes: a simple probability/decision tree table (summarized in Exhibit 6.4) that by simple multiplication and addition leads to a determination of the NPV of an option, and the use of the Nobel-winning Black-Scholes equation to calculate by a closed-form equation the value of an option. Now, why do we need to do more?

The Black-Scholes equation (BSE) is literally world famous in the academic world because of its strong theoretical economics grounding, meriting even a Nobel Prize, and in the business world because of its widespread use (with modifications) in the options and derivatives marketplace for financial assets. It has the additional virtue of being a closed-form equation, meaning that once one has determined each of the independent variables associated with the option, which in the traditional European option BSE without dividends (BSE1, as used in this book) is just five in number,[5] then the dependent variable (usually the option price commonly referred to as the call value) can be determined exactly without iteration, estimation, or approximation. Given the complexities and vagaries of financial affairs, this ability to determine a rational option value simply and exactly is really quite amazing. However, with such amazement, there is a dark side and it is this: There are a significant number of simplifying assumptions that were necessary in the derivation of BSE to achieve such a closed-form solution that are not exactly true even in the situation of financial options such as widely traded equities. So it has happened that there are many modifications and claimed enhancements of the BSE itself and how one calculates, and uses, the value for the five independent variables to account for, it is hoped, real world complications not originally encompassed in the derivation. Yet, as we illustrated with the example of Yahoo! shares, there are other kinds of underlying assumptions, such as the existence of a present rational market and that the past does predict the future, can never remove all the risk, and uncertainty.

Nevertheless, BSE and its kin provide financial analysis tools that are far better than random guessing, even with their limitations. A recent public announcement by Coca-Cola illustrates the challenges associated with the use of BSE, even in its ideal application to a financial security, and even a stable, well-known security. According to a story in the *Wall Street Journal*,[6] Coca-Cola in apparent response to investor concerns announced in July 2002 that it would begin to expense its granting of options to employees; namely, upon the grant to employees of Coca-Cola options, the company would report a current quarter expense associated with the then present value of such options even though neither Coca-Cola, nor its employee option recipients, incurred a present quarter expense for such grant. The challenge in expensing something for which no payment has been made is determining a fair valuation. Because Coca-Cola is a widely traded stock, options on such stock are also widely traded. However, the value for such options is not an exact comparable to the employee-granted options because the expiry periods (as well as other conditions, such as nontransferrability) are not the same as for publicly traded options. According to the *Wall Street Journal*, influential Coca-Cola board member Warren Buffet proposed as an alternative to using BSE or its variants to calculate such value that it obtain bids from financial institutions as to what *they* would pay to acquire the options granted to the subject employees. When this approach was provisionally adopted by Coca-Cola, it found that the bids it received from the financial institutions were essentially what would have resulted from a BSE calculation, almost certainly because that was how the institutions determined their perspective of such option value. So, Coca-Cola has resorted to simply calculating BSE option value despite "the subjective results often produced by Black-Scholes models," and "notwithstanding the method's drawbacks," and the fact that "Black-Scholes hinges on lots of assumptions."

An illustration of the effect of the assumptions is shown by the two option-value calculations cited in the article. The options granted to the senior executives of Coca-Cola in 2002 have a very long life, 15 years, which by itself leads to a high option value. However, the company assumed that for such a long time period, the volatility and risk-free interest rate would be relatively low, both of which tend to reduce option value. The net result using BSE was a 2002 option value of $19.92 a share. However, according to accounting rules cited in the story, the time period for expiry is not theoretical life but expected life, which Coca-Cola took to be 6 years, which, being less than 15 years, should reduce option value. However, for such shorter period, they assumed higher values of volatility and risk-free rate, which tend to increase option value. The result was a lower grant-date option value of $13.10 a share, which is just two-thirds of the value of the 15-year calculation. It should be noted that in all cases the share price of the underlying stock (Coca-Cola) was precisely known, as was the strike price (the grant the company gave its employees specified their cost of exercising the granted option in the future). Which number is "right?" In an economics sense, they both are because in accordance with the assumptions this is what the BSE calculation yields. In a business sense, neither one of them is "right" in the sense of their ability to foreknow the effective duration of the granted options, the risk-free interest rate during such duration, or the volatility of the underlying stock, let alone the present value of the option.

For our purposes with real options, such a dark side of BSE is even worse, nearly black, because of the absence of obtainable information that can be used to input the values of the five (or whatever) number of independent variables one needs to make the mathematical determination of present option value. In general, there is unlikely to be any market-based information that we can obtain that will lead us to understand such necessary independent variables as the present value of the opportunity (security) or its volatility, both of which are required for BSE. So, for dealmaking opportunity analysis, BSE is like $F = ma$, or $E = mc^2$, in that they are all famous and, in their realm, true but we cannot answer a dealmaking "so what?" question using them. We could, for instance, very easily calculate the moment of inertia of a room full of dealmaking team members and parties by simply knowing, or estimating, every person's weight and location; having done so: so what? Not every calculation that can be made should be made.

If the Black-Scholes pole is not sufficient, what about the other pole of simple probability tables, that will fix rational decision making and therefore NPV values? In most cases, the opportunities are sufficiently important and complex that such simple spreadsheet tables become unmanageable. This situation is parallel to the case for using Monte Carlo instead of scenario analysis; we could in principle accomplish the achievements of Monte Carlo by considering myriad scenarios and statistically analyzing their outcomes. Monte Carlo makes this analysis easier, and more comprehensible. For real options, similar tools and approaches can empower us to make easier use of the concept than constructing one by each tables with associated probabilities. And using such tools and approaches is what we now turn to in this chapter.

## EMERGENCE OF REAL OPTIONS ANALYSIS

Within the past 5 years, there has emerged a notable increase in books on the use of real options in decision making and, thereby, valuation. An example of such books, but by no means an exhaustive list, is given in the Bibliography at the end of this book. As might be expected, such books reflect the business trend in the increasing use of real options and by their existence promote even further use.

In the real options book by Copeland and Antikarov,[7] they summarize a dozen companies, ranging from Enron (one wonders as to Enron's purposes) to oil companies such as Mobil, Exxon, and Texaco, (oil companies have reportedly been using real options analysis since the 1970s) to aviation industry examples such as Airbus Industrie and Pratt & Whitney, to computer companies such as Apple and Hewlett-Packard, who have all claimed to use real-options methods. There are, of course, many other companies who have all used real options in one form or another but who may not have formally announced its use to the public.

It is instructive at this point to consider three questions: Is the practical, business use of real options expanding? If it is, why so, and in particular what meaning might this have for dealmaking? And finally, if it is expanding, is this just another business passing fad? (For those inclined to check the answers at the back of the book, here they are: (1) yes; (2) because it creates opportunities for wisdom, which is particularly valuable for dealmaking; and (3) no.)

There are several fundamental drivers for the expanded use of real options. To understand these drivers, let us consider the difference between a real option and a bet by considering a simple card game. Let us use one suit of 13 cards, say, diamonds, 9 number cards denominated 2 through the 10 of diamonds, and 4 high cards jack, queen, king, and ace of diamonds (which will hereafter be termed "face cards"). Suppose our game is this: I will sell you the right to receive $100, from some third party, if you pull out of the suit of 13 diamonds any one of the face cards on the first selection. What would you pay for acquiring such right? Well, if all 13 cards are face down and well shuffled, and you cannot peek, your chances of pulling up a face card on the first draw is simply 4 chances out of 13, or 31 percent (in round numbers). So, if you could play this game over and over, you would on average receive $31 and, accordingly, the very most you would be willing to pay for such right is, guess what, $31. Is this example a real option or a bet? It is only a bet, because within the confines of the game as constructed, there is no opportunity for increasing knowledge until the ultimate binary outcome of win or lose, nor is there an opportunity for changing the game in response to changing conditions.

Consider now a modified card game, this time using the suit of 13 spades. In the spades version, the prize and the criteria are the same. The one small difference is this: before drawing your card, leading to riches or goose egg, one card is removed from the suit, leaving 12 cards. However, you do not know which card has been removed, nor do you even know if it was a number or face card. What is this right to receive such $100 reward in the game of spades worth? At the time of drawing your card, the odds are either 4 chances in 12 (33 percent), if the removed card had been a numbered card or 3 in 12 (25 percent) if the removed card was a face card. However, these secondary calculations are irrelevant because the overall odds are not changed by the hid-

**EXHIBIT 7.1** Bets vs. Options, Games of Diamonds, Spades, and Hearts

**Face Card Payoff $100**

**Diamonds Game**

| Cards | | Probability | Pay Off |
|---|---|---|---|
| Numbered | 9 | 69.23% | $ — |
| *Face* | *4* | *30.77%* | *$ 30.77* |
| Total | 13 | 100.00% | |

**Spades Game**

| Cards | | | Intervening Event | | Overall Probability | Pay Off |
|---|---|---|---|---|---|---|
| | | | Numbered Card Removed | | | |
| | | | 8 | 66.67% | 46.15% | $ — |
| | | | *4* | *33.33%* | *23.08%* | *$ 23.08* |
| Cards | | | 12 | | 69.23% | |
| Numbered | 9 | 69.23% | | | | |
| *Face* | *4* | *30.77%* | Face Card Removed | | | |
| Total | 13 | 100.00% | 9 | 75.00% | 23.08% | $ — |
| | | | *3* | *25.00%* | *7.69%* | *$ 7.69* |
| | | | 12 | | 30.77% | |
| | | | | | 100.00% | $ 30.77 |

den removal of a card, namely, that of 31 percent, which can be seen in Exhibit 7.1.

There are four relative probabilities after the intervening event of the withdrawal of one card has occurred: there are either 4 face cards out of 12, or 3 out of 12, with the respective odds shown in the "intervening event" column for the spades example. (For clarity, all the italic entries are for face card results). The overall odds are as shown in the rightmost column, namely: There is a 46.15 percent overall probability that the intervening card withdrawn was a numbered card and the card you selected was a numbered card and 23.08 percent that it was a face card; and there is a 23.08 percent probability that the intervening card was a face card and you selected a numbered card and 7.69 percent that it was a face card. Under the rules of the game you will be paid the $100 only if you draw a face card. If the intervening event was the removal of a numbered card, you have a relatively high present value of such payoff ($23.08), whereas if the intervening card removed was a face card the resultant probability of payoff is relatively low ($7.69); however, regardless of the pathway to your payoff, you still receive $31 (rounded). The removal of the intervening card did not change the value because you did not know what it was and, so, knew nothing more or less at the time of your drawing a card than you did in the diamonds game. (One can appreciate this situation by having 12 intervening events occur in sequence by your choosing one at a time all the cards you will not select leaving the 13th card as your selection; not seeing the not-selected cards, and not having a way to change your bet, means that the effect of the game is unchanged, namely, the right to play is worth, at most, $31).

Both the games of diamonds and spades were bets, not options.

Now, let us consider a game using hearts (not to be confused with the game *of* hearts), again with $100 payoff, and a starting suit of 13 cards, deuce through ace. In this version, you can delay making a decision as to your maximum willingness to pay for the opportunity as multiple cards are removed and exposed. As each number card is exposed and removed, the value of the opportunity increases proportionately because the odds are increasing that any card selected from the remaining hidden cards will be a payoff face card. Likewise, with each face card exposed and removed, the value declines because of the reverse effect. A tabular illustration is shown in Exhibit 7.2.

Shown in the top left cell is the same starting value we considered previously: $30.77 (rounded to $31). The shaded cells in the rightmost column represent a condition of certainty and maximum value ($100) because all numbered cards have been removed, leaving as the final card a payoff face card. The shaded cells in the bottommost row similarly represent a condition of certainty but for the minimum value ($0) because all the face cards have been removed (the bottom right cell is blank because there are only 13 cards). Depending on the sequence of cards removed, more face cards or more number cards, the opportunity value goes down or up from the starting value of $30.77 as illustrated by a graphical surface mesh in Exhibit 7.3.

The starting value of $30.77 is shown on the $z$ axis for zero (starting) values on the $x$ and $y$ axes, corresponding to no cards removed. The surface, portrayed in Exhibit 7.3 by the sweeping upward and downward grid of lines, shows the opportunity value for all possible combinations of face and numbered cards remaining.

The face and number cards can be thought of in this thought experiment as representing, respectively, good news and bad news that may result from the development of an opportunity. In this model, the payoff is always assumed to be the same—$100. What is uncertain is the realizability of such payoff because of all the business factors that could come into play: the technology undergoing additional R&D could exhibit certain performance limitations that had been anticipated but not assured (a face card removed), the design for manufacture may lead to lower cost of product than had been assumed (a numbered card removed), a required government approval for product introduction could be delayed (a face card removed) or granted without extensive and expensive efforts (a number card removed), and so forth. A developing opportunity can be understood as the locus of an ever-changing sequence of good and bad news (which is one reason why people suffering from bipolar disorder could be advised to seek a different career). In a more

**EXHIBIT 7.2** Hearts Payoff Table as a Function of the Number and Kind of Cards Removed

Number of Cards Removed →→→ *Increasing Option Value*

| Face Cards Removed | 0 | 1 | 2 | 3 | 4 | 5 | 6 | 7 | 8 | 9 |
|---|---|---|---|---|---|---|---|---|---|---|
| 0 | $31 | $33 | $36 | $40 | $44 | $50 | $57 | $67 | $80 | $100 |
| 1 | $25 | $27 | $30 | $33 | $38 | $43 | $50 | $60 | $75 | $100 |
| 2 | $18 | $20 | $22 | $25 | $29 | $33 | $40 | $50 | $67 | $100 |
| 3 | $10 | $11 | $13 | $14 | $17 | $20 | $25 | $33 | $50 | $100 |
| 4 | $0 | $0 | $0 | $0 | $0 | $0 | $0 | $0 | $0 | $100 |

*Decreasing Option Value*

Cells of Certainty (Minimum value)

Cells of Certainty (Maximum value)

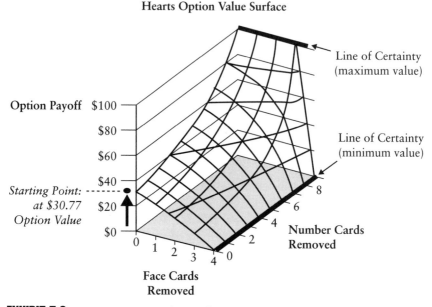

**EXHIBIT 7.3**  Hearts Option Value Surface

realistic example, the maximum payoff value is itself a variable because of these favorable and adverse outcomes, rather than the constant ($100) we used in this simple example.

Despite its simplicity, this game of hearts displays one of the principle motivations for using real options. At an early stage of an opportunity, one can make a long list of uncertainties that can affect the value and even practicability; however, beyond even such causes of uncertainty, one has to realize that it is not possible to make a list of issues that are unknown (the unknown unknowns in Defense Secretary Donald Rumsfeld speak).

There are situations where the uncertainties are simple to grasp, because the projects are themselves modest in scope, or have few and well understood uncertainties of low impact. In such cases, the simple and rational decision is to acquire, or pass, on the opportunity and get to work. When the number of uncertainty cards is either large or potentially high in impact (favorable or unfavorable), then it is a very different situation. Boldness in plunging into such opportunities can be thought of as a trait of a visionary or a leader. More likely it is a manifestation of hubris, that ancient word for unbridled arrogance and pride leading to a belief that, no matter what, chosen objectives can be reached. It is a hopeful business sign, that a significant measure of increased business humility seems to have arisen as we begin the twenty-first century, and for many industries and companies such increased humility has been growing over the past five and ten years.

Various business aphorisms have been coined to capture this idea: "don't dig big holes," "think small," "do the last experiment first," "first find a customer," "quick and dirty new product development," "stage gate product development," "phase 1 feasibility funding," "let's spend a little and learn a little (or a lot)," and so forth. All of these aphorisms have a common element of seeking to avoid making large commitments when the uncertainties are high by sequencing the opportunity in a way that makes possible relatively small investments leading to a dramatic decrease in opportunity uncertainties.

The process of creating physical structures can further illustrate this principle. If one is in need of a dog house, developing a cost model for a sheet of plywood and nails and an associated project plan or even simple drawings are not likely to be necessary. As the scale, cost, and complexity expand, it is reasonable to require a host of intermediate steps: conceptual drawings, scale models, physical tests of key components, phasing in of a building complex. During late 2002 and early 2003, the full complexity of such a building process was followed in the design and planning of the future use of the former World Trade Center site in lower Manhattan. This process has involved multiple architectural firms, visualization plans, comments from the various affected publics, including those who personally memorialize the site because of horrific personal loss. Frank Lloyd Wright, one of America's most well-known architects of the twentieth century, though he would have said of himself that his fame extended beyond any continent and any century, was sometimes required to demonstrate that his creative designs would actually work. His design of the SC Johnson headquarters in Racine, Wisconsin, has as its centerpiece a series of huge lily padlike structures with tall and exceedingly thin columns supporting large concrete pads that form a canopy high above the main building floor. Before he was permitted to build such a structure, he had to demonstrate the load-carrying capacity of such columns and pads. Near the construction site they propped up one such cast structure and loaded its lily pad with sand until failure, which was found to be 10 times the design load, and so construction was approved and a dramatic building resulted.

The point of these architectural examples is that when the uncertainty and value are both large, it is reasonable to follow multiple, and sometimes many, intermediate steps to reduce uncertainties, including redesign of said opportunities and in some instances even abandonment because of an improved understanding of a project's difficulties.

Real-option analysis is a systematic, humble way of grasping an opportunity by approaching it in steps and pieces, all the while seeking to gain an overall understanding of risk and value while expending the minimal necessary investment (consistent with other objectives such as speed to market). As discussed elsewhere in this book, the essence of wisdom is making good choices. A real-option analysis is an essential tool in enabling such wisdom.

## INTRODUCING THE BINOMIAL LATTICE FOR REAL OPTIONS

In order to apply real options in practice, we have to begin first with some bad news and it is this: There is no closed form equation that gives us the answer in the way that NPV and Black-Scholes calculations do. However, the really good news is that the calculations of real-option values, for various structures, can be done readily using the power of personal computer spreadsheets such as Excel, and even by specially developed real-options software products, as will be discussed later.

A key starting point for performing either a spreadsheet or real-options software analysis is a graphical portrayal somewhat similar to Exhibit 7.3 for the game of hearts. The key portrayal is known as a binomial lattice and it works like this. From any starting point, one envisions increasing time and decreasing uncertainty extending to the right. Going up on the page is increasing option value as a result of good outcomes associated with decreasing uncertainty, such as shown in Exhibit 7.3 when numbered cards are removed from consideration and the percentage of face cards thereby increases. Similarly, going down on our page represents decreasing option value because, for example, the answer to one or another uncertainty is bad news, though not necessarily mortally bad. We think then of this starting point as having two future points to its right, one higher and one lower because of good news and bad news, respectively.

Next, we conceive of each of these two points as themselves having two future possibilities, each having one higher state as a result of future good news and, sadly, each also with one lower state as a result of bad news. Now comes a crucial simplifying assumption inherent to a commonly used form of binomial lattices: It is assumed that the good news and bad news increments are equal in magnitude, though opposite in direction, such that there always exists a future state at the same economic value (vertical position) as the starting point arrived at either by one sequence of good news (leading upward) followed by one of bad news (leading downward), or equally by first the bad news and then the good. If these up and down increments are assumed to be equal, then every second time period has one opportunity value that is identical to (i.e., level with) the starting point. Thus, each subsequent point (or node) in the lattice becomes itself the starting point leading to two subsequent

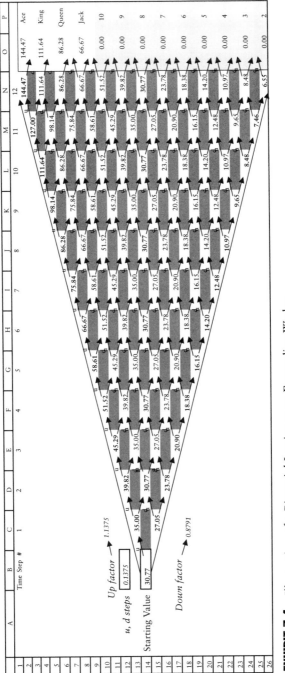

**EXHIBIT 7.4**  Illustration of a Binomial Lattice as an Expanding Wedge

points at the end of the next time step, and so forth throughout the lattice. All of this is graphically illustrated in Exhibit 7.4, created in an Excel spreadsheet.

At the leftmost cell, we see the starting value of $30.77 in cell B14, taken from our preceding examples for the game of diamonds, spades, and hearts designated by the reference Starting Value on the exhibit. For this example, we have assumed that the up and down steps have a value of 0.1375 (for reasons to be explained later). So the multiplier on each node value for *up* outcomes is 1.1375, and for *down* outcomes 0.7273 (or the inverse of 1.1375). So looking at the two matrix values in column C, namely, cells C13 and C15, we see that the favorable or up value has increased by 10.375 percent to 35.00, while the down value has decreased by 10.375 percent to 26.54.

In the subsequent time step, we have an *up* outcome from C13 to D12 and a *down* to D14; likewise we have a *down* from C15 to D16 and an *up* to D14. As it turns out, if we assume a uniform percentage for up and down changes, the value of cell D14 is identical regardless of whether it occurred as a consequence of a down from C13 or an up from C15. This process of dividing nodes into two increases the number of nodes for each time step arithmetically by one; such a lattice is called *closed* or *recombining*. If it is assumed that the up and down percentages are unequal, then each node produces two nodes after it and the lattice expands geometrically at a rate of powers of two with each time step: 1, 2, 4, 8, and so forth growing at the rate of $2^t$ where $t$ is the number of the respective time step (0, 1, 2, 3, and so forth). Such lattices are called *open* (or *nonrecombining*) and are obviously more complicated by virtue of many intermediate states. For the time being we consider only closed lattices.

Also shown in Exhibit 7.4 are 12 time steps extending from column C to N. The outcome in cell N2, namely, 144.47, is the maximum possible lattice value for the time corresponding to such 12 steps, which could be months, or quarters, or any other physical period. The value of 144.47 is conceptually analogous to the idea of the maximum Monte Carlo value for the specified number of iterations: It is the value where everything went as well as possible, within the scope of the model's assumptions, every time. Likewise, the value of cell N26 is the worst of the worst: 5.21; it resulted when everything went as badly as possible every time. The arrows extending diagonally upward and downward from the starting value of 30.77 in cell B14 encompass all possible future outcomes and can be thought of as an uncertainty wedge (or cone).

Now returning to our card game, let us assume instead that the payoff table for the opportunity is as shown in columns O and P of Exhibit 7.4. The 12 outcomes in column N, starting from the lowest value of 5.21 to the highest value of 144.47 can be assumed to represent the 13 values associated with the 13 possible remaining cards, deuce through ace, in our suit that was left after all the others were chosen in accordance with our previously assumed process. Further, consistent with our previous assumption, we will take that the utility of any outcome corresponding to a numbered card, 2 through 10, has zero value, as shown in the corresponding cells 11 through 26 of column O. (The logic of this could be simply that any opportunity worth less than 50 will be abandoned as not worth pursuing, which is the case for each of the lowest 9 outcomes; this outcome could occur, for example, if there was a subsequent cost of 50 required to commercialize after reaching the time corresponding to the 12th time step). For the face card outcomes, jack through ace, we will assume that the resulting value has the outcome value shown by the binomial lattice in column N2 through N8, namely, 144.47 to 62.96.

Now the basis for the percentage change for each up and down calculation can be described. For purposes of this example, such change was solved by using the Excel Goal Seek function such that the average of the four face card payoffs was 100, which results in the shown value of 0.1375. So, using a binomial tree, assuming that any payoff less than 50 will be abandoned and thereby have zero value, and with an average payoff of 100 for the four outcomes that have any payoff, namely, jack through ace, the 30.77 starting value is mapped to the final possible outcomes after 12 time steps using the factor of 1.1375 for up and 0.8625 for down.[8]

The binomial lattice produces a symmetrical distribution in that the node corresponding to the starting value, namely cell N14, divides evenly all possible outcomes into two equal halves: 50 percent of the time the value will be 27.44 or higher and 50 percent will be 27.44 or lower. Note that such median value is less than the starting value of 30.77. The average of the 12 payoff values in column N, prior to our abandoning all the ones below the value of 50, is 44.70. So the median value is reduced but the average value is increased compared to the starting value. This result is a consequence of a fixed percentage up or down being applied to each node. Finally, Exhibit 7.5 shows the same binomial lattice as given in Exhibit 7.4 but portrayed in a more Excel-friendly way.

By using the triangle structure, it is substantially easier to create such lattices in a spreadsheet, exploiting the available fill right and down functions. All the cell values are identical with the more easily visualized wedge portrayal in Exhibit 7.4. We can visualize these values more clearly in Exhibit 7.6, which portrays the value of each cell as a three-dimensional bar chart.

The starting value of 30.77 is shown by the frontmost bar and between 1 and 2 on the $x$ axis in Exhibit 7.6. Each subsequent bar represents one of the cell values in the binomial matrix of Exhibit 7.5 in a way similar to that shown in Exhibit 7.3. As in Exhibit 7.3, the value of the opportunity increases, or decreases, from its starting value based on the turn of intervening events; in Exhibit 7.3 such changes were affected by the relative withdrawal of numbered versus face cards, whereas in Exhibit 7.6 it is the relative occurrences of up and down changes across each time step.

u, d steps: 0.1375

Up factor: 1.1375

Down factor: 0.8791

Minimum Value Line

Maximum Value Line

| Time Step # | 0 | 1 | 2 | 3 | 4 | 5 | 6 | 7 | 8 | 9 | 10 | 11 | 12 |
|---|---|---|---|---|---|---|---|---|---|---|---|---|---|
| | 30.77 | 35.00 | 39.82 | 45.29 | 51.52 | 58.61 | 66.67 | 75.84 | 86.28 | 98.14 | 111.64 | 127.00 | 144.47 |
| | | 27.05 | 30.77 | 35.00 | 39.82 | 45.29 | 51.52 | 58.61 | 66.67 | 75.84 | 86.28 | 98.14 | 111.64 |
| | | | 23.78 | 27.05 | 30.77 | 35.00 | 39.82 | 45.29 | 51.52 | 58.61 | 66.67 | 75.84 | 86.28 |
| | | | | 20.90 | 23.78 | 27.05 | 30.77 | 35.00 | 39.82 | 45.29 | 51.52 | 58.61 | 66.67 |
| | | | | | 18.38 | 20.90 | 23.78 | 27.05 | 30.77 | 35.00 | 39.82 | 45.29 | 51.52 |
| | | | | | | 16.15 | 18.38 | 20.90 | 23.78 | 27.05 | 30.77 | 35.00 | 39.82 |
| | | | | | | | 14.20 | 16.15 | 18.38 | 20.90 | 23.78 | 27.05 | 30.77 |
| | | | | | | | | 12.48 | 14.20 | 16.15 | 18.38 | 20.90 | 23.78 |
| | | | | | | | | | 10.97 | 12.48 | 14.20 | 16.15 | 18.38 |
| | | | | | | | | | | 9.65 | 10.97 | 12.48 | 14.20 |
| | | | | | | | | | | | 8.48 | 9.65 | 10.97 |
| | | | | | | | | | | | | 7.46 | 8.48 |
| | | | | | | | | | | | | | 6.55 |

**EXHIBIT 7.5**  Binomial Lattice Shown as a Triangle

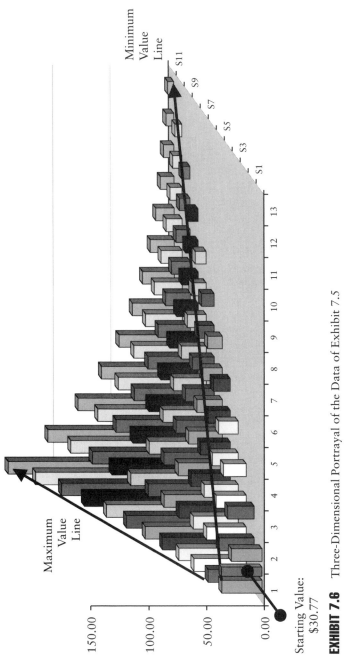

**EXHIBIT 7.6** Three-Dimensional Portrayal of the Data of Exhibit 7.5

191

## CALCULATING OPTION VALUES FROM BINOMIAL MATRICES

Using the triangular portrayal of a binomial matrix, let us now consider an example introduced in Chapter 6 having a starting value of $160.13. Further, we will calculate the value of *up* using the following equation:

$$u = exp[V \times \sqrt{(\Delta t)}] \quad \text{(and, d, is simply the inverse, namely:} = 1/u) \quad (7.1)$$

where V designates volatility as we defined and used it in the preceding chapter, and $\Delta t$ is the size of the time step between adjoining rows of the binomial lattice. The volatility must be based on the same time basis as used for value of $\Delta t$. As in the preceding exhibits, we use 12 time steps but now we designate each one as representing 1 month, or on an annual basis, each such step is 0.08333 years. Further, let us use a volatility value (based on an annual period) of 0.8036. Accordingly, equation (7.1) yields:

$$u = exp\ (0.8036 \times \sqrt{0.08333}\ ) = 1.2611$$
$$d = - exp\ (0.8036 \times \sqrt{0.08333}\ ) = 0.7930$$

Substituting these values into the format of Exhibit 7.5 results in Exhibit 7.6.

Shown in Exhibit 7.7 is the binomial lattice calculated as in the previous exhibits working left to right using the previously calculated up and down factors. The results are shown in column N at the right: maximum value of $2591 and minimum value of $9.90.

For the option to be meaningful, there must be a cost to exercise the right at the end of the option period. Let us assume that the exercise price is simply the starting value of the asset, namely, $160.13. For such value, only the highest six outcomes are "in the money," that is have option value; the lowest seven have no value because their value does not exceed the cost of exercising the right to acquire the asset. Accordingly, the option value of these lowest seven is zero. The value of the highest six is simply their value, less the cost of exercising the option ($160.13), as shown in column O.

Now the question remaining is what is the cost to *acquire* the option, as distinct from the earlier selected cost of *exercising* the option ($160.13)? To answer that question, we need to calculate backwards to the beginning time step using the final values shown in column O and a new equation, which, for the moment, we will simply take on faith. This equation calculates what is known as the risk-neutral probability:

$$\text{Risk-Neutral Probability} = [exp(RF \times \Delta t) - d]/[u - d] \quad (7.2)$$

| | A | B | C | D | E | F | G | H | I | J | K | L | M | N | O |
|---|---|---|---|---|---|---|---|---|---|---|---|---|---|---|---|
| 1 | Inputs | Volatility | T. expiry | T. steps | | | Calculation (Eq. 7.1) | | | | | | | Strike Price | $ 160.13 |
| 2 | | 80.36% | 1.00 | 12 | | | | u | d | | | | | | |
| 3 | | | | | | | | 1.2611 | 0.7930 | | | | | | |
| 4 | | | | | | | | | | | | | | | Net of |
| 5 | Time Step # | 0 | 1 | 2 | 3 | 4 | 5 | 6 | 7 | 8 | 9 | 10 | 11 | 12 | Strike Price |
| 6 | | $ 160.13 | 201.94 | 254.66 | 321.16 | 405.01 | 510.75 | 644.11 | 812.28 | 1024.36 | 1291.81 | 1629.09 | 2054.44 | 2590.84 | $2,430.71 |
| 7 | | | 126.98 | 160.13 | 201.94 | 254.66 | 321.16 | 405.01 | 510.75 | 644.11 | 812.28 | 1024.36 | 1291.81 | 1629.09 | $1,468.96 |
| 8 | | | | 100.69 | 126.98 | 160.13 | 201.94 | 254.66 | 321.16 | 405.01 | 510.75 | 644.11 | 812.28 | 1024.36 | $864.23 |
| 9 | | | | | 79.84 | 100.69 | 126.98 | 160.13 | 201.94 | 254.66 | 321.16 | 405.01 | 510.75 | 644.11 | $483.98 |
| 10 | | | | | | 63.31 | 79.84 | 100.69 | 126.98 | 160.13 | 201.94 | 254.66 | 321.16 | 405.01 | $244.88 |
| 11 | | | | | | | 50.20 | 63.31 | 79.84 | 100.69 | 126.98 | 160.13 | 201.94 | 254.66 | $94.53 |
| 12 | | | | | | | | 39.81 | 50.20 | 63.31 | 79.84 | 100.69 | 126.98 | 160.13 | $0.00 |
| 13 | | | | | | | | | 31.57 | 39.81 | 50.20 | 63.31 | 79.84 | 100.69 | $0.00 |
| 14 | | | | | | | | | | 25.03 | 31.57 | 39.81 | 50.20 | 63.31 | $0.00 |
| 15 | | | | | | | | | | | 19.85 | 25.03 | 31.57 | 39.81 | $0.00 |
| 16 | | | | | | | | | | | | 15.74 | 19.85 | 25.03 | $0.00 |
| 17 | | | | | | | | | | | | | 12.48 | 15.74 | $0.00 |
| 18 | | | | | | | | | | | | | | 9.90 | $0.00 |
| 19 | | | | | | | | | | | | | | | |

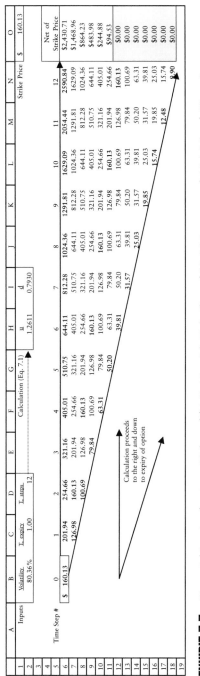

Calculation proceeds to the right and down to expiry of option

**EXHIBIT 7.7** Binomial Lattice for Asset Value of $160.13, with Volatility of 80.36 Percent and 12 1-Month Time Steps

where RF is the risk-free rate, and $\Delta t$ is the size of the time step (0.08333 years), and $u$ 1.2611) and $d$ (0.7930) are the up and down factors we defined and used before. The risk-free rate is a factor that is used in option analysis as we saw in Chapter 6. For the moment, let us use 6.19 percent (i.e., 0.0619). Substituting these values in equation (7.2) results in the following:

Risk-Neutral Probability =
$$[\exp(0.0619 \times 0.0833) - 0.7930]/[1.2611 - 0.7930] = 0.4533 \qquad (7.3)$$

Such risk-neutral probability is now used working backwards from the ending values of the lattice of Exhibit 7.7 as shown in Exhibit 7.8.

Shown in column N of Exhibit 7.8 are the final values at the end of our 12 time steps comprising our option period, as determined in Exhibit 7.7. Recall that such results were dependent only on the volatility, which is presumed to be constant and intrinsic to the opportunity under study, the size of the time step subdividing the option period whereby both the time step and option period are selected, one might say optional, values, and finally the exercise price of the option that fixes which outcomes are in the money (exercisable) and enables the calculation of their value.

Now to perform the calculations shown in Exhibit 7.8, we use additionally the risk-free probability of equations (7.2 and 7.3) as follows. The value of Cell M6 is determined as follows:

$$
\begin{aligned}
M6 &= [N6 \times RNP + (1 - RNP) \times N7] \times \exp(-RF \times \Delta t) \\
&= [2430.87 \times 0.4533 + (1-0.4533) \times 1469.05] \times \exp(-.0619 \times 0.0833) \\
&= 1895.25 \qquad\qquad\qquad\qquad\qquad\qquad\qquad\qquad\qquad (7.4)
\end{aligned}
$$

The result, 1895.25, is the value shown in M6 of Exhibit 7.8. To calculate the next cell, M7, on proceeds as previously only substituting N7 for N6, and N8 for N7, and so forth, for all the values in column M. Clearly, for cells below row 11, no calculation is necessary because the two corresponding cells in column N are both zero. The completion of the calculations of Exhibit 7.8 requires the previous process to be repeated for each column working from the right, the outcome of Exhibit 7.7, to the left. The result is the value shown in cell B6, $55.08, the option value of the opportunity, the answer we have been seeking.

Now the reason for the specific values selected for Exhibits 7.7 and 7.8 can be made clear. In Chapter 6, we consider the example using the closed-form BSE to calculate the option on a share of Yahoo! stock selling on April 3, 2000 for $160.13, such option being exercisable 1 year hence at the strike price (the cost of exercising the option) of also $160.13, an arbitrarily selected value. From the data available at the time, the risk-free rate was 6.19 percent, and the volatility of Yahoo! was 80.36 percent. With these same values in

| | A | B | C | D | E | F | G | H | I | J | K | L | M | N |
|---|---|---|---|---|---|---|---|---|---|---|---|---|---|---|
| 1 | Asset Lattice Inputs | Volatility | T.expiry | T.steps | | | Calculation (Eq. 7.1) | | | | | | Option Lattice Inputs | Risk Free | Strike Price |
| 2 | | 80.36% | 1.00 | 12 | | | | u 1.2611 | d 0.7930 | | | | | 6.19% | $ 160.13 |
| 3 | | | | | | | Calculation (Eq. 7.2) | RFP = | 0.4533 | | | | | | |
| 4 | | | | | | | | | | | | | | | |
| 5 | | | | | | | | | | | | | | | Expiry Value |
| 6 | | | | | | | | | | Calculation (Eq. 7.4) | | | | | Net of Strike Price |
| 7 | Time Step # | 0 | 1 | 2 | 3 | 4 | 5 | 6 | 7 | 8 | 9 | 10 | 11 | 12 |
| 8 | | $ 55.08 | 80.58 | 121.14 | 177.93 | 255.11 | 357.14 | 488.86 | 656.22 | 867.50 | 1134.14 | 1470.61 | 1895.13 | $ 2,430.71 |
| 9 | | | 29.58 | 47.71 | 75.21 | 115.61 | 172.92 | 251.30 | 354.70 | 487.25 | 654.61 | 865.87 | 1132.50 | $ 1,468.96 |
| 10 | | | | 14.83 | 25.36 | 42.42 | 69.17 | 109.57 | 167.93 | 248.15 | 353.08 | 485.62 | 652.97 | $ 864.23 |
| 11 | | | | | 6.24 | 11.46 | 20.63 | 36.33 | 62.22 | 103.01 | 163.48 | 246.52 | 351.45 | $ 483.98 |
| 12 | | | | | | 1.98 | 3.96 | 7.81 | 15.20 | 28.99 | 53.83 | 96.18 | 161.85 | $ 244.88 |
| 13 | | | | | | | 0.36 | 0.80 | 1.76 | 3.91 | 8.67 | 19.23 | 42.63 | $ 94.53 |
| 14 | | | | | | | | 0.00 | 0.00 | 0.00 | 0.00 | 0.00 | 0.00 | 0.00 |
| 15 | | | | | | | | | 0.00 | 0.00 | 0.00 | 0.00 | 0.00 | 0.00 |
| 16 | | | | | | | | | | 0.00 | 0.00 | 0.00 | 0.00 | 0.00 |
| 17 | | | | | | | | | | | 0.00 | 0.00 | 0.00 | 0.00 |
| 18 | | | | | | | | | | | | 0.00 | 0.00 | 0.00 |
| 19 | | | | | | | | | | | | | 0.00 | 0.00 |
| 20 | | | | | | | | | | | | | | 0.00 |
| 21 | | | | | | | | | | | | | | |

Calculation proceeds to the left and up to starting node

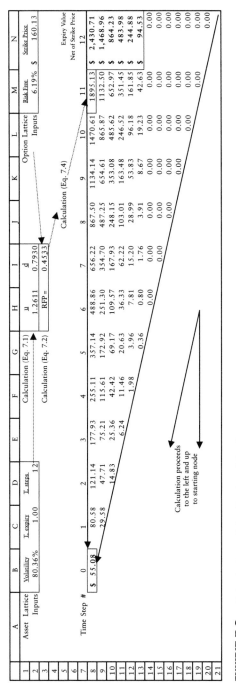

**EXHIBIT 7.8** Calculation of the Option Matrix

195

Chapter 6, we calculated the exact answer for the option price using BSE1 and obtained $53.43, slightly less than the $55.08 shown in Exhibit 7.8. The reason these two values differ is that the Black-Scholes model embedded in BSE1 is based on a continuously changing asset value that corresponds to an infinitesimally short time step. Our model in Exhibits 7.7 and 7.8 used 12 time steps, corresponding to monthly subperiods for the 1-year option period. If we shortened the size of the time steps, and thereby increased the number of such steps, our binomial matrix calculation would more closely approach the Black-Scholes exact result, at the cost of an increasing amount of calculation effort, as will be shown through the introduction of a recently available software product discussed later.

The use of the Excel model can illustrate the important effect of volatility on option value. Consider Exhibit 7.9. In this exhibit, the volatility is one-tenth of that in Exhibit 7.7. As can be seen, the values of the diverging wedge of cells do not increase, or decrease, as much as in the case for the higher volatility. Because of symmetry around the starting value, the same number of conditions leading to the exercise of the option occurs (five), but their excess value above the strike price is substantially reduced. These reduced excess values are then used in Exhibit 7.10 to calculate the option value.

As can be seen, the option value calculated is now only $10.51, compared to the Yahoo! example in Exhibits 7.7 and 7.8 where it was $53.43. Ordinarily, one thinks it a good thing to undertake a project with low uncertainties, or low financial impact of the uncertainties that exist. Why do these results, as do the ones obtained in Chapter 6, suggest the opposite? The answer lies in the value of an option. If there is no uncertainty, there is no option. There may be a payment plan for the deal, but there is no option value because there is not believed to be any up or down side on which to base such option. In other words, there is no advantage of a subsequent management decision because there is nothing to decide. In such circumstances, we are left with a simple NPV analysis. Recall, that the essence of an option is the present value of a deferrable, future decision. So, what is bad from an NPV-certainty perspective is good for real-options purposes.

## CALCULATING OPTION VALUES USING DECISIONEERING'S REAL OPTIONS ANALYSIS TOOLKIT

As discussed in our study of Monte Carlo methods, two companies make software products for this purpose: Crystal Ball by Decisioneering, and @Risk by Pallisade. For real-options analysis, at present there is known to be only one software product that is available for the PC market. It is Real Options Analysis Toolkit software (ROATS), available from Decisioneering.

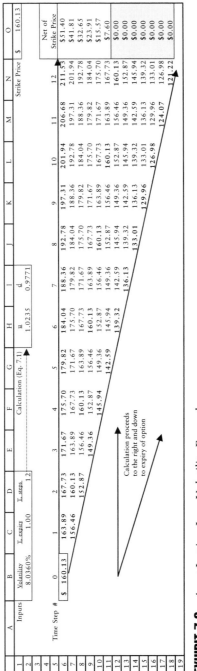

**Inputs**

| Volatility | T-expiry | T-steps | u | d | Strike Price |
|---|---|---|---|---|---|
| 8.0360% | 1.00 | 12 | 1.0235 | 0.9771 | $ 160.13 |

Calculation (Eq. 7.1)

| Time Step # | 0 | 1 | 2 | 3 | 4 | 5 | 6 | 7 | 8 | 9 | 10 | 11 | 12 | Net of Strike Price |
|---|---|---|---|---|---|---|---|---|---|---|---|---|---|---|
| | $ 160.13 | 163.89 | 167.73 | 171.67 | 175.70 | 179.82 | 184.04 | 188.36 | 192.78 | 197.31 | 201.94 | 206.68 | 211.53 | $51.40 |
| | | 156.46 | 160.13 | 163.89 | 167.73 | 171.67 | 175.70 | 179.82 | 184.04 | 188.36 | 192.78 | 197.31 | 201.94 | $41.81 |
| | | | 152.87 | 156.46 | 160.13 | 163.89 | 167.73 | 171.67 | 175.70 | 179.82 | 184.04 | 188.36 | 192.78 | $32.65 |
| | | | | 149.36 | 152.87 | 156.46 | 160.13 | 163.89 | 167.73 | 171.67 | 175.70 | 179.82 | 184.04 | $23.91 |
| | | | | | 145.94 | 149.36 | 152.87 | 156.46 | 160.13 | 163.89 | 167.73 | 171.67 | 175.70 | $15.57 |
| | | | | | | 142.59 | 145.94 | 149.36 | 152.87 | 156.46 | 160.13 | 163.89 | 167.73 | $7.60 |
| | | | | | | | 139.32 | 142.59 | 145.94 | 149.36 | 152.87 | 156.46 | 160.13 | $0.00 |
| | | | | | | | | 136.13 | 139.32 | 142.59 | 145.94 | 149.36 | 152.87 | $0.00 |
| | | | | | | | | | 133.01 | 136.13 | 139.32 | 142.59 | 145.94 | $0.00 |
| | | | | | | | | | | 129.96 | 133.01 | 136.13 | 139.32 | $0.00 |
| | | | | | | | | | | | 126.98 | 129.96 | 133.01 | $0.00 |
| | | | | | | | | | | | | 124.07 | 126.98 | $0.00 |
| | | | | | | | | | | | | | 121.22 | $0.00 |

Calculation proceeds
to the right and down
to expiry of option

**EXHIBIT 7.9**  Asset Lattice, Low Volatility Example

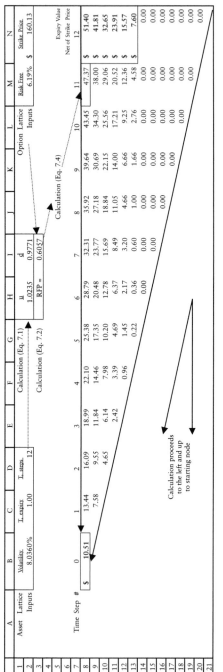

| | A | B | C | D | E | F | G | H | I | J | K | L | M | N |
|---|---|---|---|---|---|---|---|---|---|---|---|---|---|---|
| 1 | Asset | Volatility | T.expiry | T.steps | | | | u | d | | | Option Lattice | Risk Free | Strike Price |
| 2 | Lattice Inputs | 8.0360% | 1.00 | 12 | | | Calculation (Eq. 7.1) | 1.0235 | 0.9771 | | | Inputs | 6.19% | $ 160.13 |
| 3 | | | | | | | Calculation (Eq. 7.2) | RFP = | 0.6057 | | | | | |
| 4 | | | | | | | | | | Calculation (Eq. 7.4) | | | | Expiry Value |
| 5 | | | | | | | | | | | | | | Net of Strike Price |
| 7 | Time Step # | 0 | 1 | 2 | 3 | 4 | 5 | 6 | 7 | 8 | 9 | 10 | 11 | 12 |
| 8 | | $ 10.51 | 13.44 | 16.09 | 18.99 | 22.10 | 25.38 | 28.79 | 32.31 | 35.92 | 39.64 | 43.45 | 47.37 | $ 51.40 |
| 9 | | | 7.58 | 9.55 | 11.84 | 14.46 | 17.35 | 20.48 | 23.77 | 27.18 | 30.69 | 34.30 | 38.00 | $ 41.81 |
| 10 | | | | 4.65 | 6.14 | 7.98 | 10.20 | 12.78 | 15.69 | 18.84 | 22.15 | 25.56 | 29.06 | $ 32.65 |
| 11 | | | | | 2.42 | 3.39 | 4.69 | 6.37 | 8.49 | 11.05 | 14.00 | 17.21 | 20.52 | $ 23.91 |
| 12 | | | | | | 0.96 | 1.45 | 2.17 | 3.20 | 4.66 | 6.66 | 9.25 | 12.36 | $ 15.57 |
| 13 | | | | | | | 0.22 | 0.36 | 0.60 | 1.00 | 1.66 | 2.76 | 4.58 | $ 7.60 |
| 14 | | | | | | | | 0.00 | 0.00 | 0.00 | 0.00 | 0.00 | 0.00 | 0.00 |
| 15 | | | | | | | | | 0.00 | 0.00 | 0.00 | 0.00 | 0.00 | 0.00 |
| 16 | | | | | | | | | | 0.00 | 0.00 | 0.00 | 0.00 | 0.00 |
| 17 | | | | | | | | | | | 0.00 | 0.00 | 0.00 | 0.00 |
| 18 | | | | | | | | | | | | 0.00 | 0.00 | 0.00 |
| 19 | | | | | | | | | | | | | 0.00 | 0.00 |
| 20 | | | | | | | | | | | | | | 0.00 |
| 21 | | | | | | | | | | | | | | 0.00 |

Calculation proceeds to the left and up to starting node

**EXHIBIT 7.10**   Option Lattice, Low Volatility Example

The book by Johnathan Mun, *Real Options Analysis*,[9] provides a detailed overview of the theory and equations of many real-options situations and includes numerous examples from the Decisioneering product; Johnathan Mun is a vice president of Decisioneering, a finance professor, and creator of ROATS.

Exhibits 7.11 and 7.12 are screen shots from Decisioneering's Real Options Analysis Toolkit software (ROATS) for the Yahoo! example evaluated in Chapter 6 using BSE and in this chapter using equations (7.1, 7.2, and 7.4) with an Excel spreadsheet of cells in Exhibits 7.7 and 7.8 for 12 time steps.

The screen shot in Exhibit 7.11 is the calculation for a European Option; recall that such option is one that can only be exercised on the expiry date. The five input parameters are as shown in the box on the left (we have assumed throughout that there are no dividends paid during the option period). ROATS uses a default configuration of five time steps, so in the present example, each time step corresponds to one-fifth of a year (or 2.4 months). The intermediate calculations are as shown at the top middle of Exhibit 7.11: the up and down factors calculated for this five time-step year are 1.4324 and 0.6981, respectively, obtained by the use of equation (7.1). These two values are used to calculate each of the lattice nodes in the top lattice "Underlying

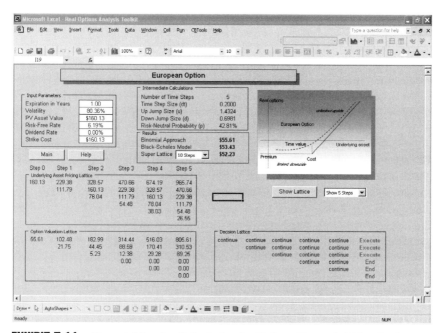

**EXHIBIT 7.11**   Binomial Lattice Calculation for Yahoo! Example Using Real Options Analysis Toolkit Software

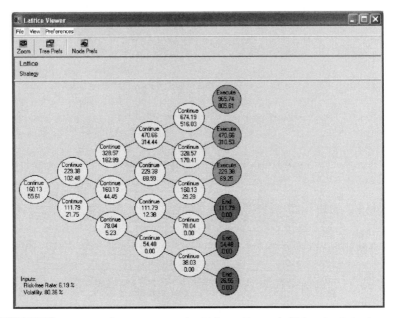

**EXHIBIT 7.12**    Binomial Lattice View for Yahoo! Example Using Real Options Analysis Toolkit Software

Asset Pricing Lattice" starting from the given initial asset value of, in this case, $160.13. The final intermediate calculation, that of the "Risk-Neutral Probability" (RNP) is determined as shown (42.81 percent) using equation (7.2); this factor is used starting from the Step 5 values of the lattice to work backward to determine the option value at the originating node as shown in the "Option Valuation Lattice" at the bottom left. In order for this option valuation calculation to occur, it is necessary to apply the decision criterion associated with the option. Otherwise, it can be shown that the result from using the RNP calculation will simply be that the option has no value because there is no choice being made.

The Decision Lattice is shown at the bottom right of Exhibit 7.11. For those Step 5 values exceeding the strike price ($160.13), then the appropriate decision is to exercise the option. This result is the situation on the highest three outcomes. For the lowest three outcomes, the strike price exceeds the ending step values and no rational option holder would do anything other than abandon the option.

Exhibit 7.12 is a nodal view available in ROATS that shows the results of all three lattices within each circle.

Real Options Analysis Toolkit software also shows in Exhibit 7.11 option value results for the Black-Scholes calculation ($55.43), which we calculated in Chapter 6, and the value for binomial lattices with a larger number of time steps. Shown is the value for 10 steps ($52.23). Real Options Analysis Toolkit software has built in choices of 5, 10, 50, 100, 300, 500, 1,000, and 5,000 steps. As the number of steps is increased, the binomial lattice calculation yields values ever closer to the Black-Scholes result. As discussed elsewhere, the importance of precision should be considered in the context of all the uncertainties associated with a dealmaking opportunity and the direct benefit of a more accurate result. When investing in financial options such as equities, precision is extremely important because small differences are what make the difference between profit and loss. For the use of real options with opportunity dealmaking, the relatively large number of uncertainties, some recognized and some not, make it unnecessary to seek a high level precision from the use of a large number of small time steps.

## USING REAL OPTIONS ANALYSIS TOOLKIT SOFTWARE IN DEALMAKING

Using Decisioneering's ROATS let us now consider how it could be applied to dealmaking. Many underlying opportunities have the following three attributes:

1. There is a relatively short period (compared to the lifetime of the opportunity being dealt) after deal consummation during which time many questions relevant to opportunity value will be answered. Such questions could include:

   ■ The creation of initial, or expanded, patent protection as evidenced by new patent applications filed and obtaining allowance of claims by the U.S. Patent and Trademark Office.

   ■ Completion of certain R&D tasks critical to a product's final design, and its feature-function capability and value.

   ■ Market research and testing including possibly placement of alpha or beta prototypes with lead users, early adopters, or long-term company clients.

   ■ Design for manufacturability with possibly initial yield data and improved understanding of what will be the ultimate cost of goods sold.

   ■ Government approval(s) for manufacture or use, or the disposal for waste products.

2. There are numerous opportunity expansion options typically available. In Chapter 4 we considered how a certain new polymer technology could be applicable to:

   ■ Multiple product application such as could be made available via multiple field of use options.

- Multiple territories, such as North America, Western Europe, Japan, or Oceania (which would include multiple Far East countries, Australia and New Zealand) and now increasing opportunities in what formerly was considered Eastern Europe as a block of countries, and China, India, and Russia.

- In addition to the previous examples, options to expand could include the right to sell to specific customers or customer segments within a territory, or to sell greater than a specified number of units, and many other possibilities.

3. A dealmaking Box could provide value to the buyer even if the underlying technology or associated market fails to be realized, a form of salvage value.

   - The patent(s) could partially or wholly pertain to and protect other products or processes of the buyer, or patent enforcement or cross-claim opportunities for the buyer, namely, third parties, entirely apart from new product opportunities. Such protection could be estimated and provide a floor on the deal value that can be thought of as salvage value.

   - Land, facilities, or equipment made available to the buyer with the deal Box could be of value to the buyer in other business applications as a fallback outcome in the event going forward with the originally planned new product later turns out to be insufficiently attractive.

   - Key and other employees who join the buyer's firm as a part of the transaction who could be valuable to the buyer in the pursuit of other, later-determined business applications.

   - A close customer relationship that is transferred could be valued for other commercial purposes unrelated to the narrowly defined deal subject matter.

   - The underlying technology of the deal could be viewed as important and foundational to the buyer's future business even apart from the transacted opportunity as a kind of organized master class into the future of a certain manufacturing approach.

These three features of a broad class of options can be treated by ROATS using the available "American Option to Expand and Abandon." The European Option can only be exercised at the expiry date. The American Option, which is more realistic for most dealmaking contexts, can be exercised at any time *until* expiry. Exhibit 7.13, taken from ROATS, illustrates how such option may be applied.

In this example, the expiration period is assumed to be 3 years; so for the five step lattices, each step represents a time period of 7.2 months. The

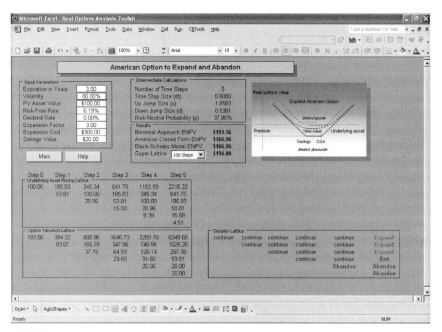

**EXHIBIT 7.13** Dealmaking Real Option Example

present value of the Box in its basic, unoptioned form, is $100 million. The risk-free rate is taken as 6.19 percent, which is an estimated value of a government bond that corresponds to the term of the option. We have assumed no dividends, namely, no value extraction opportunities available to the buyer during the period of the option. The expansion factor is shown to be three. This expansion factor could correspond, for example, to the option right for the buyer to elect additional fields of use or territories at any time during the 3 years of the option, where the NPV of such additional rights are presently believed to have a present NPV of $300 million or three times the base NPV value. Finally, the salvage value is assumed to be $20 million. Such value could arise because of other forms of value that will incur to the buyer even on the failure of the subject opportunity.

Entering these values in the respective input cells yields the results shown in the middle of the exhibit. Real Options Analysis Toolkit software defines expanded NPV/(ENPV) to represent the present value of the opportunity given the assumed available options. That is, according to this model, a fair value for the opportunity would be $193.56 million, or $93.56 million more than the $100 million present value of the baseline or nonexpanded opportunity. As seen in this exhibit, if the calculation had used 100 steps the ENPV value would change only slightly to $194.00 million. Also shown are the closed-form results obtainable from Black-Scholes and another equation specific to American Options. However, the specific options of this particular example do not even closely conform to the assumptions underlying these closed-form solutions, so in this and in most cases, the results of the binomial lattice are taken to be more reliable.

The decision lattice also shown in Exhibit 7.13 shows all four possible (within the framework of the assumptions) buyer elections: continue, end, expand, and abandon. The abandon option is chosen for those option lattice nodes whose value falls below $20 million, as is the case for the bottom two nodes in Step 5 and the bottom node in Step 4. Effectively, this salvage value assumption as used in this example has two aspects. Implied in the example is the *abandonment* of the direct implementation of the deal opportunity because it has fallen below $20 million in value, and so, is not worth doing as a business setup. However, despite such abandonment, the residual value of having pursued the opportunity is understood to have provided $20 million in other value as discussed in the text. Under these circumstances, the value of the options associated with nonuse of the Box opportunity are less than those associated with abandonment, assuming that these are mutually exclusive choices. The three top nodes in Step 5 are expand choices because the respective value of the opportunity is sufficiently large that even the substantial additional cost of exercising such expansion option ($300 million) is justified. For instance, the NPV for the most-favorable outcome in Step 5 is determined to be $2.216 billion (rounded). According to the assumptions, the expanded value is three times this value, or $6.664, less the cost of expansion ($300) yielding the shown net value of $6.349. For each of the top three outcomes in Step 5, such calculation yields a positive value, thereby justifying the option to expand.

The fourth highest outcome in Step 5 has a value sufficient to merit going forward with the basic opportunity, as opposed to the (assumed mutually exclusive) option of abandonment and the earlier considered expansion option.

Before considering other structures for evaluating real options, let us consider an important input to all these calculations: volatility.

## CALCULATING (OR ESTIMATING) OPTION VOLATILITY

As seen in all the exhibits in this chapter starting with Exhibit 7.4, we have in some form used an estimate of volatility to calculate option value. And one such value is used throughout the option period for each time step and every intermediate outcome to calculate the outcome at the next time step. As we have seen, as the volatility diminished, the option value and the value of options decreases to the limiting value of the NPV of the deal. So, volatility is a good thing for real options. How, then, do we determine its value?

First, let us review how volatility is determined for a financial option such as on an equity, such as Yahoo!. As discussed in Chapter 6, the volatility of a particular stock or even an industry of stocks can be determined by calculating the standard deviation of the historic log-normal rates of returns by using, for example, the closing daily price of the stock for some period such as 30 or 90 days. Because these values are easily known, the volatility can be directly calculated for any period sought. Because the relevant volatility is that which is in the future, which, of course, cannot be presently known, it is generally better to use as short and as most-recent period as possible. Balancing this need is to avoid having the calculation be inaccurate because the time period is too brief or too recent such that it does not include turbulent earlier fluctuation-causing events.

Alternative to performing the standard deviation calculation is to infer the market-determined volatility using the widely available public markets for equity options to solve for volatility value using the BSE or its modification.

For project opportunities neither of these approaches is available because there is neither a history of returns on which to make a log-normal calculation or a public market of options based on the opportunity. Therefore, we should not be surprised that this estimated value is difficult to calculate and subject to substantial uncertainty itself.

Johnathan Mun devotes an appendix in his book (his Appendix 7A) to methods of making such volatility estimates.[10] In yet another book by Mun,[11] he provides additional approaches to estimating volatility (in his Chapter 4). In the Copeland and Antikarov book there is an entire chapter (their Chapter 9) on determining volatility.[12] In ROATS there is a module for assisting in a calculation of volatility. Here, we briefly review several potentially applicable approaches.

As in many business contexts, a useful method for developing a key assumption is reasoned judgment of an individual or an expert panel. Given the mathematical sophistication of real options, it is a little underwhelming to rely on an opinion, however obtained, as a key input. Yet, we have to recall that the future is unknowable to us. All the inputs into all our business models involve some aspect of judgment even if is only the selection of the market study on which we will rely, for example, to forecast future revenues. Until something is actually ready for manufacturing, we cannot be sure what its final performance will be. Until something is made and ready for shipment, we cannot know what it costs to make. Until someone buys what has been made, we cannot be sure what the market's willingness to buy and to pay will be. Filling out these cells requires judgment. Similarly, when we calculate DCF and NPV values, we have to select a discounting value (risk-adjusted hurdle rate or weighted average cost of capital or some other basis). These values are also judgment calls. So, we should not object to the concept of a reasoned selection based on experience applied to a specific opportunity.

In the card suit example of hearts used earlier in this chapter, we considered a situation in which there are 12 uncertainties represented by cards that are revealed during the course of the option period. Each numbered card removed from the suit represented the elimination of an unfavorable factor affecting the opportunity's value, and conversely for the elimination of a face card. By considering all the reasonably important factors affecting opportunity value, quantifying the respective value, and assessing the probability, all steps that are needed for a DCF or probability tree analysis can also be used to estimate volatility.

Such estimates can then be made in several ways. One traditional way is to develop a database of one's experience based on many prior opportunities, each with its unique uncertainties and knowledge of how it turned out. For companies with many opportunities of broadly comparable scope, such a database of experience can be used to make a good, or at least a reasonable, estimate for the subject opportunity. For instance, seasoned venture capitalists could easily have had the experience of participating in 20 or 50 or more investments. Based on the key variables (such as the startup's management team), venture capitalists are paid to extract such judgment to apply to new opportunities. Some have the knack for doing so.

A simple way to quantify volatility is the use of such management judgment using Crystal Ball or some other Monte Carlo software. Recall that in creating a Monte Carlo model, it is necessary to input assumed probability distributions for each of the independent variables. One can use such an assumption function for this purpose of quantifying volatility. As we discussed log-normal distributions occur in many real-life situations. By taking the logarithm of a normal distribution, the result is skewed slightly but importantly in that no negative values are permitted but remains unbounded at the upper limit. Exhibit 7.14 shows two distributions each for normal and log-normal assumptions:

As can be seen, for large standard deviations (volatilities), the normal distribution assumption yields negative NPV values. From a DCF perspective, this result could of course be valid because, as one knows all too well, opportunities can exhibit negative NPV values. However, from the perspective of real options, the future value of an opportunity cannot go below zero (not including the up-front payment made to secure the option) because a rational buyer will let its option expire at that point. However, log-normal distributions cannot have negative values even for large values of volatility.

Exhibit 7.15 shows how using Crystal Ball's log-normal distribution function a management of volatility can be easily calculated. The left panel of this exhibit shows the modeling of a log-normal distribution using the estimated NPV values for the 90 and 10 percentile outcomes. As shown in this example, for a mean NPV value of $100 (rounded), and a 90 percent probability that the NPV value of $50 will be exceeded, the corresponding 10 percent probability is $162. So, for this example, one assumes that there is a 10 per-

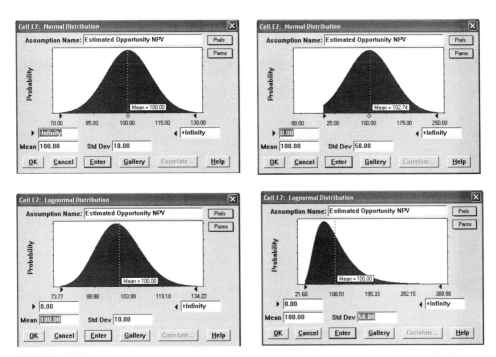

**EXHIBIT 7.14** Comparison of Normal and Log-Normal Distribution Models Available in Crystal Ball

cent probability that the opportunity will be worth between zero and $50, and also a 10 percent probability that it will be worth more than $162 with no specific upper bound. The mean (weighted average) of all such possibilities for a log-normal distribution is then simply the $100 (rounded). It should be noted that using such functionality in Crystal Ball has nothing to do with obtaining a Monte Carlo simulation; we are only using the built-in assumption capability to obtain a graphical portrayal of our assumptions and the direct calculation of log-normal volatility. The same outcome could be accomplished in Excel using its built-in functions and the Goal Seek capability. By iterating with various values of NPV for the mean, 10 percent probability, and 90 percent probability, compared to other calculations, including Monte Carlo models, that have been made, a distribution can be chosen that seems to best fit the expected range of outcomes. Then, by using the "Parms" input on the log-normal distribution screen, one can select other views such as the second panel in Exhibit 7.15 showing, for example, 20 and 80 percentile values, namely $61 and $132 (rounded). As discussed in Chapter 5, buyers and sellers may gravitate to values in the range of 20 to 30 percentile outcomes. If these values do not look like best estimates, then further adjustments can be made or other percentile points selected. Once this value looks reasonable, then again using the Parms input, the calculation for log-normal standard

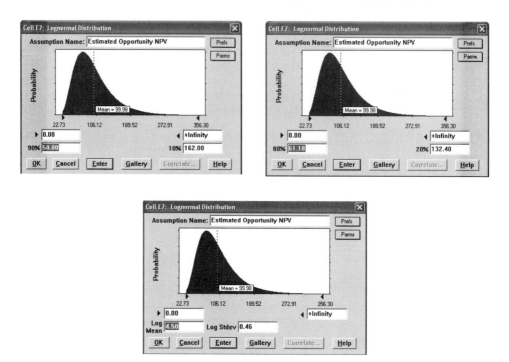

**EXHIBIT 7.15**   Example of Using Crystal Ball to Estimate Log-Normal Volatility of a Project

deviation (which is simply our volatility) can be found as shown in the final panel of Exhibit 7.15, namely, 0.46 (or 46 percent).

An alternative to the above management estimation (which may or may not be based on an underlying Monte Carlo model) is to perform a calculation using Monte Carlo to convert a time series estimate of future cash flows to an estimate of outcome volatility. According to Mun,[13] this approach was first introduced by Copeland and Antikarov.[14] The way this approach works is as follows. For each time period, one makes an estimate for the cash flows as is normally done in any DCF analysis. Summing all such cash flows, and discounting by a rate appropriate to a Monte Carlo approach as discussed in Chapter 6, yields an estimate of present, time zero, value. The process can be repeated to calculate such NPV value at the end of the first time step. So one now has two values of NPV: one at time zero, and one at the end of the first time step used in estimating cash flows, which is usually a year. The ratio of the NPV1 (at the end of the first time step) divided by NPV0 is less than one and is designated for convenience by X. Next, one performs a Monte Carlo simulation on NPV2, calculating the value of X for each such iteration, yielding a distribution of values for X. The Crystal Ball determined deviation of such distribution values for X is then the estimate of opportunity volatility.

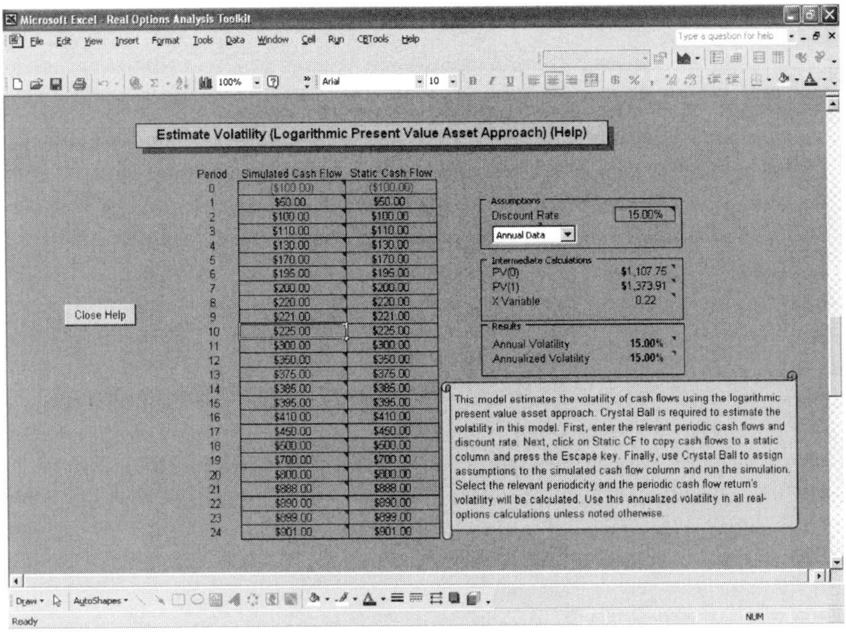

**EXHIBIT 7.16** ROATS Estimate of Volatility Using Results of Monte Carlo Analysis

In ROATS this calculation has been included as a separate, easy-to-use function as shown in Exhibit 7.16. The reader is referred to Mun's book and ROATS and Copeland and Antikarov's book for further details on this method.

An approach to using an expert panel together with benchmark equity (financial) options was recently described in a presentation by the author to a meeting of the Licensing Executives Society.[15]

One of the principal assumptions being made regarding volatility is the use of a single value for all possible outcomes at each time step and for all time steps. The latter assumption can be relaxed at significantly increased complexity by using another feature in ROATS that permits the assumption of multiple volatilities. Exhibit 7.17 illustrates how this can be done.

The left panel of Exhibit 7.17 shows the input screen for calculating option value when dealing with multiple volatilities. The difference in this feature is the ability to specify different volatilities for different time periods. In the example shown, a relatively low volatility of 20 percent has been used for the first year, increasing to 40 percent for the second year, and 60 percent for the third, fourth, and fifth years of the option to its expiry. The right panel of Exhibit 7.17 shows how the lattice appears (the image has been reduced to fit it on the page making the node values difficult to read). As can

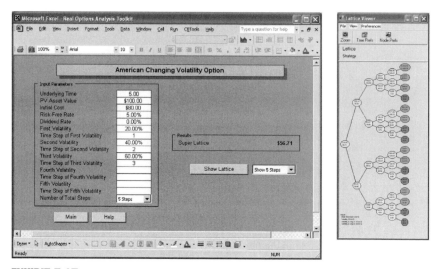

**EXHIBIT 7.17**   Capability within ROATS of Performing Option Value Calculations for Multiple Volatilities

be seen from the appearance of the lattice, the constant volatility period starting with the third time step causes it to appear in a convention-recombining lattice as we saw in our earlier exhibits. As this calculation shows, the value of the option so calculated is $56.71. Had we repeated the calculation but at constant volatility, we would have determined such value to be $39.95 (all periods at 20 percent volatility), $50.79 (at 40 percent), or $62.31 (60 percent). As before, the option value increases with higher volatility because the lower bound is zero with no upper bound. Having the stepwise volatility as shown in Exhibit 7.17 predicts an option value approximately midway between the result for a uniform volatility value of 40 and 60 percent.

## CALCULATING THE OPTION VALUE OF OPTIONS ON OPTIONS

In all our discussion so far in this chapter, we have considered what might be called a two-layer approach: There exists an underlying opportunity with its perceived value and overlaying it is the option value associated with such opportunity. Well, such overlaying option value can itself have an option value. One can literally offer an option on an option.

Let us first consider a simpler situation, that of two simultaneous options. This corresponds to the granting of the option right to choose A or B, in

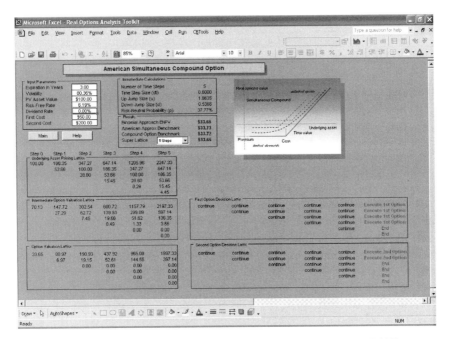

**EXHIBIT 7.18** Example of Calculating an Option on an Option in ROATS

which A and B represent discrete business opportunities that could be pursued by the buyer of the opportunity. This scenario is illustrated in Exhibit 7.18.

As can be seen from the input panel in Exhibit 7.18, it is assumed that the volatility is 80.36 percent, and the risk-free rate is 6.19 percent, both annual values over the option period. The option period is 3 years. The best estimate of the NPV is $100 million. The cost of exercising the first option, which may correspond to the right to apply the opportunity in a particular field of use, is assumed to be $50 million. The cost of exercising the second option, which may be the right to sell products worldwide, is assumed to be $200 million. The results calculated in ROATS are as shown: the present value of the combined option is $32.65 million, and there are estimated to be four chances out of six that the first option will be exercised and just two out of six that the second option will be exercised.

We can use the assumptions in Exhibit 7.18 to consider a sequential option, in which the exercise of the second option is contingent on the exercise of the first option, as shown in Exhibit 7.19.

As can be seen in the panel designated "intermediate option valuation lattice," five out the nine outcomes shown in the final time step have sufficient value to warrant being exercised given the assumed cost of exercise of $50 million. For such five outcomes, the bottommost panel relating to the

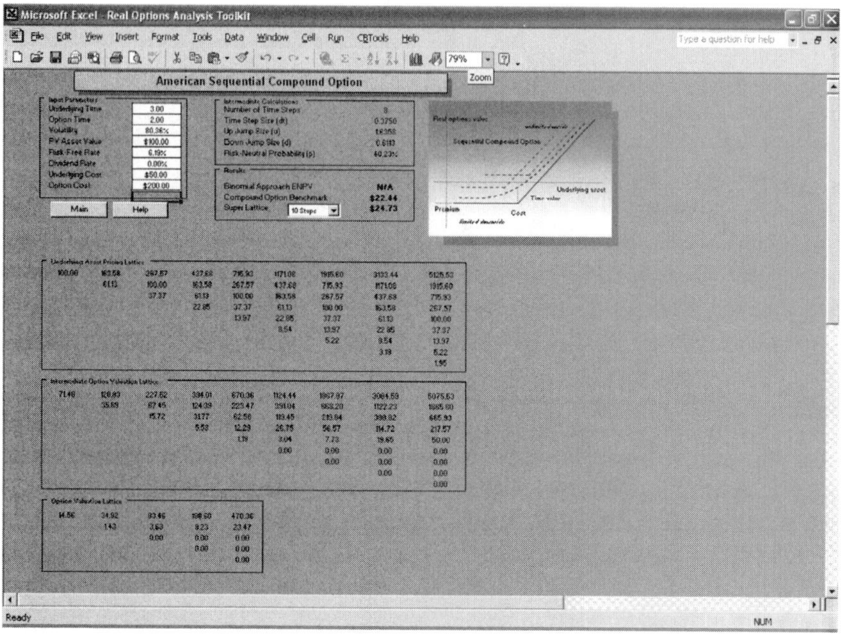

**EXHIBIT 7.19** Example of Sequential Option Calculation Using ROATS

"option valuation lattice" shows that in two of such outcomes is the opportunity expected to yield a value that warrants exercise given the assumed cost of exercising such second option of $200 million.

All the previous calculations done using ROATS can be accomplished in Excel using the two-step approach shown earlier in this chapter and in Exhibits 7.7 through 7.10. However, the availability of the software makes it easier to consider many possible "what ifs" and to portray the lattices graphically. Although neither approach has the virtues of a closed-form equation, such as Black-Scholes, they have other, better virtues: one can by trial, judgment, and experience gain a better understanding of the unlocked value in an opportunity, and the consequences, both good and bad, of different levels and kinds of uncertainties.

## CONCLUSIONS AND OBSERVATIONS

What we have sought to accomplish in this chapter are two things: developing a different framework for looking at structure and value of an opportunity and showing how to implement this framework in the practical world of dealmaking.

Every price on every thing can be thought of as an option. And many such options have options. So, an opportunity Box may have been configured and valued based on scenario analysis, probability trees, simple DCF, Monte Carlo, or some other methodology, and determined to have a best-thinking, expected present value of $100. Because such $100 is for an opportunity that emerges in the future, as opposed to, say, a very nice dinner to be consumed in the next hour, what can be offered is an option on such $100 Box. Depending on the configuration of the real option Wheelbarrow (term of the option, exercise price), the nature of the opportunity itself (volatility) and the business environment (risk-free investment alternatives), an option value can be calculated. So every Box can be offered in an option structure, valued and negotiated as such.

Further, each such $100 Box can be offered in components through options on such components, in which components could be the opportunity for the buyer to acquire additional rights such as fields and territories (or alternatively to shrink its rights). Carried to an extreme, this optioning on options approach can create an unmanageable level of complexity. But, again, there is the principle of the reasonable mean. For opportunities that are high in potential value, with high uncertainties that have a significant potential effect on value, and with practicable ways of implementing subsequent management decisions to expand, contract, switch, or abandon, real options affords a real opportunity to do better dealmaking.

## NOTES

1. The entire verse is: *"Do not turn to mediums or seek out spiritists, for you will be defiled by them. I am the Lord your God,"* from Lev. 19:31, New International Version (NIV).
2. The two words translated by the NIV in Lev. 19:31 by mediums and spiritists are worthy of further consideration. The word translated by mediums literally means ventriloquists or, more likely, necromancers; namely, one who echoes without understanding what is heard spoken or shown in another realm. The word translated as spiritists derives from the Hebrew word for "knowing one"; this translation conveys the idea of someone who, by the use of magical arts and only by such use, can know something not humanly attainable. From time immemorial, humans have been tempted, and have succumbed, to gain advantage by seeking knowledge by supernatural, supernormal, means. This temptation, of course, has created a not-so-small industry of charlatans of many varieties. It is well to remember that real options and the other methods and tools considered in this book are not likely to be useful to ventriloquists or their audiences, because the power of such methods is not in producing a number but a framework for understanding. Further, it is not the intention of teaching such methods to create the opportunity to disadvantage the other parties to a dealmaking opportunity. So the knowing aspect of the use of these methods is certainly appropriate, but secret knowing is neither necessary nor generally advantageous.

3. Tom Copeland and Vladimir Antikarov, *Real Options: A Practitioner's Guide* (Texere Publishing, 2001).

4. Johnathan Mun, *Real Options Analysis* (New York: John Wiley & Sons, 2002).

5. They are (1) $S_0$, the present market price of the security (opportunity), (2) $S_1$, the future price one chooses to pay to acquire the security (the so-called strike price), (3) the risk-free hurdle rate, (4) the date of the expiry of the option, and (5) the volatility of the underlying asset.

6. Jonathan Weil and Betsy McKay, "Coke Developed a New Way to Value Options, But Company Will Return to Its Classic Formula," *Wall Street Journal*, 7 March, 2003, Sec. C, p. 3.

7. Copeland and Antikarov, Ibid.

8. The binomial tree example does not directly correspond to the circumstances of the card suit examples. In these examples, the favorable and unfavorable outcomes by drawing and removing each card were not equal: the removal of a face card caused a larger decrease in the value of the opportunity, because there are only four face cards that are "in the money." For a closed binomial tree, we must have the favorable and unfavorable outcomes equal as a percentage.

9. Mun, *Real Options Analysis*. Johnathan Mun has also authored another recently published book: *Real Options Analysis Course: Business Cases and Software Applications,* John Wiley & Sons, 2003. Additional information from Decisioneering on real options is available at: www.decisioneering.com/realoptions.

10. Ibid.

11. Johnathan Mun, *Real Options Analysis Course: Business Cases and Software Applications,* John Wiley & Sons, Inc., 2003.

12. Copeland and Antikarov, Ibid, p. 198.

13. Mun, Ibid.

14. Copeland and Antikarov, Ibid.

15. Additional information is available at "¹Dealmaking" resources on the Author's Web site: www.razgaitis.com.

## APPENDIX 7A: REAL OPTIONS EQUATIONS

In Chapter 7 we use various equations to calculate the various lattice nodes of the underlying asset and, by backward calculation, of the option value. There is a well-developed mathematical basis for these equations. However, the presentation of the derivations are beyond the purpose of this book and they are well developed in books by Johnathan Mun[1] and Copeland and Antikarov.[2] What follows is a section from Johnathan Mun's book that provides a more basic understanding of the basis of the equations used in Chapter 7 to develop the binomial lattices and used in ROATS to calculate the outputs that have been shown here; the permission of John Wiley & Sons and Johnathan Mun to include this section is gratefully acknowledged.

### Binomial Lattices

In the binomial world, several basic similarities are worth mentioning. No matter the types of real options problems you are trying to solve, if the binomial lattice approach is used, the solution can be obtained in one of two ways. The first is the use of risk-neutral probabilities, and the second is the use of market-replicating portfolios. Throughout this book, the former approach is used. An example of the market-replicating portfolio approach is shown in [Mun] Appendix 6B for the sake of completeness. The use of a replicating portfolio is more difficult to understand and apply, but the results obtained from replicating portfolios are identical to those obtained through risk-neutral probabilities. So it does not matter which method is used; nevertheless, application and expositional ease should be emphasized.

Market-replicating portfolios' predominant assumptions are that there are no arbitrage opportunities and that there exist a number of traded assets in the market that can be obtained to replicate the existing asset's payout profile. A simple illustration is in order here. Suppose you own a portfolio of publicly traded stocks that pay a set percentage *dividend* per period. You can, in theory, assuming no trading restrictions, taxes, or transaction costs, purchase a second portfolio of several *non-dividend-paying* stocks and replicate the payout of the first portfolio of *dividend-paying* stocks. You can, for instance, sell a particular number of shares per period to replicate the first portfolio's dividend payout amount at every time period. Hence, if both payouts are identical although their stock compositions are different, the value of both portfolios should then be identical. Otherwise, there will be arbitrage opportunities, and market forces will tend to make them equilibrate in value. This makes perfect sense in a financial securities world where stocks are freely traded and highly liquid. However, in a real options world where physical assets and firm-specific projects are being valued, financial purists would argue that this assumption is hard to accept, not to mention the mathematics behind replicating portfolios are also more difficult to apply.

Compare that to using something called a risk-neutral probability approach. Simply stated, instead of using a risky set of cash flows and discounting them at a risk-adjusted discount rate akin to the discounted cash flow models, one can instead easily risk-adjust the probabilities of specific cash flows occurring at specific times. Thus, using these risk-adjusted probabilities on the cash flows allows the analyst to discount these cash flows (whose risks have now been accounted for) at the risk-free rate. This is the essence of binomial lattices as applied in valuing options. The results obtained are identical.

Let's now see how easy it is to apply risk-neutral valuation. In any options model, there is a minimum requirement of at least two lattices. The first lattice is always the lattice of the underlying asset, while the second lattice is the option valuation lattice. No matter what real options model is of interest, the basic structure almost always exists, taking the form:

$$\text{Inputs}: \ S, \ X, \ \sigma, \ T, \ rf, \ b$$

$$u = e^{\sigma\sqrt{\delta t}} \text{ and } d = e^{-\sigma\sqrt{\delta t}} = \frac{1}{u}$$

$$p = \frac{e^{(rf-b)(\delta t)} - d}{u - d}$$

The basic inputs are the present value of the underlying asset ($S$), present value of implementation cost of the option ($X$), volatility of the natural logarithm of the underlying free cash flow returns in percent ($\sigma$), time to expiration in years ($T$), risk-free rate or the rate of return on a riskless asset ($rf$), and continuous dividend outflows in percent ($b$). In addition, the binomial lattice approach requires two additional sets of calculations, the up and down factors ($u$ and $d$) as well as a risk-neutral probability measure ($p$). We see from the equations above that the up factor is simply the exponential function of the cash flow volatility multiplied by the square root of time-steps or stepping time ($\delta t$).

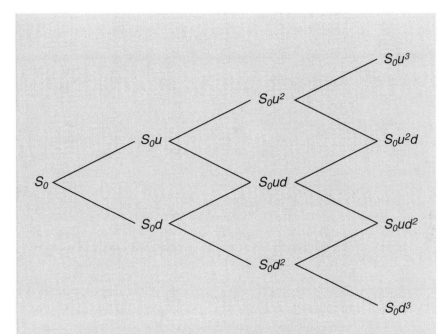

Time-steps or stepping time is simply the time scale between steps. That is, if an option has a one-year maturity and the binomial lattice that is constructed has 10 steps, each time-step has a stepping time of 0.1 years. The volatility measure is an annualized value; multiplying it by the square root of time-steps breaks it down into the time-step's equivalent volatility. The down factor is simply the reciprocal of the up factor. In addition, the higher the volatility measure, the higher the up and down factors. This reciprocal magnitude ensures that the lattices are recombining because the up and down steps have the same magnitude but different signs; at places along the future path these binomial bifurcations must meet.

The second required calculation is that of the risk-neutral probability, defined simply as the ratio of the exponential function of the difference between risk-free rate and dividend, multiplied by the stepping time less the down factor, to the difference between the up and down factors. This risk-neutral probability value is a mathematical intermediate and by itself has no particular meaning. One major error real options users commit is to extrapolate these probabilities as some kind of subjective or objective probabilities that a certain event will occur. Nothing is further from the truth. There is no economic or financial meaning attached to these risk-neutralized probabilities save that it is an intermediate step in a series of calculations. Armed with these values, you are now on your way to creating a binomial lattice of the underlying asset value, shown in [the figure on previous page].

*Binomial lattices can be solved through the use of risk-neutral probabilities and market-replicating portfolios. In using binomial and multinomial lattices, the higher the number of time-steps, the higher the level of granularity, and hence, the higher the level of accuracy.*

Starting with the present value of the underlying asset at time zero ($S_0$), multiply it with the up ($u$) and down ($d$) factors as shown below, to create a binomial lattice. Remember that there is one bifurcation at each node, creating an up and a down branch. The intermediate branches are all recombining. This evolution of the underlying asset shows that if the volatility is zero, in a deterministic world where there are no uncertainties, the lattice would be a straight line, and a discounted cash flow model will be adequate because the value of the option or flexibility is also zero. In other words, if volatility ($\sigma$) is zero, then the up ($u = e^{\sigma\sqrt{\delta t}}$) and down ($d = e^{-\sigma\sqrt{\delta t}}$) jump sizes are equal to one. It is because there are uncertainties and risks, as captured by the volatility measure, that the lattice is not a straight horizontal line but comprises up and down movements. It is this up and down uncertainty that generates the value in an option. The higher the volatility measure, the higher the up and down factors as previously defined, the higher the potential value of an option as higher uncertainties exist and the potential upside for the option increases.

*Source: Real Options Analysis: Tools and Techniques for Valuing Strategic Investments and Decisions by Johnathan Mun, © 2002 John Wiley & Sons, Inc. This material is used by permission of John Wiley & Sons, Inc.*

## NOTES

1. Johnathan Mun, *Real Options Analysis* (New York: John Wiley & Sons, 2002).
2. Tom Copeland and Vladimir Antikarov, *Real Options: A Practitioner's Guide* (Texere Publishing, 2001).

# CHAPTER 8

# Knowledge and Uncertainty

*Do not boast about tomorrow, for you do not know*
*what a day may bring forth.*[1]

**W**hat can we know? and *How we can know what we can know?* are two foundational questions of Western thought and, really, any rational thought. Earlier we considered the representational dilemma, namely, that what we grasp to study, model, simulate, test does not fully conform to what is "out there." In this life we are encased in an epidermal layer that does not give us unmediated access to what's outside us (and Freud would argue that we cannot even get unmediated access to what is *inside* us and Proust would say this also of our own memories of *our* experiences). Our characterizations of our representations, such as Monte Carlo or Real Option analysis, will be, at best, complete and comprehensible depictions of such representations. We do not, and cannot, have the assurance that these representations portray in their full complexity the real world.

In this chapter we consider a different aspect of our knowledge limitations and consider how this might guide our practical use of these negotiation methods and tools.

## FUTURE KNOWLEDGE

The representational dilemma can be thought of as the problem of fully grasping some reality at this moment. For situations of any reasonable complexity, my need for a representation creates a mediated—not direct—access to such reality even when time (past or future) is not complicating matters. When I consider other times, the knowledge problems compound. Let us first consider the past.

Because, as they say, the past cannot be changed, we naturally tend to think of the past as knowable. We may recognize some historic limitations because people die with events known only to their unique memories and, so, there is a loss to all of us remaining about what can be known. Further, records become lost or the characterizations (words or structures) become less and less accessible to us. Even our ability to decipher the hieroglyphics of ancient Egypt, only possible since the nineteenth century analysis of the Rosetta Stone discovery, does not enable us to recreate the full imagery of life then. What about the recent past? Do we really *know* it? The answer is no. There have been many studies of eyewitness accounts that show how unreliable our memories can be when drilling down below just high-level recall. In a famous multivolume novel by Marcel Proust (1871–1922), *Remembrance of Things Past*, he shows in a literary form how our present representations of the past elude not only any comprehensive understanding but also unbiased precision in particulars. In business contexts, this selectivity, mistyness, and outright distortion of the past should cause wonder about what we think we have learned and now know.

When considering the future we face other challenges. Some aspects of the future may seem to be within our predictive control. We certainly assume that the rules of mathematics accepted today will be equally true tomorrow; when we recheck a previously developed spreadsheet model, we do so for errors but not because today we have learned that 2 + 2 = 4.01. Likewise, we hold to laws of physics being the same tomorrow and the underlying physical constants of the universe staying, well, constant; we do not get out of bed in the morning gingerly because we admit to the possibility that the gravitational constant has changed for today. Even very changeable experiences such as the weather change slowly and infrequently; someone has studied the weather and concluded that there is, on average, an 82 percent chance that tomorrow will be just like today (but it is that 18 percent that makes weather interesting). Life has a rhythm that feels not only smoothly continuous but also generally predictable. But like the weather forecast example, it is the 18 percent that businesses are about because dealmaking opportunities are generally about effecting a change, making something new, creating or serving a new market, perhaps also by a new business model even using a new technology. Simultaneous with the changes that our deal team envisions by the subject opportunity, there are literally thousands of other product managers, new business developers, entrepreneurs, inventors, and others envisioning change and opportunity on their behalf. We are not dealing with a steady-state business universe that awaits only the change to be caused by our opportunity.

Because this confidence we tend to have about future knowability is so engrained, let us further consider another somewhat complicated example. One of the great achievements of science, one can even say the founding of science, at least rational science, was Isaac Newton's recognition that the force affecting the motion of heavenly bodies is the same one that pulls down the proverbial apple from the tree to the ground. He was able to express this force in a simple equation and introduced the idea of a universal gravitational constant, which later investigators were able to determine experimentally. Everything with mass creates any apparent attractive force with every other thing with mass. When you jump from a fence it is literally true that both you and the earth move and meet, though because of your small relative mass the movement of the earth was unobservable (or it would be a very wobbly existence here). Newton's discovery opened the way to the study of the motions of the organized masses in the universe (planets, moons [large objects that orbit planets], asteroids [rocks], comets [dirty ice balls], and stars [such as our sun]).

It turns out that when considering what is known as a two-body problem, say only the earth and the moon, all future motions of both bodies can be determined by the equations of motion developed by Newton. Similarly, if we treat the earth and moon as one mass (body), then we can also know the motion of the two-body system of the earth-moon and the sun. That is, when only two bodies are considered, exact, certain solutions are available, and the future is knowable. One of the amazing discoveries however is that when three bodies are considered, say earth-moon, Jupiter, and the sun, there is no exact certain solution possible.[2] What this means is that even for the very simple and powerful equations of physics that govern the relative gravitational interactions and the motions of just three bodies, it is not possible to know their future positions with certainty. When we think about the hundreds of major bodies in our solar system, one star, 9 or possibly 10 planets, many moons (Jupiter has more than 20), and numerous large rocks in the asteroid belt between the earth and Mars, there is no way to predict what effect they will have on one another let alone consider the effect of an interloper mass paying us a repeat or one-time visit.[3]

## DEALING WITH UNCERTAINTY

Certainty eludes our grasp unless the question amounts to tautology. (We can say with certainty that all unmarried males are bachelors, but we have only said we are certain that the word *bachelors* means unmarried males; we cannot be certain how many bachelors there are, say, in New York City at any given moment, or how many there will be a year from now.)

In philosophy, this important subject of knowability goes by the name *epistemology* and has a very rich, 2,500-year history in Western literature. It began with Greek pre-Socratics such as Thales, Anaximenes, and Anaximander. Socrates who lived in Athens in the fourth century B.C., spent much of his life leading inquiries through dialogues, recorded and later published by his pupil Plato, in pursuit of very exact answers about what is or can be known. Socrates was ultimately put to death in 399 B.C. by the vote of the democracy of Athens because, in large part, he had shown by discourse how the founding of their many held convictions was based on something other than knowledge; and here's a tip: People do not normally appreciate the moment of realization of their ignorance. His philosophic acolyte, Plato, wisely fled Athens and pursued knowledge of unchanging, otherwordly truths (the so-called *forms*, which led to his famous metaphor of men in caves seeing shadows thinking they are seeing what is real); apparently, this was sufficiently incomprehensible to neighboring polities that Plato appeared to live out his days in peace. Plato's student, Aristotle, and teacher of Alexander the Great, made the philosophical earth-turn and focused on what is knowable here in this world. So influential was Aristotle in logic and approach that his writings became the text of Western scholarly thought and academic learning, along with the Bible, for nearly 2,000 years, until the so-called Enlightenment. For most of that long scholastic period, so influential was this individual that any reference to "the Philosopher" in literature throughout this period is understood as reference to Aristotle himself. Our purpose in this little history lesson is to introduce an important Aristotalian idea useful to us in 'Dealmaking, namely: the ideal of the mean.

First, let us consider an example. How might we define *courage*? Socrates would ask Athenians such questions and force them to give him answers that met the "only and every" test, namely, that the answer describes only *courage* and it defines every application of *courage*; on some sleepless night, try your own answer on a yellow pad in front of a fire and you will feel the utility of having available the power of capital punishment. Aristotle developed another way of looking at such questions. He reasoned that one response to danger/risk would be avoidance at all costs; we might call that the fearful-flee response. At the opposite extreme, he reasoned there could be the action we will call the impulsive-engage response. Although at first one might be inclined to answer our courage inquiry by saying the first response is cowardice and the latter is courageous, but Aristotle says no. The impulsive-engage response is in many ways just the same as the fearful-flee one. They are both driven by unreasoned reactions, in the one case away and in the other case toward, whatever danger or risk is confronted. Aristotle would ask, do we really call the impulse to engage in any and all dangers *courage*? There is a wild black bear who lives not far from me. If he shows up, would it be *courageous* to confront and show him in no uncertain terms who owns this property? In New York City, just 60 miles away, there are 8 million people of various persuasions regarding human engagement. Is it *courageous* to confront always anyone who expresses some uncharitable opinion on my human worthiness and right to live? Aristotle would say it is as foolish to posses an impulse-engage character, as it is for its opposite of fearful-flight. *Courage*, Aristotle would say, is the ideal mean between impulse-engage and fearful-flight in which one has reasoned what battle must be engaged and how.[4] So the expression of *courage* would be a reasoned response in the context of a real option to flee, and of the dangers and costs and prize associated with engagement. Courage would then be expressed with both knowledge and fear-feelings and when engagement is determined it is enabled by mind over emotion. And when nonengagement is the determined course, it is likewise enabled by mind over emotion, both the emotion to engage and the emotion to flee. Or, as Aristotle himself put it:

> For the man who flies from and fears everything and does not stand his ground against anything becomes a coward, and the man who fears nothing at all but who goes to meet every danger becomes rash; and similarly the man who indulges every pleasure and abstains from none becomes self-indulgent, while the man who shuns every pleasure, as boors do, becomes in a way insensible; temperance and courage, then, are destroyed by excess and defect, and preserved by the mean.
>
> Book 2, Chapter 2, *Nicomachean Ethics*

> For in everything it is no easy task to find the middle, e.g. to find the middle of a circle is not for every one but for him who knows.
>
> Book 2, Chapter 10, *Nicomachean Ethics*

This *courage* lesson has some relevance to ʿDealmaking negotiations because confrontation is likely to be part of negotiation and a proper response may in some circumstances be the engagement, regardless of the emotional tugs, or the concession, regardless of its emotional tugs. Our primary purpose for the Aristotalian "ideal of the mean" concept is answering this chapter's question: What can we know, and what can we know about what we know? At one extreme we could respond that we cannot know much of anything; at the other, that we can reach some nirvanic grasp of true and complete Knowledge. If the despair of unavoidable ignorance is our response to complexity, then we become either immobilized by our lack of knowing or impulsive and "doing whatever." There is a widely used metaphor in business that dates back to colonial rifle teams: "Ready, Aim, Fire!" in which "ready" was preparing one's muzzle-loaded weapon for its next discharge (no M-1s then), "aim" was when the weapon was loaded and one had to await one's entire rifle line to be ready, and "fire" launched the one-bullet fuscillade and restarted the sequence. Using this metaphor, the one extreme on the ignorance–certainty axis, namely, that of unavoidable ignorance, is like being "ready" handling one's business (weapon) but never deciding, never acting, never changing, because certainty is not possible; it's tantamount to the hope that all the potential enemies surrounding me will similarly find their amusements in handling, but not using, their weapons, and we can all sit on the ground and have a career-long picnic, or more likely a short career and a long picnic.

The other extreme, that knowledge certainty is both available and necessary, is the "aim" position. This perspective drives us to paralysis by analysis. There is always one more piece of research data to find, another spreadsheet model to create, another meeting in the pursuit of all knowledge and certainty. From this abyss nothing ever emerges because certainty is beyond our grasp in all nontrivial opportunities.[5] Using our rifle warfare metaphor, this is the "aim" pole, where all that goes on the day long is taking aim, more aim, better aim, aiming for fun, aiming for work, aiming in the morning, and in the evening, and probably in nighttime dreams as well.

There are many companies who went from greatness to not-so-great, average, and out-of-business from both the "ready" and "aim" pole positions. In many cases, such business decline and failure is expressed by the inaction response to a (false) belief in total ignorance or an equally false belief that certain knowledge is attainable. Another failure mode would be utter despair because of these two unacceptable extremes and take a different type of probably harmful act: because we have to do something, and we know nothing (because it is not knowable or because we have not yet completed our perfect analysis), then let us do *anything*. Extending our metaphor one last time, this is the "fire" position without a "ready" or "aim." It is exhibited by companies on the prowl for a deal, any deal, at a price, any price. They are going to buy something, or sell something, and at whatever the price because action is better than no action.

The ideal of the mean principle would say there is a valuable place of knowledge at the mean between these two poles. At such a mean, there is knowledge but not certainty, opportunity but not security, ambiguity but not darkness. But where along that continuum between the poles is the *ideal* mean? Consider one example of the death penalty. In the case of Socrates, it took only an Athenian majority, after a trial that could not last longer than one day. And before we mock that decision making, consider how long various populations—from working groups in a business to the entire United States—give to the focused consideration of a decision. In our capital offense trials, we have a knowledge standard that has become popularized in movies and TV: "beyond a reasonable doubt" unanimously held by all the jurors (usually 12); this seems to correspond to something even higher than 99 percent certainty. That is an extraordinarily high standard to apply to knowledge. If one of the 12 says, "I actually think he is guilty as sin, but I can't be sure beyond all reasonable doubt," then we say the jury is "hung." We as a society accept this standard even though we understand that it means many guilty will never be convicted of a capital crime because it is important to us to avoid the other error, which nonetheless can occur and has occurred, namely, falsely convicting the innocent. In civil trials, such as contract or patent litigation, a lower standard is used: "the preponderance of the evidence," which seems to correspond to something like 51 percent. Between these 2 legal standards, there is yet an intermediate one applicable in certain matters, such as determination of patent invalidity: "clear and convincing evidence." This is a higher standard than "preponderance" but lower than "any reasonable doubt."

For ¹Dealmaking, is knowledge "beyond a reasonable doubt" the appropriate standard? How about "preponderance of the evidence?" In most business circumstances both these standards seem to fall short: The first one is too high, and almost no opportunity would pass, and the second one is too low, causing perhaps too many marginal opportunities to pass. In reporting of engineering data, an interesting standard has emerged, promulgated by the American Society of Mechanical Engineers (ASME). When submitting a paper for publication in any of the highly regarded professional journals of ASME, the authors are required to show uncertainty bands around the data they purport to reflect some aspect of the physical world. In order to determine the bounds of such uncertainty bands, a mathematical approach is used that can be summarized as follows: Based on an analysis of the data scatter, the uncertain bands should span to encompass 19 out of 20 measurements. In other words, if we repeated exactly the experimental data (a so-called replicate), there would not be more than 1 time out of 20 when such replicates would be measured outside the shown band. This result can be termed a 95 percent confidence level. This level of uncertainty is deemed acceptable for the publication of engineering data.

However, as another example, the ASME also has a role in setting the standards for boiler design. The rapid growth of the industrial revolution was largely powered by steam generated under pressure and used to drive engines and machines. Such pressurized steam was held in boilers. In the eighteenth and nineteenth centuries many tragedies occurred as these boilers exploded with sometimes fatal consequences because of the high pressures and scalding temperatures. Today, exploding boilers are almost unheard of. This situation is partly due to improvement in the manufacturing process (welding versus riveting, better control of steel properties, more powerful inspection procedures, more reliable overpressure relief valves, and so on), but an important role is played by a standard developed by ASME. They established the requirement of a "proof" test in which the subject boiler is pressurized to validate the boiler design and manufacturing methodology, to demonstrate that its burst pressure is at least four times its design pressure. So, for engineering data, ASME says that 95 times out of 100 is fine, but for boilers it wants a demonstration that it operates at not more than 25 percent of its failure pressure, which experience has shown that, with all the various vagaries of life, results in no boiler (for practical purposes) exploding. When human lives are at stake, we look for 100 percent certainty (no boilers exploding)[6];

when we are trying to grasp the world at the engineering and research stage, 95 percent confidence is fine, and in many cases is even more than necessary.

## STANDARDS

In the business world, it does not appear that anything as exact as the certainty characterization example for engineering has emerged. Let me suggest five such possible standards.

1. When a business is seeking senior-most, investor-grade debt, namely, the first lender in line to recover physical assets in the event of default of financially strong companies, such lender will not make such loans, even secured, unless it has a very strong belief that failure is extremely unlikely. Let us call this the "boiler standard," which is effectively certainty (though even the highest-ranked bonds do evidence some small percentage of default, so nothing is ever 100 percent).

2. When a business is seeking ordinary (nonsophisticated) investor funding, the financial projections are going to be relied on by people who do not have access to the full body of business information and probably also lack the business competence. What appears to be a standard is a confidence level far better than 50:50, but still short of the "boiler standard." I would estimate this as being in the 75 percent to 90 percent range, say, 82 percent, like our weather or, possibly, "clear and convincing evidence" example, and characterized as the "investor standard."[7]

3. When a business is making an internal decision by an investment committee to pursue a new opportunity funded by retained earnings proposed by a senior manager, the level of certainty can be substantially less than the "investor standard." Depending on the comparative magnitudes of investment and potential reward, in the context of the next best alternative (including saying "no" or deferring the decision), such decision makers could use a standard in the range of 50 percent to 90 percent, that I will characterize as "investment committee standard."[8] The likelihood of failure is generally higher because such an investment is a single project as distinct from an investment in the entire company, which is a portfolio or mutual fund of projects and products.

4. When a business is deciding on an R&D project, a decision made by an R&D committee or by the R&D head or sometimes by an R&D "fellow" (a individual contributor with a highly regarded track record), the standard is typically lower than the above levels because, after all, it is "R&D." Depending on the nature of the project the standard can be from approximately 20 percent to more than 50 percent. In a survey article

published in *Scientific American*, the success of various candidate new drugs going through FDA trials was analyzed for the period 1976–1978 shown in Exhibit 6.5. Only about 20 percent of the drugs that entered the trials succeeded in being approved for sale to the public. A widely held perception is that, in these more short-term thinking days, the R&D standard has crept up because of the increased need for short-term successes, so perhaps for some companies it is 33 percent to 75 percent. There is a legend among Green Beret and other commando teams, that they are willing to undertake a mission that has as low a success probability as 20 percent. In honor of such spirit, and perhaps as an echo of earlier days, let us call this level of certainty, say 20 percent to 67 percent as the commando standard.

5. Finally, let us consider the science or breakthrough investment decision, which may be done by a government agency such as the National Science Foundation, the National Institutes of Health, or DARPA (the Defense research agency). For new science that could lead to breakthroughs, the standard of success is very low in terms of probability. In the example of major league baseball, a team typically actively scouts 500 highly skilled amateurs each year; from this pool they will sign 50 (10 percent), and of these 5 will one day make a major league club (10 percent of 10 percent, or 1 percent of the starting pool). Taking another example, in 2001, the U.S. record industry introduced 6,422 new music CD titles. The normal standard of success in that industry is 500,000 copies sold, because the production, marketing, and star management costs are significant. Of the 2001 class of 6,422 titles, only 112, or less than 2 percent, exceeded that 500,000 copies standard, and the album *Glitter* was not among them. The Industrial Research Institute (IRI) reported in a study of industrial innovation that it took some 3,000 initial ideas to lead to (on average) one commercial success. Some have estimated that if one measures new drug success starting at the identification of a new molecule, that it takes 10,000 such molecules tested to find one that makes it all the way to a drug. (Earlier we cited the 20 percent statistic of those drugs that started down the approval track that made it through FDA approval but before that stage more than 99 percent of all the molecules examined had already been deemed failures.) For this standard, which approximately corresponds from 20 percent down to 1 percent, let us call it 5 percent and refer to it as the breakthrough standard.

In summary, we have created five confidence level categories: (1) boiler (99+ percent, virtual certainty), (2) outside investor (ca. 82 percent, failure would be a major and adverse surprise), (3) investment committee (50 percent to 80 percent, likely to very likely to succeed), (4) commando (20 percent to 50 percent, reasonable chance of success but many projects are terminated), and (5) breakthrough (ca. 5 percent, remote, but conceivable, chance of success and if it occurs the impact is expected to be significant). How might we use such segmentation with our ¹Dealmaking tools to prepare us for negotiation?

One obvious way is to use these values to select the corresponding net present value (NPV) forecast values as determined by the Monte Carlo method. In Chapter 6, we showed how the use of a 20- to 30-percentile standard would lead to an opportunity valuation. If we can develop a model for the risk character of that opportunity, such as given in the previous discussion, we could select other appropriate percentiles as valuation standards. In a dealmaking context, there is the added risk associated with the transfer of the opportunity from the seller to the buyer. Although possession by the buyer may actually reduce the overall risk, because of its technological prowess or market reputation and presence, there is often a compensating, or more than compensating, risk the other way that because of the "handoff" and an incomplete understanding of all the problems one will face (there are unknowns that we can know are unknowns, but there are unknowns we do not even know we do not know).

Appropriate standards of uncertainty can also be usefully applied to the Real Options method. As shown in Chapter 7 and in this chapter, characterizing the future probabilities of success directly affect the value of the option to the opportunity.

Francis Bacon (1561–1626), who in many ways began the scientific revolution with his influential book *Novum Organum*⁹ (1620), said this: "If a man will begin with certainties, he shall end in doubts; but if he will be content to begin with doubts he shall end in certainties." He intended the reference to the achievement of certainties as the result of what became known as the scientific method of ordered induction. In the business world our only certainties are the results that are achieved. So we can recreate Bacon's idea for our purposes as follows: If a person begins with the need for certainty, he or she will find only doubts; if he or she accepts uncertainty, doubts can be overcome by sufficient actionable knowledge." *Hubris*, another great word from Classical Greek, means overbearing arrogance or pride. In Classical Greek literature its emergence in a character is a certain indication of that person's impending fall and doom; it is effectively the universal "fatal flaw" in that genre. At its root, an important element of hubris is the present certainty of something about which one cannot be certain. So, we may think of hubris as being the antithesis of the Aristotelian mean between certainty and ignorance and as he noted:

If we are to be always deliberating, we shall have to go on to infinity.

Book 3, Chapter 3, *Nicomachean Ethics*

Monte Carlo and Real Option methods are, in business terms, likewise antithetical to the hubristic approach of present value certainty based on a single analysis.

## WHAT ABOUT TRUTH?

Well, what about truth? Or as the Roman Governor Pontius Pilate put it: "What is truth?"[10]

In business contexts, "truth" generally is freighted with two meanings. First is the idea that that which is claimed to be true accurately represents reality. As has been discussed, we represent reality as best we can, appropriate to an acceptable level of uncertainty and depth of analysis. Yet, our representation is not "truth" in the sense of exactly conforming to some deep reality, especially a present view of a future reality.

There is a second sense in which "truth" is commonly used. Starting from a representation of reality—some model or analytical framework—we seek that the character of the assumptions be logical and consistent, that our analytical methods and calculations be valid, and that our work be error free. In short, we want our representation done in a "truth preserving" way, meaning that having accepted the realization that our model, any model, is not a perfect reflection of reality, we still aspire to having everything within our representation done without the introduction of ill-formed reasoning, inconsistent assumption, or even mathematical mistakes.

For models involving sophistications such as Real Options and Monte Carlo, this latter aspiration can be almost as illustive as the representational problem. Just as in computer program "bugs," and book text "typos," errors seem to diffuse into analyses and defy discovery. Do their presence invalidate the analysis? Not necessarily. Not every bug, typo, or error is meaningful in hindering the overall objective. In business modeling activities, our primary purpose here, it is usually a good practice to use multiple approaches as reasonableness tests (aka: "sanity checks"). These additional steps do not assure one that the model has been error free, but it increases the likelihood that the effect of a significant error in reasoning, modeling, or math has been discovered, and so, avoided.

## NOTES

1. Old Testament, or Hebrew Bible, Prov. 27 versus Prov. 1, New International Translation.
2. For those not already lost or bored by this example, there is a special case of exact three-body solutions known as Lagrangian points. Every two-body system has five specific locations where a third body can be placed and for which a certain

prediction of all future positions can be obtained. Several of these Lagrangian points have been proposed, for instance, as the location for a large, long-term space station.

3. Predictions of the future positions are made despite this limitation by making certain assumptions, such as reducing n-body problems to two-body problems and, more commonly, by numerical (computer-based) simulation, whereby future positions are incrementally calculated in thousands or even millions of tiny time steps. Such calculations are how predictions are made about some particular asteroid approaching the earth by such and such a distance on some future date. But these are all computer approximations and even these have used some important simplifying assumptions. The fact is we have a present estimate of the future state of our n-body universe, but not certain knowledge, which is unattainable. The universe may well be in some configuration that could cause dramatic future changes.

4. It should be noted that by the idea "mean," Aristotle did not mean some midpoint between the extremes. Rather it represents that wisely selected position somewhere between the extremes.

5. Because I know that many readers of books with "real options" in the title are resistant to this challenge to certainty, please consider this example. Is the population of the United States knowable and if so, how would it be known? The quick answer is "yes" and "by counting," which in fact we do every 10 years. But how do you count approximately 4 million people in the United States who keep dying or disappearing each year, and while new people keep showing up in nurseries and at borders? The key to answering the knowability question is to ask what is really asked by "the population of the United States?" For government officials it means something far from knowing the existence of every human in the United States at some moment in time. For most practical, even trivial questions, certain, complete knowledge eludes us. As a final test: how many pair of socks (stockings) do you own? Can you answer that with certainty? (If you can, it is only because it is a very small number, and even then, I am confident there exists at least one pair, buried somewhere, that you will find someday, that escaped your count; if you are stuck on certainty, I hope for your sake that you discover that missing pair soon.)

6. In 1905, a most horrific boiler explosion occurred at the Brockton Shoe Factory in Massachusetts killing 58, injuring more than 100, leveling the factory. This event led to a proliferation of codes that began to be harmonized by ASME's initial publication of the code in 1915.

7. During this period of seemingly daily revelations of examples of biased and utterly self-serving industry investor advice, such 75 to 90 percent certainty range characterization seems quaint. Nonetheless, such is the aspiration of the best of those in that business.

8. Affecting such standards is the common business situation in which because of multiple considerations, the business feels the need to take greater chances. Such a circumstance could arise from a chain-of-consequence fear in which, for example, senior management concludes that it if doesn't enter this particular market it will

be closed out of the successor markets, which would have catastrophic effects on other parts of its business. In which case, the certainty level could be much lower than 50 percent, because they are, or believe they are, in a "must have" situation. Similar impulses are known to occur when management is responding to a CEO's pet project, or a CEO to an investor- or government-led tumult on some issue.

9. Latin for *New Engine*, a great title, and a prescient prediction.

10. Gospel of John, Chapter 18, Verse 38. This question was Pilate's final words to Jesus.

# CHAPTER 9

# Deal Pricing

U p to this point, we have focused on methods and tools of characterizing an opportunity based on its projected worth from various perspectives based on various assumptions. This process is often termed *valuation*. *Pricing* is the process of concretizing and communicating a valuation, in the context of a deal structure, to the other side. Valuation is what I think it is worth, and pricing is an offer.

Why are these not the same thing? In simple situations, such as a one-time, lump-sum payment for a simple asset, they could be the same or differ only in that an appropriate gap might be used to initiate negotiations. However, as discussed in Chapter 3 and elsewhere, each opportunity can be created in multiple ways from the seller's contribution (the Box) and from the buyer's contribution (the Wheelbarrow). Further, for each given combination of asset and payment structures, there are multiple perspectives for multiple possible business models that could be created. Yet further, there are ways of structuring such payments that adjust the risk sharing between the seller and buyer that are all part of the valuation model. So by *valuation* we normally mean a comprehensive array of models, assumptions, perspectives, and structures among which some are more attractive to the seller and some to an individual buyer. Pricing is about making a specific proposal, based on a Box and Wheelbarrow, and a business model with its attendant assumptions.

## SIMPLE PRICING

Let us assume a simple situation in which the content and context of a negotiation will closely conform to the valuation model. We also assume that there is only one logical Box to be considered. And, further, that such valuation model leads to a "best estimate" of $10 million as the one-payment number. What pricing strategy might be followed?

An obvious one might be called "here's the number" pricing, namely, the price is $10 million, firm, fixed, and final, take it or leave it. Another, at the opposite extreme, might be called "guess my number" pricing, namely, I will not state a price, but invite your offer, and if it is at or above my $10 million number, we will have a deal. A third, intermediate, strategy is "number mark up" pricing, namely, the price is X (some increase above, or multiple of the $10 million number), characterized in some way (such as "but we're flexible") and invite negotiation, discussion, and counteroffers; this could also be called the "third-world street vendor" pricing strategy, as every tourist has learned.

So, which is the right strategy? Here's the Number, Guess My Number, or Number Mark-Up?[1] In answering that question, let us first consider the power of persuasion. Winston Churchill, the twentieth century giant in inspirational communication[2] once said: "the essence of a truly great speaker is to _____." What do you suppose goes in the blank? Eyebrow wink? Ice-breaking humor? Posture? Blue, designating sincerity, business suit? What? Before answering that question, let us consider some data of the number one factor that juries cite as the basis for accepting and relying on an expert that they have heard testify. Here are the top four factors cited by juries[3] who have been studied to determine how they assess credibility:

1.  He/she seemed to _____.
2.  Was prepared.
3.  Explained it so I could understand it.
4.  Answered questions.

What do you suppose is the number one factor leading to credibility? It is the same one Churchill cited. The answer in both cases is this: *believe what you are saying.* It is an important principle in developing a pricing strategy to realize that your own credibility depends on your own convictions. There are, no doubt, people who are skilled at creating an appearance of believing "their number," when they hold no such belief; after all, they give actors Academy Awards for making us believe they are somebody else. But a serious negotiation is more than a 110-minute movie and your real beliefs are likely, ultimately, to be perceived. A loss of a deal manager's credibility tends to lead to increased doubts as to all the other representations made, regardless of their comparative fidelity.

One of the many virtues of the Monte Carlo and Real Option methods is that they can support a believable basis for asserting a price that may be different from a bottom line number that could still be acceptable. For instance, a Monte Carlo analysis for a particular opportunity in full consideration of the context and in particular the risks may lead the seller deal team to conclude that the 30th percentile would be an appropriate price point and genuinely hold that conviction, namely, that a reasonable buyer believing the business model we have developed in support of this negotiation would conclude that such percentile was a fair deal. Yet, the seller could also conclude that it would be prepared to concede price down to, say, the 25th-percentile value if all the other deal terms were accepted as proposed. On such a basis, a seller could well be in a position to believe, propose, and defend a 30th-percentile price and still have a bottom line number corresponding to the 25th-percentile level.

Although this discussion was done from the seller's perspective, it mirrors what the buyer could do as well in developing its own first estimate or price, or its response to hearing the seller's initial offer.

## BOX PRICING

As discussed in Chapter 3, sellers—and buyers—need to make an initial, provisional configuration of the Box, the complete identification of what is being sold (or licensed). There is a very corny vaudeville joke that I will reword to make it politically correct: a woman was asked, "How's your husband?" to which she replied, "compared to what?" Valuation and pricing must be done with reference to something.

The initial Box configuration may be inappropriate for an optimum deal between the seller and negotiating buyer. It may contain elements that represent value to the seller but do not represent value, or only little value, to the buyer. By having pricing communications in the context of a Box, it is more likely that these elements can be discerned and potentially removed from consideration or included but in some way that provides the buyer only what is important and allows the seller to retain some of what it values highly.

The initial Box configuration may be less than ideal because of what is not included. The seller may have left something out of the box inadvertently or because of a belief that such was of little or no value to the subject buyer or because of some internally perceived constraint. Again, a pricing negotiation on the Box, and what might be added that would increase its attractiveness to the buyer, can potentially increase the value of the deal to both parties.

In practice, Box additions and subtractions may be both possible and value enhancing, and can take the form of horsetrading which, in exchange for something that the buyer wants added the seller identifies something that has to be withdrawn, under a provisional presumption that the price is staying the same. Generally, such reconfiguring is not done at constant value or price. The underlying hope, often realized, is that there are potential Box contents that are more valuable to one side than to the other. It is this very hope that underlies the value of any trade, namely, each side must believe that it is better off by virtue of having done the trade or (in an arm's length situation) no trade would occur. So the trade must be a value-increasing event. Each reconfiguration negotiation is an opportunity to create additional deal value.

## WHEELBARROW PRICING

Just as the Box can be reconfigured, so also the Wheelbarrow of consideration to be provided by the buyer can be structured differently. In the sections that follow we consider, as examples, ways of doing such reconstruction and the effect it could have on pricing.

### Total Cash Payment

The most obvious Wheelbarrow adjustment is the total cash payment to be made by the buyer. This approach alone can be problematic. The seller wants more cash paid, the buyer less; the contrary positions are as old as time, maybe older. The auction format, formal or informal, is the historic solution. If the seller offers the opportunity to many prospective and qualified buyers, it normally has a reasonable basis for belief that it received a fair price. When in a one-on-one negotiation, each side may attempt to assert an auction model as a fairness of standard for its respective offer: The seller contending that its proposed terms would be considered reasonable by one or more prospective buyers if the offer were to be taken to them, and the buyer contrarily asserting that although it cannot represent the nonexistence of an irrational buyer willing to pay more, it is presently offering what would be the winning bid in a context among rational buyers.

As discussed in Chapter 10, the seller and buyer are advised to have respective Plan B opportunities under consideration and even pursuit to support their respective analysis of and confidence in their above assertions. Accordingly, one resolution procedure to an unresolved negotiation gap is for the respective parties either with mutual agreement or independently to pursue such other opportunities with the possibility but not the assurance that they may yet return to negotiate further. For the seller the risk is that if it returns, the buyer will logically conclude that it is the high bidder and may use the occasion to reduce its offer or possibly to reassess the opportunity because of a new found fear of a hidden flaw. For the buyer the risk is that the seller will "have gone to school" on at least how one buyer responded to the opportunity and may be genuinely able to receive perhaps even just a nominal amount larger from a seller Plan B alternative.

Another resolution approach would be for the parties to reexamine their respective financial models even to the point of exchanging their models with the other side with a "show me where I'm wrong" perspective. If done with honest intent, this often can lead to a key assumption or modeling difference that can then be reexamined more carefully by both sides. In such circumstances, there may be a variety of steps the parties can take to resolve such difference in perspective. There may be a market study or other third-party report or white paper respected by both sides that could be secured and studied. The parties could jointly fund an "honest broker" third party who may critique each side's assumption and suggest a reasoned alternative. Such a third party could also be used to develop independently a financial model and valuation and defend it to the seller and buyer. Sometimes a key value-affecting assumption can be tested by additional research. The seller, or the buyer, or both could invest in an investigation aimed at gaining a better understanding of such factor and moving the parties to agreement with either the seller's or buyer's position. This solution only works if both deal teams can agree that they can be persuaded by new information. For an ¹Dealmaking approach, this agreement to agree should be achievable. However, if either side is constrained by the "number/nut/bogie," then there is not likely to be any change in position based on facts, which is yet another reason why imposing a number on a deal team, or a deadline, is an ill-advised practice. Co-funding such further investigation is a way of testing for a side's inability to reason. Unwillingness to do so may be such an indication.

Another traditional technique is known as "splitting the difference." So, if the seller has reduced the value to a number, say, $10 million, and the buyer has concluded the most it wants to pay is, say, $6 million, the parties may accept $8 million, each concluding they conceded as much as the other side, which has a feeling of fairness. However, everyone knows about the splitting-the-difference approach. If one side suggests it, it immediately calls into question whether that side has deliberately kited their starting price to account for this gambit (for instance, the buyer was genuinely prepared to pay $8 million, but feared being drawn up to $9 million, so asserted the $6 and in the end got the $8 that it originally sought). For this reason, the respondent to the side offering to split the difference typically counters with something like this: In the above example, the seller hears the buyer's proposal for a deal at $8 million, and says, "So you are prepared to pay $8 million, but I am not prepared to go that low; I'll tell you what, we'll split *that* difference and agree at $9 million." Halfway in dollar terms is not necessarily splitting the difference, especially if one side has gamed the gap. Also, a $2 million adjustment in payment represents a 25 percent increase for the buyer and a 20 percent decrease for the seller, from their proposed terms. The midpoint may represent a disproportionate shift in percentile outcome based on the Monte Carlo model. A more rational splitting could be to split the difference in the proposed percentile standard if the parties can agree on a common Monte Carlo model.

Another approach is to bring in on both sides new voices to the deal team. Sometimes a more senior person can bring a higher-level perspective to bear on the assumptions, the model(s), the risk characterization, the Plan B alternatives, and the nature of compromise. Another candidate for a new voice is a retiree who brings the wisdom that sometimes only years can provide. Such new voices can also provide something else that may be very important. Once a gap has become frozen, it can become very difficult to have either side budge because of a loss of face. In such situations the deal manager can be, or feel, unable to make concessions without creating a poisoned atmosphere and legacy on his or her *own side*. This new voice, senior "upward" (rank) or "longitudinally" (age/experience), can provide a respected perspective and make possible an acceptance of the other side's reasonable proposal and preclude, as much as possible, the possibility that the story that will necessarily follow the deal team, and especially the deal manager, will not be negative. It requires courage to accept the power of a better argument and a senior wise man or women can be of enormous help.

From ancient times the aftermath of major battles are recorded on vertical, stone surfaces, frequently in the form of stele (pronounced "stel-ah").[4] Such stele have been the joy of archeologists because they are often a unique, preserved source of writing. The Rosetta Stone, is perhaps the most famous of these.[5] Earlier we considered the issue of retrospective, historical understandings governing deal negotiations. Each new deal itself becomes yet another component of such retrospective perspective. Deal teams, and especially deal managers, understand this well and it looms over them. How will *their* story read when engraved in some form of corporate stele? There is a verse from the Book of Proverbs in the Old Testament (Hebrew Bible) that at least on the surface applies to this subject: "Bad, bad says the buyer; then he goes his way, then he boasts."[6] This interpretation may not be a canonical one, but the doubled "bad" in this verse may have a double meaning. It is clear why the buyer may be inclined to "bad" the opportunity to the seller. But the second "bad" could have been directed for the buyer's side. When preparing for a negotiation, there is a strong temptation for the buy-side deal manager to talk down the deal opportunity to his or her own side, meaning that it expects to pay a substantial sum to acquire the opportunity. Then when the deal closes at a price less than had been expected, it brings hero status, so it may be thought, to the deal manager.

Managing the deal stele is a fact of life for both the seller and buyer. When a negotiation gap exists because of "stele fear" on either side, the deal closure issues get more difficult. There may be an opportunity for the deal manager on the other side to create some alternative deal constructions to facilitate a solution. Discussion between a senior counselor on the troubled side and creativity on the other side, perhaps in a sidebar discussion, may enable a creative solution acceptable to all parties.

Generally the most fruitful way of closing a total cash payment impasse is to make corresponding adjustments in other elements of the Wheelbarrow as we consider now.

## Cash When

The simplest way to solve a negotiating gap on the cash payment is to explore ways of moving cash payments to occur on various triggers. The simplest such trigger is the calendar. Moving some payments from the time of closing to subsequent days, even adjusted upward to account for the opportunity value of the delayed payment, may increase the perceived fairness of the price. This situation could occur if the buyer is cash constrained such that a $10 million payment is perceived to be substantially more than $4 million more than their $6 million offer. The expectation of significant future cash infusion can have a dramatic effect on perceptions. Also, if the agreement has a termination and exit provision, the buyer may in effect be viewing a deal with $6 million paid now and, say, $5 million to be paid a year from now as being in effect a real option.

Another trigger could be a progress measure such as the achievement of an external milestone. One common example in the pharmaceutical industry where new drugs go through prescribed stages (Phase 1, 2, and 3 clinicals, and the filing of an NDA, New Drug Application). Deferred payments to such milestones have the effect of real options, assuming there are buyer termination options.

## Cash Maybe

Closely related to "cash when" solutions are "cash maybe" approaches. Such payments are triggered not on a termination event but on a level of economic performance. For instance, the parties could agree that there will be three payments a year hence: $4 million minimum, $6 million if the technology or product achieves some minimum standard of performance, and $8 million if it exceeds a high standard. Such metrics could be a measure of manufacturing cost, or product performance, or a market success measure, or some other measure limited only by the creativity of the parties.

Because these payments vary based on a future event, they create the effect of a real option to the buyer and hence increase the deal value. They also have the effect of risk sharing with the seller such that if the result turns out at the high end of the expected range, the seller participates in the increased value, and vice versa.

## Cash As

Royalties are a common means of solving negotiation gaps and may be a preferred form of payment for both parties. Royalties are payments made, usually quarterly, by the opportunity buyer to the opportunity seller expressed as some proportion of the buyers actual commercial use of the subject opportunity. A very common royalty is a percentage of the revenues obtained by the buyer through sales of its products using the subject matter of the deal. However, there can be many ways royalties can be constructed. There can be different rates for different uses or products, or for different levels of revenues achieved, or for different periods (for instance, a reduced rate in later years), or for different outcomes in the marketplace (such as level of achieved market share), or for securing certain intellectual property rights (issuance of now-pending patents), and so forth, and in combination.

The flexibility and the direct tie to commercial use make such scaled, conditional payments a powerful mechanism for reaching fair agreements. If the revenues from use are substantially larger than expected, then the seller gets more and vice versa. Also, the buyer is paying as it is paid, which is usually perceived to be more affordable, though some buyers may prefer to limit the royalties in some way. Such limits, or caps, are typically unacceptable to sellers, but it is another negotiation mechanism. The reader is referred to another book I have written for a fuller discussion on these matters: *Valuation and Pricing of Technology-Based Intellectual Property*, John Wiley & Sons, 2003.

## Cash Substitutes

One cash substitute is the use of equity-based payments, particularly with restricted stock or from a nonpublic buyer. As with royalties, this payment can be expressed in many different forms. Stock can be issued to the seller in some proportionate way to commercial use either directly, as options, or as warrants.

There are many other cash substitutes. The buyer can enter into a supply agreement whereby it provides product to the seller at no cost or under favorable terms. When this feature is used, it is commonly a product that the seller needs for some purpose and is related to the opportunity being negotiated. However, the agreement could be for some unrelated product made or sold by the buyer. Another product-based payment as a substitute for cash is a purchase agreement, whereby the buyer agrees to pay the seller above-market rates for some product made or sold by the seller. Future intellectual property, such as patents be they improvement patents or patents related to some other technology, could be another form of cash substitute. Likewise other buyer assets in the form of intangible or tangible property, or services, could be used. As discussed earlier, the ideal negotiation closure opportunities occur when one side can offer something that costs them little and the other side values it much.

## TERM SHEETS

A term sheet can be considered as the pricing work product. It is the succinct codification of what offer will be made to the other side. Normally there is a simpler, option-free version known as the "external term sheet" that is made available, at the appropriate juncture, to the other side. In addition, there is an "internal term sheet" used by the offering deal team that may include variants on the external term sheet such as alternate Boxes and Wheelbarrows or alternate configurations for payment within the same Wheelbarrow framework.

The objective of the term sheet is to provide the parties a basis for an early discussion on a deal framework. It is normally presented by the seller as its version of the deal. However, the buyer can also initiate a term sheet either because it wants to frame the discussion, or because the seller is inviting initial offers. In either case, it is an important opportunity to understand at least one side's perspective of what it will take to close the deal.

The term sheet is normally succinct, usually just a page or two. The important elements of the Box and Wheelbarrow are specified, including the key financial terms. Lesser important terms can be included in an unspecified way such as "minimum annual royalties to be negotiated will be required."

As discussed in Chapter 3, there may be many possible deal configurations acceptable to the seller as the initiator of the term sheet. Generally, there is no practicable way to express all such if/then pricing configurations. Unless there is a well recognized either/or condition known to the parties, it is usually better to keep the initial term sheet simplified to a baseline, reasonably centrist configuration.

In addition to the central purpose of determining if there is a basis for in-depth negotiation, the term sheet also provides a vehicle for optimal deal discovery. As discussed earlier, deal value can be enhanced when something exists of high value to one side that is low in cost to the other. A term sheet defining the key deal elements can begin that process of mutual discovery. Accordingly, it is a good idea not to create or present the term sheet as fixed, final, and non-negotiable unless the seller is locked on the idea of obtaining bids from multiple prospective buyers on an asset the seller wants to package in only one way. A summary of the advantages of uses of term sheets is shown in Exhibit 9.1.

The term sheet may be expressed in spreadsheet software such as Excel. This method can be particularly useful for the internal term sheet as it can contain all the other tabs comprising the negotiation workbook discussed in Chapter 8. The actual term sheet value can be tied directly to cell values in

**EXHIBIT 9.1**   Negotiation Value of Using a Term Sheet

- Defines the Box and the Wheelbarrow
- Creates internal clarity, congruence, and commitment
- Frames negotiation planning
- Enables *valuation* and *pricing*
- Qualifies prospective buyers
- Distinguishes proposed transaction from historic practices
- Provides checkpoints negotiation
- Commences dealmaking
- Frames negotiations/dealmaking
- Provides checkpoints negotiations/dealmaking
- Creates eye on the prize perspective
- Enables Plan B

other worksheets such as the example of the 20th percentile with a Monte Carlo model. This method can be useful when in negotiations the deal team wants to consider the impact on the term sheet by making different assumptions or restructuring the model or a counterproposal from the buyer or multiple prospective buyers.

## NOTES

1. I have excluded another pricing strategy sometimes, regrettably, used by sellers, which could be called: "propose a number" and give me a dollar so I can buy a clue.

2. In 1940, in the early days of WWII, and after the shocking surrender by the French and Belgian governments, and in anticipation of a likewise English capitulation, Churchill galvanized his countrymen by his conviction expressed by his "we shall never surrender" speech.

3. Based on data taken and presented by Courtroom Sciences, Inc., Dallas, TX.

4. Or "stela." A stele is a vertical slab of stone (usually) used for grave inscriptions and other commemorative writings of significance. They have been found throughout Greece, Egypt, Mesopotamia (Babylon and its environs, including the famous Code of Hammurabi, circa 1800 B.C.), China, and the New World (the Mayan culture in Mexico and Central America). It derives from the ancient Greek words *stayko* for "stand" or "stand firm" and *stayrizo* "to establish or set up" or "make a firm resolve."

5. Discovered by French troops under Napoleon in 1799 near the Egyptian town of Rosetta, hence the name, and now in the British Museum, it was recognized to describe a historic event in three parallel languages: Greek, which was known, and hieroglyphic and demotic Egyptian scripts, which were lost languages. This stone was used by Jean Francois Champollion (1790–1832) to recapture the ancient Egyptian written language (1821).

6. Prov. 20:14, New American Standard Bible.

# CHAPTER 10

# Negotiation Perspectives and Dynamics

In this chapter, we consider a few points relating to the various perspectives parties bring to a negotiation and the effect those perspectives have on the dynamic process of negotiation.

## NEGOTIATION PERSPECTIVES

Returning again to a subject introduced at the beginning of this book, what exactly are we trying to accomplish with the valuation methods and tools presented? Is it to determine a "fair price," meaning that we act from a God's eye view on the deal and compute its value regardless of whether we find ourselves on the buy side or sell side? Or are we trying to find the extreme price point of the other side, the most a buyer would be willing to pay or the least a seller would be willing to take, so we can determine what we will offer to take advantage of such understanding?

In many cases, the power of the valuation methods considered here will result in a negative answer to both of these questions. The reason for this negative answer is that by these methods we are able to assess and value the aspects of the deal that are unique to the other side as well as to us, and as such are not likely to reflect the deal value that would be calculated with a third party.

Let us consider a Shakespeare quotation on valuation from the play *Troilus and Cressida*. Troilus asks: "What's aught but as 'tis valued?" Hector replies: "But value dwells not in particular will, it holds his estimate and dignity as well wherein 'til precious of itself as in the prizer."[1] Troilus's perspective seems to be that there is no value except in the valuer; this is akin to the tree makes no sound when it falls in the forest unless there is someone to hear it. Troilus thus appears to be the market-is-always-right man. Hector, whom

I would take to be the idealist, appears to express the contrary belief that value resides intrinsically, which bears as much consideration as the value perceived by any external entity. So who is right, Troilus or Hector (recognizing that Troilus was betrayed by his loved one and ultimately killed)?

As a seller my concern is always "who is my buyer?" For ease in collecting statistics, let us consider for the moment only buyers in the United States. If I presume that my buyer is a business, U.S. census statistics suggest that there are 5.8 million potential buyers if we consider all firms with employees regardless of their legal form. With the frightful possibilities made available by commercial e-mail lists, I could presumably acquire the means to send a deal proposal with one mouse click to 5.8 million inboxes. Assuming for a moment that such a proposal would be at least viewed, what would be the reaction of this universe of prospective buyers? Well, of course, the almost universal value ascribed would be even less than zero, meaning that, were it possible, this vast group of *nonbuyers* would consider or acquire the opportunity only if they were paid to do so simply because they have no business interest in the area.

Next we would find a category of *nominal buyers* who would have sufficient interest to invest in reviewing the opportunity but their interest and the opportunity fit is such that their perceived value, at the last, would be nominal or zero. Were the opportunity offered for free, or near-free, they could be interested; but realizing that such is not likely to be a realizable outcome, they know enough not to pursue the valuation, due diligence, and negotiation process.

Next we would expect, but cannot be assured, that there would be a comparatively small category of *target buyers* who, because of the business benefit associated with the opportunity, would immediately perceive this offer as something worth pursuing.

Finally, one might find a single, unique *ideal buyer* for whom this opportunity fits like a key into an extraordinary valuable door lock available only to that company. This scenario is the business-to-business equivalent of the metaphorical "soul mate" concept used in human affairs.

These four categories—nonbuyers, nominal buyers, target buyers, and ideal buyer—are illustrated in Exhibit 10.1.

As will be discussed in the next chapter on "Plan B" development and issues, it is a wise dealmaking practice for a seller to have multiple potential buyers under consideration. Using the above categorization, this means that of the population of "target buyers" and the one, or very few, "ideal buyer(s)," a selection must be made as to the population that will be targeted for contact and discussion. There are two temptations that generally should be resisted: seize on one and only one target buyer, or, at the other extreme, make a very long list and pursue them all. The ideal, as in much of our discussion in this book, is the golden mean between extremes. Here such a mean could

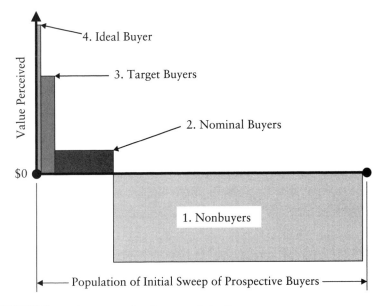

**EXHIBIT 10.1**   Valuation in the Context of the Buyer

be 5 to 10 potential buyers. The list is short enough that an appropriate level of analysis on each prospect is manageable that will enable an intelligent contact and follow-on discussion to occur. Yet, providing the opportunity is itself attractive and the selection of the target list has been done well, there should be enough prospective parties interested that an appropriate use of Plan B can be accomplished, as will be discussed.

Returning now to our Troilus and Hector debate on the source of value in the context of the picture of Exhibit 10.1, we can see that the issue of intrinsic versus market value depends on the buyer category. For Category 1 nonbuyers, the opportunity has no "prizer" or market value although it does (in our example) have intrinsic value. For Category 2 nominal buyers, they see only nominal, or opportunistic value. If we can assume that there will be a sufficient number of buyers in Category 3, these buyers as a group can establish a market value by, for instance, some form of auction. The Category 4 ideal buyer by our hypotheses can extract the most value from the opportunity by virtue of its unique positioning and assets. However, because the ideal buyer is (in principle) unique, such a buyer is reasonably likely to assert that the opportunity is worth what the Category 3 target buyers perceive it to be and the excess value above that belongs to the unique contribution by the Category 4 buyer.

So, one could conclude that the market value is what the Category 3 buyers establish it to be, assuming there is a sufficient population on which to make such a determination. In consideration of a deal, such a market-established price should approximate the opportunity's intrinsic value. The alternative intrinsic value would be the value to the seller if it retained ownership of the opportunity and used it in some way itself. The presumption in a dealmaking context is that if there exists a Category 3 population, then the value associated with a deal will exceed the value to the seller's retaining it. There could be exceptions to this expectation, which is why a Plan B analysis, as discussed in Chapter 11 includes Plan B options for retaining the opportunity.

## NEGOTIATING SEQUENCING

The process of going from deal conception to deal consummation has many steps for opportunities of any significance. The normal sequence involves starting internally with one's own organization and developing a framework for a negotiation, the specific terms that will be and can be offered (expressed through term sheets), and a plan for communicating with, and it is hoped, engaging someone interested in pursuing the negotiation. That plan for communicating and engaging is what we want to consider next.

Where does one start? One possibility is to open with a few pleasantries and pastries and then provide the other side with a fully executable contract for the purpose of "walking" them through the proposed agreement, from "whereas" to "dotted line." This plan generally does not work well, although we consider later circumstances where, as heavy-handed as this feels, a variant could be an appropriate plan.

If we do not normally start with the final agreement documents, then where should we begin? Well, just like a formal meal, there is no written rule that says one cannot start with dessert and coffee, followed by, say, appetizers, then a main entrée, and conclude with soup, crackers, and palate refresher. However, if you invite your friends and business associates to such an experience, they will talk about you, and likely worry about you as well. There is a meal etiquette that probably has an evolved social rationality behind it that makes it worth following but there is also the incentive that it makes people comfortable.

In a negotiation, the main sequence is usually something like the following 10 stages:

1. *Initial screening for potential interest.* Such screening occurs without formal written documents (although table napkins have an illustrious history). It can occur in an informal, even chance encounter, or over a meal or some other occasion (golf outing or event attendance), or by telephone.

2. *Nonconfidential, brief, writing that characterizes the "scene" of the opportunity.* Writing creates something concrete that can be pondered on in private and shared with others whose opinion will matter. Such writing, which I refer to as an Opportunity Memorandum (distinguished from the formal Offering Memorandum), gives the readers a perspective that fits with their business operations and their customers. It provides some weight behind the Stage 1 discussion to answer the always present "so what?" question.

3. *Confidentiality agreement specific to the opportunity.* It is customary in business communications to keep confidential the communications with other parties about prospective opportunities as a matter of professional courtesy and ethics. However, there are some good reasons for such agreements, such as protecting the seller's ability to pursue future patenting, maintaining a valuable trade secret, preventing premature disclosure of an interest in selling, providing competitors with advantageous information, and so forth. The scope of such an agreement should be proportional to the significance of anticipated disclosure in Stage 4.

4. *Confidential writing that discloses key elements of what is contended to be proprietary to the seller.* This disclosure could be done at a face-to-face meeting or by letter. Such a disclosure should have the purpose of creating awareness in the seller as to why a negotiation is necessary to secure the business benefits characterized in Stages 1 and 2. Normally the seller does not disclose everything confidential or all the facts behind the opportunity because it is still not clear how serious the interest is.

5. *Term sheet(s) and detail disclosure.* Prospective buyers often seek to understand the seller's proposed terms prior to "deep dives" into the opportunity. Sellers may share a similar interest for a similar reason— to avoid wasting time. However, sometimes sellers want to wait until there is a deeper context developed from which such terms can be better understood.

6. *Initial negotiation and due diligence.* To reach Stage 6, the prospective buyer should have concluded that (1) this opportunity fits their business, (2) the opportunity makes sense, and (3) there appears to be something proprietary to the seller that would be worth acquiring. Both the buyer and seller should have reached a common understanding on at least this level prior to beginning initial negotiations or due diligence. As in Stage 5, these two activities are paired because they can occur in either order (diligence first or last) or semi-simultaneously. If there are some key business terms that either party is seeking that, based on the term sheet in Stage 5, appear to be key deal issues, then it is often a good practice to work on them first to gain confidence that, if the due diligence is satisfactory, an agreement is likely to be possible. However, until due diligence

is completed, there is often substantial uncertainty as to the total value, and even all the prospective deal issues. Although due diligence is a common term of art for a buyer's activities, in many business deals there can be important due-diligence activities by the seller.

7. *Detailed negotiations and formal agreement drafting.* As previously, these two activities are paired because they can occur sequentially or semi-simultaneously. Lead negotiators who are also attorneys appear to prefer detailed negotiations by means of formal agreement drafting. Lead negotiators who have sales and marketing in their backgrounds and orientations generally prefer to detail negotiations *instead of* (at least for their part of the dealmaking) formal agreement drafting.

8. *Final negotiations and agreement.* In Stage 7 activities, which can last over many weeks, there is commonly a list of items that requires either side to consider with other parties within their respective organization or there has been incomplete assent by both parties (or even outright disagreement). In Stage 8, all these areas are to be communicated and resolved or the dealmaking process will be stalled or even terminated.

9. *Execution and asset transfers.* This stage should normally be a straight-forward process of dotting i's and crossing t's, but there are often last-minute issues that arise either because some matter had been forgotten, or some issue already resolved has returned, or legal wrangling occurs regarding making the English and legal language work in conformity with the agreed provisions.[2] There is a phenomenon of "buyer's remorse" known to all automobile salesmen. Shortly after a purchase commitment has been made, it is human nature to wonder if one did the right thing. Before the purchase, the buyer had the universe of possibilities in front of him or her, and now, by making a commitment, that universe has shrunk. Seller's can experience the same thing, though it appears to occur less often, perhaps because sellers are typically the initiators of the entire dealmaking process. Both parties can have the internal churning of "did I get the best deal I could have?"[3]

10. *Agreement maintenance.* Complicated deals commonly have after-deals, just as earthquakes have aftershocks. They can range from informal clarifications to the need for a formal amendment or even (according to at least one side) to a complete renegotiation.

All ten stages are important to a negotiation. Our focus in this book, and specifically here in a discussion of sequencing, is the heart of the negotiation process that takes place in Stages 6, 7, and 8. Of all the deal issues that require mutual assent, how should they best be sequenced in a negotiation? There are four possible strategies:

1. Start somewhere, anywhere.
2. Start from page 1.
3. Work from the easiest to the most difficult issues.
4. Work from the most difficult to the easiest issues.

The start-somewhere strategy reflects the belief that it is not particularly important to choose or sequence but to get started.[4] Start from page 1 is the strategy favored by the checklist oriented, especially when working on standard deals such as license agreements. The more interesting sequencing strategies are the final two. Is it better to work the most difficult issues first or last?

The argument made in support of saving the most difficult issues until last is to create momentum by agreeing on some simpler matters. The idea is to first lift the 5-pound weights, get comfortable doing so, let the blood flow to warm those muscles, and then move to the 10 pounders. By the end of the process, you will be prepared to chalk up, notch up, and try to heave up some Olympic weights. For me the compelling counterargument is that little of significance is established by lifting 5-pound weights if one's goals are Olympic; we would be better off getting to the really important issues first, reaching agreement on these matters or, if no agreement is possible, seeking another way to reconfigure the entire approach to make agreement become possible, or moving on to Plan B (discussed in Chapter 11).

A way of creating a synthesis of these last two approaches is shown in Exhibit 10.2. The synthesis solution is to select a few issues that should be easy for both sides to adjust their stated positions to accommodate reasonable interests of the other side and then commence on what appears to be the most difficult issues.

## ISSUE EXPLOSION

Some negotiations experience an emergence of many issues separating agreement between the parties. In some instances, the mere large number of such issues can be a signal to the parties that agreement is not likely within the presently envisioned framework of the agreement. In other cases, such issue explosion could arise because of motives, perhaps not altogether pure, by one side of the negotiation. Such a strategy is generally a bad-faith effort by the issue-proliferating side to create a blizzard of objections, or concerns, for the purpose at some later stage of conceding on many or even all of them as bargaining ploys to gain certain concessions from the other side on a very major issue. The underlying idea is that one side concedes many issues and creates a concession bank account that it can then draw on, perhaps in one

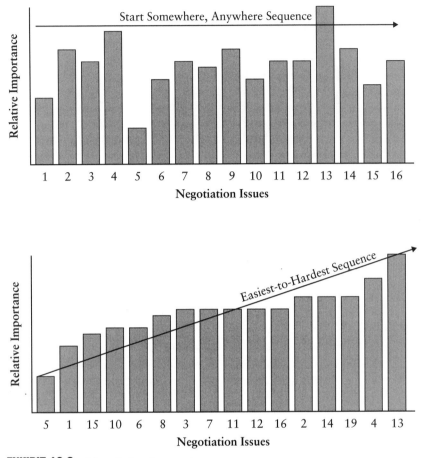

**EXHIBIT 10.2** Negotiating Sequencing

massive withdrawal, to achieve the concession it really seeks from the other side. This strategy is sometimes called the "bones" strategy, as in throw the dog a bone to keep it happy, and is equivalent in moral standing to the now widely discredited "cookie jar" strategy of some companies in managing their reported earnings by recognizing a revenue (a cookie) at convenient moments each reporting quarter to manage investor illusions.

However, a particular agreement framework for a particular opportunity for particular parties can genuinely lead to a vast number of legitimate negotiating issues that could be disproportionate to one side. In such cases, the sheer number of issues should cause the parties to reconsider the big picture before attempting to go through any resolution sequence. Generally speaking, there are three possible sources for legitimate issue explosion:

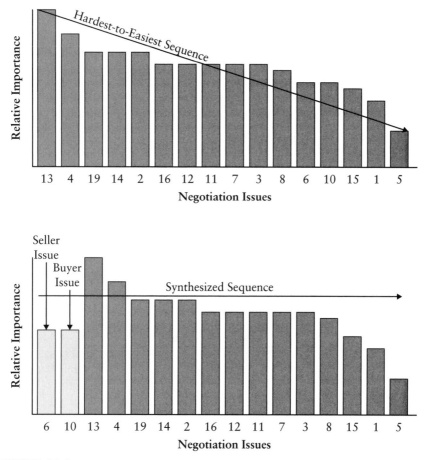

**EXHIBIT 10.2** *Continued*

1. Wrong parties for the given opportunity
2. Wrong opportunity for the right parties
3. Wrong framework for the right opportunity for the right parties

These scenarios are akin to the situation of a poorly performing employee. One possibility is that the employee simply *is* the wrong person for the job. However, the problem could be a good employee in a wrong job. Finally, the employee and employer and the job could all be made to work well if the job is restructured in some way. In a similar way, issue explosion is a sign to deal managers that something is wrong either with respect to the pairing of these two particular parties, or the deal framework, or both.

## NEGOTIATING VALUES

The three A's of professional services sales are: Ability, Availability, and Affability. We tend to overlook the third one: People buy from people they like, whenever they are able to do so. Jerry Mulen, producer of *Jurrasic Park* and *Schindler's List* and many other movies, talks of negotiating with prospective directors and story tellers as "sitting down and listening to their [the collaborator's] heart" and "assembling a team to tell a story you have a passion about" and "friendships that survive the project." This point drives the seeking of win–win deals

Communication fidelity is always an issue when dealing with individuals and groups who negotiate on behalf of their self-interest. The challenge is not the silence, namely, what you are not told about the other side's position (although as discussed in Chapter 11 silence can inhibit opportunity discovery), it is the truthfulness of the communications received. Over the years, there have been many attempts to find simple attributes that can, without raising suspicions, detect an untruthful statement. Eye movements and blinking, for example, have had popular adherents. An interesting study was performed with subjects to see if one ear or the other could detect truthfulness; amazingly, one study reported that there was a left-ear advantage to recognizing the truthfulness of a statement.[5] Until some technology is developed that is accepted for dealmaking, we will have to rely on more traditional measures. Although I am not aware of studies that have been done in the context of business negotiations, I believe that deal teams interacting with each other in multiple encounters do, in fact, become attuned to communication fidelity. Loss of trust, deserved or not, is normally very damaging for deal closure prospects.

## DEAL/AGREEMENT COMPLEXITY

Deals that involve conditional future consideration, such as milestone payments, or royalties, or royalties that are subject to future adjustments, or any of the other ways of configuring the Wheelbarrow, or even the Box, create additional agreement complexity. Such additional complexity may be sufficiently important to one or both parties because of future uncertainties that it is a good idea to include the feature. However, if each deal compromise, or each idea by a deal-team member, results in a new feature for the Wheelbarrow, the agreement can get unmanageably complex.

As with our Einstein quote of making things as simple as possible but not simpler and the Aristotelian idea of the mean, a good agreement is one that can be grasped by both parties, administered by individuals not present at the negotiations, and respond to future events as the parties intended. As shown

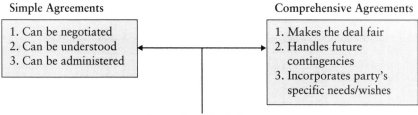

| Simple Agreements | Comprehensive Agreements |
|---|---|
| 1. Can be negotiated<br>2. Can be understood<br>3. Can be administered | 1. Makes the deal fair<br>2. Handles future contingencies<br>3. Incorporates party's specific needs/wishes |

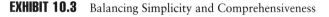

*What is the right balance?*

*"Make it as simple as possible, but not simpler."*
(*A. Einstein*)

In any situation consider:
1. Reporting criteria/format
2. Auditability

**EXHIBIT 10.3** Balancing Simplicity and Comprehensiveness

in Exhibit 10.3, the advantages of simplicity need to be weighed against the benefits afforded by adding complexity.

A final point of advice is on the aspect of flexibility. The point of deal-making is developing and using tools and methods to enable deals done, not apriori positions to be defended. In the play *Antigone*, Sophocles has the character Haimon appeal to his father, King Creon:

> "I beg you, do not be unchangeable: do not believe that you alone can be right. The man who thinks that, the man who maintains that only he has the power to reason correctly, the gift to speak, the soul—a man like that, when you know him, turns out to be empty. It is not reason never to yield to reason!" (Haimon to his father Creon who has sentenced Antigone his betrothed to death.)

*Antigone*, Scene III

## NOTES

1. *Troilus and Cressida*, II ii., based on a medieval legend that retells the fall of Troy to the Greeks, originally told in Homer's *Iliad* and *Odyssey*. Troilus was the son of the king of Troy and Cressida was the betrayer of his love, whereupon Troilus was killed in the Trojan War. Alas.

2. A great quote, for which I do not recall the citation, complicates much of Stages 8 and 9: "English resists meaning."

3. There is even a pathology that poisons dealmaking whereby one side concludes that if the other side has agreed, they must have been willing to make it more favorable,

which leads to the contradiction that the only time I know that I have gotten the best possible deal is if the other side walks away!

4. This strategy could also be called the Mt. Vernon strategy. George Washington's home, available for touring, is maintained by an approach called "Mt. Vernon method." It consists of starting wherever one starts, and keeping going through the room you are now in, cleaning and fixing as necessary, and then progressing from room to room. Wherever you stop at the end of that day, you just pick up the next day, and so on in perpetuity.

5. F. Fabbro, et al., "Hemispheric Asymmetry for the Auditory Recognition of True and False Statements. *Neuropsychologia* 31 (1993): 865–870. The experiments were done with 48 right-hand adjust subjects, 24 males and 24 females.

# CHAPTER 11

# Plan B

Everybody needs a Plan B. And, the best time for one is before you need one.

## AUCTIONS AND BETROTHALS

Before developing a plan for Plan B, let us first consider two polar negotiating situations: auctions and betrothals. Auctions, in which any seller can be presented with many prospective buyers considering and making offers, are as old as commerce and as new as www.ebay.com. Auctions are a well-established business process for (1) price discovery, because there exists (in principle) a genuine market-based determination from buyers; and (2) liquidity, because the buyer with the highest accepted bid pays what he or she bid. The format of the auction, whether open outcry as on a traditional stock exchange floor, a silent closed-bid auction, or now-prevalent forms of electronic auctions, is less significant than the observation that all auctions are designed for the purpose of avoiding particularized negotiation between a given seller and buyer. An auction enables any seller to be pursued by many prospective buyers and, by an auction's structure, any buyer can pursue multiple sellers with similar or different opportunities. Auctions, as we traditionally think of them, work because of this mutual personal indifference. The transaction and its value are dependent solely on the defined product and the bidder competition to become the product's owner. However, such a transaction is possible if and only if the product being offered can be valued without significant due diligence with respect to the individual transaction. For instance, a buyer interested in buying stock in, say, 3M or Yahoo!, may do significant analysis on the respective company's management, products, financial performance, competitive positioning, and future prospects. In doing so, the buyer may well create scenario-based discounted cash flow (DCF) models, Monte Carlo models, and various Real Option analyses (which may lead to participation in the auction of "puts" and "calls" in lieu of immediate stock ownership). However, in the auction process such a prospective buyer seeking a block of stock is not concerned with who the particular seller may be or the circumstances of why they are selling. The title and the product are simple and proscribed: a share or block of MMM or YHOO. It is this transaction simplicity that makes stock markets liquid and inherently rationally priced.

The seller of MMM or YHOO who is in need of immediate liquidity may simply take advantage of such market determination of price and avoid doing any analysis. However, most sellers are performing the same type of analyses in anticipation of the range of possible bids, together with an analysis of the alternative investments that could be made on achieving liquidity from the subject sale. So ahead of the transaction, there is, or should be,[1] an appropriately detailed negotiation-planning analysis even though the deal consummation is done simply, quickly, cheaply, and with third parties.

This stock market example would work about as well for a tanker of crude oil, a trailer of bananas, or a collection of Pez dispensers (which was the impetus for the creation of eBay), given the few product specifications that any buyer would need to know, such as how old are those bananas. For opportunities that are not fungibles, such as oil and bananas, there is an increasing need for deal specifics, particularly when the subject matter is not a single asset being sold whole, such as would occur with a transaction involving a license to related intellectual property, the right to recruit and hire certain key people, access to know-how and special customer relationships, and a supply or purchase agreement.

For high-value, high-ambiguity transactions, traditionally constructed auctions or even electronically enabled auctions are not likely to be practicable.

Now, let us consider the polar opposite of auctions: "betrothal" dealmaking. By the term betrothal negotiations in dealmaking is meant that, for reasons and forces (apparently) beyond the control of the deal manager, there is a preestablished expectation that Seller X and Buyer Y will negotiate, value, and consummate this deal. This XY betrothal may be at the behest of the infamous lunch or golf outing or Outward Bound bonding of CEO-X and CEO-Y who agree to agree and assign down the responsibility to get the dealmaking done. The temptation for the deal team in this situation is to resignedly accept the mission and get the best deal possible. However, in general, even with such expectation constraints, it is still a good idea to develop a Plan B analysis, as will be discussed later. For instance, one of the most constraining of deal constraints is litigation between X and Y that CEOs have directed their teams to settle. Is a Plan B possible in such a case? Yes, and the side that does it better has an advantage. In this case the Plan B is simply to point out the costs, rewards, and risks of not settling and either continuing to pursue the litigation or creating some alternative form of dispute resolution to a negotiation. Without a Plan B what can one side do to a fabulously unreasonable and fixed position taken by the other side, which then just waits for acquiescence?

Two other common sources of betrothal negotiation are the favorite Company Y for Seller X and the so-called match made in heaven (which may also be called the "soul-mate deal"). In the favored company example, there is some favorable working history or perhaps ongoing collaborations that create a context that is attractive to one or both sides. Such trust and experience is helpful in overcoming many communication hurdles and may also be useful in valuation or agreement construction by referring to and using previous transactions. However, opportunities tend to be opportunity specific. It may well be, and probably is, that in this specific instance companies X and Y will determine, if they each perform a Plan B analysis, that one or both will conclude that this opportunity has greater value with some third party. Without such Plan B analysis, it is almost certain that a suboptimal though easy deal will result. And if it does subsequently become disadvantageous to either side, then the deal will in fact have harmed the relationship.

The other example, the soul-mate deal, occurs when what looks to be the ideal buyer Y, from the perspective of seller X, has independently concluded that its ideal opportunity is the subject opportunity being offered by X. This situation is that of the seller of a Buckminster Fuller hard-to-sell geodesic house in rural nowheresville finding a prospective buyer who has been searching all his or her life for a Buckminster Fuller geodesic house in nowheresville. Should such parties still do a Plan B? Yes, although in this example the seller would probably be advised to do his or hers quite quickly. The experience in dealmaking, like marriage, is that initial appearances may not correlate well with ultimate experience. Further, a soul-mate buyer characteristically comes to that realization and discerning the absence of a seller, Plan B will be inclined to exploit the advantage (CFOs on deal teams are typically quite skillful at providing such buyer voicing).

## PLAN B ANALYSIS AND TOOLS

The essence of a Plan B is the analysis of present value of the conceivable alternatives to a deal, as envisioned, between X and Y. From a buyer's perspective, the alternatives are often clearly vast. Since a buyer is characteristically interested in maximizing investor return, and because there are typically many potential avenues that could be pursued, the alternative to the subject negotiation can be acquiring a very different kind of asset.

For the seller, the scope of possible Plan Bs is also large. In addition to finding other prospective buyers, the seller may be able to simply retain the opportunity and continue its development and commercialization, or the transaction framework for the given opportunity and the Plan A buyer could be fundamentally restructured. One of the most useful and creative acts of a deal manager and team is the early formulation of a Plan B.

The starting point for a Plan B is the creation of a universe of possibilities. It is surprising how rarely (and poorly) this is sometimes done. One possible reason is the thought-constraining experience of education in which we tend to learn that there is always a best answer, and that the teacher is the one who knows it. There are creativity experiments done with early elementary school students, such as third graders, in which they will be asked to suggest how a particular problem can be solved. What follows is something like an explosion of ideas, often with humor, and normally with enthusiasm. (If you are a parent with children in this age range who, say, want a horse; just ask them, seriously, "How could we keep one here?" and you will be amazed at the range of answers.) However, in these same experiments done with late elementary school students, say, seventh graders, the creativity is (commonly) curtailed and classes tend to think of no or only marginally variant alternatives. This change has been attributed to a general transformation from joy and wonder to fear and judgment (which may be the ultimate meaning of Cervantes' *Don Quixote*).

In business contexts, especially when a lot is at stake, and especially when a senior company official is present, this combination of fear and judgment can constrict the creation of a list of options to the few obvious and timid suggestions. How to stimulate creativity is beyond the scope of this book, but following are four suggestions:

1. Create a draft list of possible Plan Bs by involving a few stakeholders or even nonstakeholders and start a deal-team meeting with such list.

2. Retain a facilitator who, using an unstructured process, leads or forces the deal team to create a long list of options and to prioritize the opportunities.

3. Focus a meeting on creating a list of criteria for a suitable Plan B candidate for the purpose of tasking a subgroup to bring back an ordered list of candidates and how they meet or exceed the criteria.

4. Have a series of one-on-one discussions with people of good judgment within and possibly outside the company with open-ended questions such as "If you were me, what would be your top three deal alternatives?" In case of particularly sensitive preparations, it still may be possible to sanitize the context that useful ideas can be shared without compromising secrecy needs.

An extremely useful tool for Plan B analysis is spreadsheet software, such as Microsoft's Excel, illustrated in Exhibit 11.1. Each considered alternative is given its own row. Columns to the left of the identity of the Plan B alternative

**EXHIBIT 11.1**   Illustrative Spreadsheet for Rating/Ranking

| | | | Considered Alternatives | | | | Metrics of Alternatives | | | | | | |
|---|---|---|---|---|---|---|---|---|---|---|---|---|---|
| Rating/Ranking Score | | | | | | | | | | | | | |
| C1 | W1 | WC1 | C2 | W2 | WC2 | Score | Rank | Cat. | Grp | ID | Company | Rev. $ | CAGR % | GM % | EBIT % | R&D $ | Deals | Contacts |

| Rank | Cat. Grp | ID | Company | Rev. $ | CAGR % | GM % | EBIT % | R&D $ | Deals | Contacts |
|---|---|---|---|---|---|---|---|---|---|---|
| 1 | A | | | | | | | | | |
| 2 | A | | | | | | | | | |
| 3 | B | | | | | | | | | |
| 4 | B | | | | | | | | | |
| 5 | B | | | | | | | | | |
| 6 | B | | | | | | | | | |
| 7 | B | | | | | | | | | |
| 8 | B | | | | | | | | | |
| 9 | B | | | | | | | | | |
| 10 | C | | | | | | | | | |
| 11 | C | | | | | | | | | |
| 12 | C | | | | | | | | | |
| 13 | C | | | | | | | | | |
| 14 | C | | | | | | | | | |
| 15 | C | | | | | | | | | |
| 16 | C | | | | | | | | | |
| 17 | C | | | | | | | | | |
| 18 | C | | | | | | | | | |
| 19 | C | | | | | | | | | |
| 20 | C | | | | | | | | | |

can be created and used for classification and ranking purposes; columns to the right are then used to provide key facts about the candidate such as annual revenues in relevant markets, profitability measures, deal history examples, complementary patents, and so forth. With Excel there is essentially no limit to the ability to generate, delete, and move columns, and later hide columns, and because of its ubiquity it can be easily shared with team members without having to learn database coding. Shown in the two-three-headed columns to the left in Exhibit 11.1 are rating/ranking criteria and math: C, the scored criteria; W, the weighting on such criteria; and WC the result obtained by multiplying the first two columns. An example of C1 could be the ability to dominate the market(s) that are relevant to the subject opportunity and C2 could be the ability to master the underlying technology(-ies) that will successfully convert the subject opportunity into a finished manufacturing operation. If the criteria are deemed approximately equal in importance, then the weighting column can be eliminated, thereby simplifying the analysis. Alternatively, if the relative importance of the various criteria is simple, then the weighting can be done at the time of calculating the final score. The use of such rating/ranking columns is discussed in more detail in the remainder of this chapter.

Shown in the columns grouped to the right in Exhibit 11.1 are the highlights of the key facts and observations about each of the candidates. Shown, as examples, in the first of these columns are the annual revenues, the growth in such annual revenues (compound annual growth rate [CAGR]), gross margin and earnings before interest and taxes (EBIT), and spending on research and development (R&D) (and perhaps other measures of the company's ability to make new investments). Shown in the rightmost columns are more subjective measures such as deal rate or reputation and the level, magnitude, and/or significance of existing contacts at the subject alternative company. The idea of this table is to separate facts and value. The columns to the right are reserved for metrics that are fact-based, but can and should include subjective matters. There is necessarily judgment involved in choosing what gets included and how it is portrayed, especially for the more subjective matters. But the purpose is to collect in a summary fashion the key metrics associated with each candidate, and keep that separate from the judgments reached about their suitability and potential value insofar as pursuing negotiation.

For important candidates, a separate, subsequent tab can be dedicated entirely to facts about the company such as its publicly filed financial statements, or even the results of market surveys. Excel allows you to build a Plan B Workbook of text and financials that can be very useful in negotiation planning. Opportunity marketing information, such as key deal-team contacts and background information, can also be conveniently placed within dedicated Excel worksheet tabs. Once such a Plan B Workbook exists, it generally stimulates new suggestions even if they were slow in coming at the beginning.

The middle columns of Exhibit 11.1 show the group to which the company belongs, its ranked order (when the rating/ranking process is completed), and its dealmaking priority (Plan A versus Plan B versus a distant possibility Plan C). Often when a long list of candidate companies are considered, they can be usefully distinguished as belonging to different types or subgroups. For instance, a new software opportunity could be of interest to a large software company that sells integrated multiproduct solutions such as an IBM, or a large company primarily focused on a particular segment, such as PeopleSoft, or a company that may be interested in being a service provider rather than a software product seller, or a small startup company. Grouping the companies according to some taxonomy can be useful for multiple purposes. The rating/ranking criteria and weighting might change because the appropriate business model for a deal could be different for one group of companies. When observing a highly ranked candidate it is useful to think of other possible companies that might belong to the same group and that had been overlooked in an initial assessment of deal alternatives. It is generally a good practice to include in the list of alternatives some that do not include a deal with any third party. For instance, one alternative is simply to wait for some prescribed period, say a year. Another alternative is to retain the opportunity and develop it further or completely. Other alternatives could include aggregating the opportunity with something larger, such as a technology being aggregated with a product line or a division, and offered only as a whole; another alternative could be to deaggregate the opportunity and offer for sale or license, say, just the rights to certain patents or other intellectual property. These nondealmaking alternatives may simply have been a priori ruled out. Still it is useful to include them here as a benchmark by which to gauge the relative attractiveness of various alternatives. Including these alternatives is especially valuable when Plan A has not worked out and one is forced to consider various dealmaking Plan Bs. The question often arises, is such pursuit really worth doing? Keeping at the ready nondeal alternatives, even including a financial model for such alternatives, establishes the value or cost of the alternative to any deal.

The key tool for use in such Plan B analysis is "rating/ranking."[2] Rating/ranking is a widely used method for contrasting and comparing multiple alternatives that differ from each other in different ways. A common example is the frequent publication of the best place to live or start a business or retire. There is even at least one Wb site that is dedicated to the use of rating/ranking for determining a best location for some purpose: www.bestplaces.com. At this site one can find rating/ranking examples and results on all sorts of decision making. The Web site even provides ratings/rankings of third-party ratings/rankings (such as might be published by *Forbes* and *Money Magazine*). There are many more everyday examples of the use of rating/ranking. *US News and World Report* regularly publishes its ratings/rankings of academic programs offered by colleges and universities and hospitals by specialty. In a specialized and emerging form of rating/ranking, hospitals themselves are now widely using a 10-point pain rating/ranking, the so-called fifth vital sign, using graphics to assist patients in self-analysis: from smile faces (0 for "no hurt") to crying frown faces (10 for "hurts worst"). Edmunds (www.edmunds.com) provides a ranked valuation of every automobile, new and used. In the wake of the terrorist attacks of September 11, 2001, there now exists a Transportation Security Agency (TSA). One of its actions is to develop a screening tool for risk potential. In response to another kind of adversity, Charles Schwab, the financial services company, has developed a proprietary rating/ranking tool that groups some 3,000 publicly traded stocks into five categories: 10 percent top ranked stocks as "A" stocks, 20 percent high ranked stocks as "B," 20 percent as "C," 20 percent as "D," and 20 percent as "E." According to the company, it uses a computer program to assess automatically these stocks based on 24 different criteria. Morningstar rates some 10,000 mutual funds (since July 1, 2002) in 48 distinct sectors by the assignment of stars: the top 10 percent receive five stars, the next 22.5 percent get four stars, the next 35 percent three stars, the next 22.5 percent two stars, and the bottom 10 percent one star. Value Line has for many years used its own proprietary rating/ranking approach enjoined with some measure of human judgment.

Moody and Standard and Poor's (S&P) ratings of commercial bonds are example applications of rating/ranking to guide debt investors. In such a context, the higher rated/ranked bonds are associated with lower risk. In the middle of the rating/ranking categories there is a demarcation between the upper categories, which are generally termed "investment grade," and the bottom categories, which are popularly known as "junk bonds" but are more accurately simply high-risk/high-yield bonds. The market in response to such scoring, and accounting for any other factors, then accepts lower expected rates of return (yield) on such highly rated/ranked bonds. The following table shows the default rate on the payment of such bonds over the past 15 years as a function of the original S&P bond rating, in which those rated BBB or better are investment grade.

**Default Rate on S&P Bonds over Past 15 Years[3]**

| Original Rating | Default Rate |
|---|---|
| AAA | 0.52% |
| AA | 1.31 |
| A | 2.32 |
| BBB | 6.64 |
| BB | 19.52 |
| B | 35.76 |
| CCC | 54.38 |

Rating/ranking does not perfectly correlate with defaults; in the bond example, every rating category experienced defaults. Even with investment grade bonds (BBB), more than 1 out of 20 rated bonds goes into default; but nearly 19 out of 20 perform as promised.

As with the rating/ranking of bonds, the evaluation of diverse alternatives is likely to require making apples-to-oranges comparisons because of intrinsic differences among them. The way this is performed is to determine the key characteristics that would affect the attractiveness of a particular candidate for negotiation. This ranking could include their ability to afford substantial up-front payments, or their reputation for honest dealings or dealmaking alacrity, or their market position or technology prowess with respect to the subject opportunity, and so forth. Depending on the issues that affect attractiveness from your side's perspective and the range of alternatives being considered, there may be just three or four rating factors or as many as 10 (or even more). As with the Einstein principle discussed in a previous chapter, every analysis should be as simple as possible, but not simpler.

Once the key factors have been identified, or at least provisionally so, then an assessment of their relative importance should be made. If any of the factors are notably more important than others, they can be accounted for by weighting such factors by a multiplier such as two for those perceived to be twice as important in determining overall attractiveness, and so forth. The next step is to score each of the factors for each of the alternatives using a defined scale. One of the commonly used scales is a 1 to 5 scale where a 3 is considered average, 4 good, and 5 excellent. This scale is generally known as a Likkert Scale. The advantages of a Likkert Scale are:

- Clearly scores opportunities above and below a reference benchmark, such as the Plan A alternative.

- Can create any number of levels above and below the reference point (a 5-point scale has two above and below, a 7-point has three above and below, and so forth), allowing any level of precision desired or warranted.

- Numerical normalized result can be used to create priorities when considering multiple Plan B alternatives.

- The individual scores on each of the factors can be used in preparing for negotiation.

Some issues with the use of Likkert Scale are:

- It does not overtly reflect the catastrophic effect a fatal flaw can have on value. Suppose on an intellectual property (IP) protection score, an opportunity receives a "1" because it has none, but it scores high on all other factors. Just determining a weighted average score will obscure the fact that the opportunity could have no (or little) value.[4]

- It can too easily let mediocrity slide by on each of the factors so that the results are commonly "better than average" (like Garrison Keilor's *Lake Wobegon*, where all the kids are above average), something like gentlemen C's.

- Too much can be made of the significance of the absolute value of the final score or small differences in score. Despite its quantification, the method rests on judgments that are not always defendable with mathematical exactitude.

One way of complementing the Likkert scoring is to use a four-color rating/ranking scheme in combination with it. Such a scheme uses red for a fatal flaw (and avoids the mediocrity phenomenon), yellow for serious concerns, green for good, and blue for excellent. The various cells with scores can be colored to reflect judgment on the significance of the individual score or on an overall basis. Alternatives with even one red should normally be discarded from further consideration. Those with multiple yellows are unlikely to be worth pursuing. Plan A, meaning the one or few primary dealmaking alternatives, should be, if possible, those with primarily green, as many blue cells as possible, and few or no yellow cells. Alternatives with yellow cells may warrant drill down assessment to force them into either green or red categories. One of the benefits of such coloring is that the results are easily communicated among deal team members.

However the principle benefit of the scoring and coloring is that it is likely to show multiple, attractive Plan B alternatives. As with DCF, Monte Carlo, and Real Options, the tool can be "gamed" to make it come out in some prescribed or politically correct way. However, when used with judgment, and an honest search for good decisions, it can be very helpful when used to correlate the perspectives of the various deal-team members and the available quantitative data. Rating/ranking, like many human activities, is about making reasoned, systematic a priori judgments with the belief that such choosing is justified over most of the time, or a least an economically significant percentage of the time. To gain a more elevated appreciation of the rating/ranking method, we can rightly claim it as an expression of an important philosophical concept that is succinctly expressed in Latin as *mutatis mutandis* (derived from the word *mutate*, the phrase means, literally: "things having been changed that need to be changed," namely, we have adjusted, or mutated, as needed to make things applicable); so if someone reacts to this method as being ad hoc, you can reply, "ah, contrare, *mutatis mutandis.*"

And, it helps to remind ourselves of the Aristotelian mean:

> we must also remember . . . [to] not look for precision in all things alike, but in each class of things such precision as accords with the subject matter, and so much as is appropriate to the inquiry. For a carpenter and a

geometer investigate the right angle in different ways; the former does so in so far as the right angle is useful for his work, while the latter inquires what it is or what sort of thing it is; for he is a spectator of the truth.

Book 1, Chapter 7, *Nicomachean Ethics*

## PLAN B IMPLEMENTATION

How, then, might one appropriate the insights from the above Plan B analysis? One way is to create a short list of the most attractive candidates, such as three to six companies, and pursue them in parallel, equally ready to enter into negotiations for the purpose of closure with any member of the set. This approach has a high marketing and negotiating cost because of the multiple, parallel, equally important avenues being pursued, and it may tax available deal-team resources. But it has the advantage that it is more likely to provide the earliest indication of market interest, deal issues, and valuation ranges. It is possible for a seller pursuing such a short-list approach to create the effect of an auction with multiple interested parties bidding on the opportunity. When there are multiple equally attractive alternatives, then such a short-list approach avoids having to select a Plan A negotiating opportunity; in effect, Plan A addresses in parallel the highest-ranked candidates, which innately provides a Plan B alternative.

Alternatively, we could use the results of our Plan B analysis to assure ourselves that our Plan A is indeed the one that appears the most attractive, considering all the alternatives and relevant factors, and to identify those who are highly ranked but are distinctly less attractive. This approach would be the more traditional sense of Plan B. Even with this approach it is normally a good practice to begin discussions early with one or more candidates from the Plan B list. This approach avoids having a significant delay in overall negotiating time in the event Plan A fails, and also obtains an initial measure of interest from one or more Plan B alternatives.

One of the virtues of having a Plan B is that an analysis of potential deal value can be made and compared with the Plan A value or with other members of the Plan B population. Such comparisons among alternatives is a type of scenario analysis. Such comparisons may point out ways to improve the assumptions or model used. Also, the value of the best Plan B alternative should, in principle, be the floor of the terms that should be accepted with the Plan A alternative.

The other virtue of creating a Plan B is having in place a disciplined process for decision making among alternatives, as shown in Exhibit 11.2. Consistent with earlier comments, the appropriate level of analysis reflects a balance between too much (which can reduce to "aim, aim, aim" as shown) and too little ("fire, fire, fire").

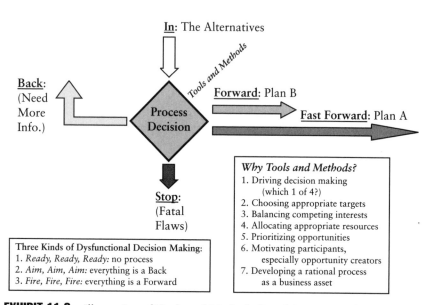

**EXHIBIT 11.2**    Illustration of Tools and Methods-Based Decision Making

## PLAN B CAUTION

As with any good practice, there can be a dark side to having a Plan B. One obvious one for Plan B analysis is that one can become stuck in analysis, as in paralysis by analysis. There can be too many alternatives under serious consideration. Or there can be too many factors being scored and weighted. Or there can be too long a debate as to the significance of the differences in scoring. When the opportunities are potentially significant and the future opportunity can be difficult to characterize or widely varying in value depending on the perspective used, then a serious effort in such analysis is appropriate and warranted. But time is often a critical factor. So having established procedures and trained deal teams and even access to outside consultants, together with a reasonable standard of certainty, is important to keep the opportunities from being sidetracked by study.

Another less obvious caution is the loss of deal focus. Most high-value, high-complexity deals experience times of discouragement bordering on despair. Issues thought to be resolved seem to reappear. Hard issues for which there appeared agreement on a resolution principle or process cannot seem to be resolved. Harsh words or other foul behavior can sour relationships. Feelings known as post-deal remorse (as in buyer's remorse) can appear even before deal closing is in sight, perhaps expressed late at night as "Why are we even thinking of doing this deal?" Having a ready Plan B, which is a good thing, can in such cases cause a deal manager or deal team to give up at the point of adversity on what would otherwise, with determination, have been a very good deal. At this stage, the Plan B alternative(s) can appear better than they are simply because you have not begun the hard work of negotiating with such fresh faces.

Having quantified at least the top candidates on the Plan B list can be useful at such junctures to reinforce the reason why this particular opportunity was your Plan A in the first place. Difficulty in negotiation may be just that—difficulty.

## PLAN B FROM THE BUYER'S PERSPECTIVE

Although much of the previous discussion has been in the context of the seller's perspective, a Plan B is important for prospective buyers as well. Without such alternatives, the buyer deal team can assume that their very careers are on the line such that no deal means no career because there is no alternative in view. Although such a scenario can be usefully motivating, it is also a dangerous practice that will cause deal teams perhaps to ignore red flags, and/or overpay. We witnessed in high-visibility technology companies numerous acquisitions that in retrospect were simply not well considered.

When the buy-side deal team has been charged with acquiring the best available X, in which X is a technology or product, creating alternatives and a Plan B rating/ranking is very similar to the process described for the sell-side deal team. When the alternatives are very disparate investments with perhaps loss of deal-team cohesion, it becomes more difficult.

## PLAN B AND LIFE

Exhibit 11.3 is a reproduction of a black and white painting by Raphael Soyer,[5] perhaps incongruous in a book on negotiation, but worth your careful reflection. Depicted are two women shown on a common black floor but silhouetted against two very different vertical panels, one black (the unopened shade) and one an unshaded, light-transmitting window. The ballerina on the right is dressed for ballet practice, with her hair up; the one on the left is dressed in street clothes with her hair down. One has her head down, looking into the practice room, the other's is up and looking outside. One is holding with both hands what appears to be a garment associated with her work, the other is holding the shade with one hand, almost like a wave (or a salute?) and reaching outward with the other. On the third vertical panel, the rightmost one, is a second white panel balancing the panel with the "outward"

*Painting by Raphael Soyer, courtesy of the Seattle Art Museum.*

**EXHIBIT 11.3** *Ballerinas* by Raphael Soyer

*Source:* © The Seattle Art Museum, gift of Mrs. Helen Eisenberg. Reprinted with permission.

woman on the left; on this third panel is some sort of message, which echoes in the outward woman's also light panel and contrasts in the "inward" ballerina's dark panel. The inward ballerina appears almost weighted down by the dark panel, as if it were pressing her into the dark floor; even her shoes, shown as dark, appear almost like weights that have locked her into the practice room. The outward ballerina, in contrast, has white shoes that not only contrast with the floor but she is shown barely within the confines of the floor and the shoe color suggests that a freeing break has been made.

And, so? We are processing in this picture a deep idea of response to imposed, dramatic change. Why two ballerinas, as opposed to two, say, writers or welders? Because, I think, there comes a time, usually surprisingly soon, when the ballerina's profession shuts off the professional opportunity for employment, for compensation, for expression; the calendar is simply less kind to ballerinas than to writers or welders. What happens at the moment of the "writing on the wall" when the realization occurs that Plan A can no longer work?[6] This painting conveys the two basic responses available to us: the inward resignation versus the outward, new-opportunity perspective. In this book centered on options, albeit investment options, it is appropriate to close with a deeper look at what options should mean.

ᴵDealmaking is about dealmaking. For high-value, high-complexity dealmaking, this endeavor can become an all-consuming pursuit. It is not uncommon that as a result of forces beyond one's control or anticipation, the negotiating process can take a track that seems to require dealmaking at any price, the anthithesis of ᴵDealmaking, or it can lead to a deep feeling of despair because the track is leading to nowhere, regardless of price. That perception is the inward ballerina, stuck in the room, hands almost bound to what no longer can work, dressed for no other purpose, eyes on no other prize.

There is another perspective possible. Somewhere there is a shade that can be undrawn, and a window that opens to something else. There exists a Plan B. A cornerstone idea of ᴵDealmaking is that there are other opportunities, always, hidden behind drawn shades that can, and should, be considered. Look one last time at the outward, now-former ballerina at the window. Between her and that window, a small barrier in front of her feet, is pictured a radiator, shown by the alliteration of light and dark vertical lines. Those lines convey an image of miniature jail bars. With the shade drawn, those lines could have looked like tall bars hidden by the shade; with the opened shade, they are seen for what they really are—a small barrier.[7]

So, in the spirit of this book, I envision a new symbol posted on that bulletin board in the rightmost panel: $\exists$B. The symbol $\exists$, is used in mathematics to designate existence, literally, "there exists" as in: $\exists$ an even number greater than two. ᴵDealmaking is about posting $\exists$B in front of every analysis: beyond this opportunity, which we are hotly pursuing, there does exist a Plan B. Its existence, though solely perceptual, has a reality because of the conviction that it can be made to exist experientially. The inward ballerina, perhaps as her first step toward acceptance, may be less imprisoned by the garment in her hands and more conducting a funeral and placing the remnants of Plan A in what looks very much like a miniature sarcophagus. Perhaps that is always the necessary first step.

The balance between undivided commitment to Plan A, without which demanding opportunities usually cannot be realized, and being open to a Plan B goes to the innermost place of our motives and our character. There is the famous story of Julius Caesar, a Roman general of the time, leading an invasion on Britain in 55 and 54 B.C. who orders the burning of the Roman landing boats to create the reality for both invaders and invadees that there is now no Plan B.[8] A homier example is this simple story of Scott Smith:

"Maybe the best manager I ever had was the guy who taught me to sell Fuller Brushes in the summer between my freshman and sophomore years, when I was poor, scared, happy and already a father. We were ringing doorbells on Northampton Street in Easton, PA. We had run into the proverbial brick wall. No one was home or no thanks or go to hell and take that college kid with ya. 'Just one more, kid,' he said, 'Just keep ringing one more bell, and when you don't even think about it anymore, that'll be the door. Some woman will buy your case out.'"[9] Getting your Plan A realized can require a determination that does not allow the allure of Plan B as an escape from the present difficulty to dishearten or defocus your enthusiasm and hope.

And there are some, few situations where ∃!A (namely, there exists uniquely/only Plan A). So the heart and soul must be in pursuit of Plan A, that is what makes it "A." And without such pursuit, one becomes a dilettante, always dabbling, never realizing the difficult opportunities. But the commitment to A must be sheltered by the B. Such realization leads to better execution of the A, and the courage to know when to "fold 'em" and pursue the B. And for dealmakers, a good deal accomplished is a very sweet experience: *fosan et haec olim meminisse jivabit* (perhaps one day it will please us to remember even this).[10]

## NOTES

1. We are not considering here long-term allocation investing in which one may well do no such calculations but take as reasonable the price determination by *others* who are presumably doing a rational analysis. Such piggy-backing generally works well for patient investors providing the purchase price of the market basket of stocks purchased was determined rationally in such market, which is not always a reliable assumption.

2. There is a chapter on rating/ranking in *Early Stage Technologies: Valuation and Pricing*, by Richard Razgaitis (John Wiley & Sons, 1999) and in *Valuation and Pricing of Technology-Based Intellectual Property* (2003) that has a purely valuation focus based on its use with market comparables.

3. Data is from Standard & Poor's Corp, reported in *Business Week*, April 8, 2002, p. 40.

4. This issue can be overcome, to a degree, by multiplying each of the factor scores instead of adding them. This method has the effect of splaying out the differences and rightfully punishing an opportunity that scores only a "1" on one or more factors. However, the numerical result is not easy to normalize and visualize meaning.

5. 1945, the original is in the Seattle Art Museum, Seattle, Washington.

6. I see the note on the right panel, as the writing on the wall, as being the list of the ballerinas selected for the performance season and neither ballerina in our picture made the "cut."

7. The vertical lines also convey to me the marking of time, somewhat as a prisoner might do by ticking off the days and years of confinement.

8. Whereupon, it is said, the British defenders, who had an alternative to death, immediately surrendered rather than face a Roman army with no alternative to death.

   The "burning boats" story is also ascribed to Caesar's later crossing of the Rubicon (49 B.C.), effectively declaring war on his own Roman Republic, to Hernando Cortez landing in 1519 at Vera Cruz to attack the Aztec Empire, and to numerous ancient Greek landing parties. These stories, some or all, may be apocrophal; nonetheless, the imagery and metaphor are useful and widely used.

9. Story of Scott Smith, quoted in *Business First*, Columbus Ohio, March 8, 1988.

10. Roman poet Virgil (70–19 B.C.), Book 1 of his epic *Aeneid*.

# CHAPTER 12

# Conclusion

*It may work in practice, but it will never work in theory.*
Reportedly said by a French economist.

It is difficult sometimes to determine what should be chosen at what cost, and what should be endured in return for what gain.

Book 2, Chapter 1, *Nicomachean Ethics*

In this concluding chapter, we want to develop a perspective on deal values. Although most of our considerations in this book have focused on monetary values, and for good reason, it is important to recall that there are other values that cannot be counted in the same sense as money. For inventors, there is commonly a strong feeling of wanting to see their creation made real and useful. For sellers with "orphans," a deal can clear the slate of something that was not going to be important so there is now room for something that is. For deal managers, there is the delight in the pursuit and closure associated with dealmaking and the sense that, all things considered, this was a "good deal." For deal managers in enlightened moments, there is an immeasurable satisfaction at seeing the other side also feel that this was a "good deal." That is the essence of *dealmaking*.

## IN THEORY, IN PRACTICE

In theory, there is no difference between theory and practice. But, in practice, there is.

Jan L.A. van de Snepscheut[1]

The nature of books is to collect and convey principles and generalities expressed as methods and tools. Our goal here is to develop a discipline that is founded on method but is practical and realistic. But as there are limitations on methods as there are on all representations, so there are on the ability to connect in the everyday world.

There is a term of art not widely used today that is relevant here: "learning the trade." Its use dates back to the age of apprenticeship in which one learned one's craft by working with a master craftsman. Over extended years and experiences, one gained the insight that is unique to each profession. The word *trade* is particularly appropriate in this closing chapter because that practice that is to be learned is the trade of trade (dealmaking).

No mere book by itself can replace the experience of learning by the real world observation of more-advanced practitioners. Professional societies such as the Licensing Executives Society (www.les.org) can provide both educational programs and even more importantly networking opportunities directed toward dealmaking on specific opportunities but also the sharing of experiences of dealmaking as a trade. I encourage you to get that experience.

## VALUE CREATION BY DEALMAKING

If we were in the earth's orbit looking outward into the furthest reaches of the universe, with views now afforded by the amazing Hubble Space Telescope (HST), we would be, or should be, struck by several amazing questions. Perhaps the most famous question is why is there something instead of nothing? This question is beyond the scope of this book, but there is a second foundational question that we do want to consider: Why is the something pulled together in bodies, groups, and clusters?

Specifically, let us consider the HST picture shown in Exhibit 12.1. This absolutely spectacular picture was taken by the HST on April 1 and 9, 2002, as part of a NASA servicing mission. The elongated shape that dominates the picture is a galaxy of stars popularly known as the Tadpole Galaxy (UGC10214). That galaxy is located 420 million light years[2] from us in the direction of the constellation Draco. The elongated tail of the Tadpole is 280,000 light years long, which is more than a million trillion miles, just that line right there in this book. There are two particularly remarkable features of this particularly remarkable photograph that we want to point out. First, that long tail was caused by something else in this picture. In the upper left portion of the main body of the Tadpole Galaxy can be seen a small, compact interloper galaxy shown by the arrow. These two galaxies have had a close encounter. Despite their vast dimensions and open spaces, the forces exercised by the stars and other matter in each galaxy are believed to have unwound, partially, the spiral arm structure of the Tadpole into that amazing tail.

are of the same place, New York City taken in 2002.[4] The one on the left was taken at night. Even in these relatively low-resolution pictures, one can see the three primary New York airports (JFK, LGA, and EWR) and the large outer belt highway into New Jersey (I-287). Now, why are these pictures in this book?

Just as the deep space pictures evidenced an attractive force that creates clusters instead of chaos, so the earthward pictures show the same general effect. But instead of gravity from principles of physics, there is an attraction from the principles of economics. There is no reason for New York City to exist as we see it. People have not crammed themselves into this high-rent district to be within fortified walls as with medieval cities; it is quite the opposite as the events of September 11, 2001 have shown us. Why are they there?

The answer for this city, and the countless others, is to pursue opportunity. New York City began as a place for traders, originally Dutch traders. It expanded and grew because that city, like the United States itself, welcomed many others who sought the opportunity to trade. Commonly the trade was their labor for the liquidity to buy from those markets whatever they desired. In these New York City pictures but not clearly visible, or well remembered, is little Ellis Island, where millions of immigrants, my parents among them, came to America with the dream of pursuing opportunities, their opportunities. The terrorist attacks on September 11, 2001 were horrific in their human toll. And the targets were the World Trade Centers, places created and energized by creating such dealmaking opportunities that benefit both sides of the deal.

There is a gravity for dealmaking (trade) that draws us to one another under the belief that what I can give you, you will so value, that you can see the equity in giving to me what I will value. There are some solitary souls out in the woods converting string-bean hulks into shoe laces by some laborious process. We wish them well. But, for most of us, we would rather do what we do best so that with a tiny portion of our earnings we can buy a lifetime's supply of shoe laces, among other things of value, and go forward with more interesting pursuits.

There is, then, something special in dealmaking. As a seller you are of high value to a buyer and vice versa, because what you can offer can create greater value in the hands of the ideal partner, given an ideal deal. It does not always work out that way, between all combinations of sellers and buyers and all opportunities, but it does often enough that it attracts us to one another seeking additional (and better) opportunities. In the global, mobile, 24 by 7 village we now share, this dealmaking gravity additionally exists in the form of voices over wire and fiber, printed sheets of paper that stream out of little, cheap boxes located on 100 million tables, of bits parsed into an Internet protocol that echo thousands of miles in only seconds and essentially for free to any of nearly a billion unique web addresses. Nothing replaces face-to-face dealings, at least not yet. But the communications revolution enables us now to do better, faster, and cheaper what we have gravitated to do all along.

## A FINAL (TRUE) STORY

I began this book with a dedication to my late colleague Bruce Sidran. I would like to end it with a story about my mother, Valeria, who had come through Ellis Island in 1920 on her way to Chicago with less than a first-grade education. In the early 1950s in her 50s she learned to drive and in 1954 bought a new Chevrolet Bel Air. This car, that was her treasure, would shed its right rear hubcap with some peculiar regularity. Leaving the vehicle at 30 mph in Chicago, this hubcap was the 1950s version of Star Wars-like attacks. Replacing that hubcap was a regular Razgaitis family experience. Tiring of paying retail, I recall vividly my mother taking me to Maxwell Street, a world famous Chicago street of barter of every imaginable good. As a young boy, the tumult of this experience was both galvanizing and unsettling. After some journeying we found a street merchant with an amazing collection of hubcaps and only hubcaps. I even believe I saw our missing right rear one forlornly attached to his temporary display. I remember his opening price like it was yesterday: "75 cents, take it or leave it." I was relieved because I thought she would just pay the man and we'd get out of this place. But to my dismay, she had just begun to negotiate. They went back and forth in gestures and languages unfamiliar to me, but when it was over I recall a very happy woman with a slightly banged up 35-cent hubcap under her arm. What I understand better now is that there was also a happy street merchant with 35 cents in his pocket and one less hubcap to haul around. Some years later, when I was able to drive that very car, that very hubcap came loose and disappeared. I always believed that that hubcap merchant on Maxwell Street had another opportunity for dealmaking with it. I doubt that he used Monte Carlo, but if he saw my mother at his booth, he knew he was in for another opportunity-creating experience. (And if you were at the corner of Kimball and Diversey in Chicago in about 1960 and had to dodge a 30-mph spinning hubcap off a rust-colored Chevy, I am really sorry.)

## NOTES

1. I am indebted for this quote to a Web site of interesting quotes collected by Dr. Gabriel Robins at: www.cs.virginia.edu/~robins/quotes.html.
2. A light year is a really long way. The moon is just over a light second, that is, it takes light about 1.3 seconds to reach the earth from the moon. Our sun is 8.3 light

minutes away, meaning if the sun turned off at just this moment we would not see it go off for 8.3 minutes because there is a 93 million mile spherical shell of photons always present and streaming outward. So a light year is about six trillion (i.e., million million) miles, an incomprehensible distance.

3. Again calling on Dr. Einstein, he discovered in his work on relativity that what we call the force of gravity is the effect of space curvature caused by local masses. So stellar and other masses curve the space around them off to infinity and such curvatures in space cause the masses to move not in straight lines, which we interpret as the result of gravitation.

4. The slight blurring just below the southern tip of Manhattan is a consequence of a small cloud in the picture that coincidentally and approximately spans the distance between Manhattan and the Statue of Liberty.

# Bibliography

## GENERAL BOOKS ON STRATEGY, UNCERTAINTY, AND NEGOTIATION.

Dixit, Avinash K., and Barry J. Nalebuff. *Thinking Strategically*. New York: W.W. Norton and Company, 1991.

Dixit, Avinash K., and Robert S. Pindyck. *Investment Under Uncertainty*. Princeton, NJ: Princeton University Press, 1994.

Raiffa, Howard. *The Art and Science of Negotiation*. Cambridge, MA: Harvard University Press, 1982.

Ury, William, and Roger Fisher. *Getting to Yes*; *Getting Past No*. Cambridge, MA: Harvard University Press. [Drs. Ury and Fisher are also the developers of and have been frequent presenters at the Harvard executive education short courses on negotiation.]

## REAL OPTIONS

Amram, Martha, and Nalin Kulatilaka. *Real Options: Managing Strategic Investment in an Uncertain World*. Boston, MA: Harvard Business School Press, 1999

Copeland, Tom, and Vladimair Antikarov. *Real Options, A Practitioner's Guide*. Texere Publishing, 2001.

Moore, William T. *Real Options & Option-Embedded Securities*. New York: John Wiley & Sons, 2001.

Mun, Johnathan. *Real Options Analysis, Tools and Techniques for Valuing Strategic Investments and Decisions*. New York: John Wiley & Sons, 2002. [This book is effectively a companion text to Decisioneering's Real Options Analysis Toolkit software; Dr. Mun is an employee of Decisioneering.]

## FINANCIAL OPTIONS

Chriss, Neil A. *The Black-Scholes and Beyond Option Pricing Models*. New York: McGraw-Hill, 1997.

Chriss, Neil A. *The Black-Scholes and Beyond Interactive Toolkit*. New York: McGraw-Hill, 1997.

Lowenstein, Roger. *When Genius Failed: The Rise and Fall of Long-Term Capital Management*. New York: Random House, 2000. [Not a book on real options methods, but a compelling history of a company, Long-Term Capital Management, founded to create market-beating returns using derivatives based on options value by Black-Scholes type of analysis.]

## GENERAL FINANCE TEXTS

Brealey, Richard A., and Stewart C. Myers. *Principles of Corporate Finance*. New York: McGraw-Hill, 1988.

Luenberger, David G. *Investment Science*. New York: Oxford University Press, 1998.

## WEB SITES RELATED TO OPTIONS AND NEGOTIATION

www.razgaitis.com, and "ᶦDealmaking resources" where I will maintain an updated list of resources.

www.decisioneering.com/realoptions

www.cadence.com

www.real-options.com

www.corpfinonline.com

www.idealmaking.com and www.razgaitis.com